Securing Your
Financial Future

Securing Your Financial Future

Complete Personal Finance for Beginners

Chris Smith

ROWMAN & LITTLEFIELD PUBLISHERS, INC.

Lanham • Boulder • New York • Toronto • Plymouth, UK

Published by Rowman & Littlefield Publishers, Inc.
A wholly owned subsidiary of The Rowman & Littlefield Publishing Group, Inc.
4501 Forbes Boulevard, Suite 200, Lanham, Maryland 20706
http://www.rowmanlittlefield.com

10 Thornbury Road, Plymouth PL6 7PP, United Kingdom

British Library Cataloguing in Publication Information Available

Library of Congress Cataloging-in-Publication Data

Smith, Chris, 1955–
  Securing your financial future : complete personal finance for beginners / Chris Smith.
      p. cm.
  Includes bibliographical references and index.
  ISBN 978-1-4422-1422-4 (pbk. : alk. paper) — ISBN 978-1-4422-1423-1 (ebook)
  1. Finance, Personal. I. Title.
  HG179.S5495 2012
  332.024—dc23

                                                                2011047879

∞™ The paper used in this publication meets the minimum requirements of American National Standard for Information Sciences—Permanence of Paper for Printed Library Materials, ANSI/NISO Z39.48-1992.

Printed in the United States of America

Contents

Preface

This book is about how to manage your personal finances responsibly and successfully. Unlike most books on this subject, it is specifically intended for those who are just starting out in their financial life, or who will be soon. It covers the essential principles that are important for just about everyone to know. Even though the concepts are fundamental ones, most people have never had a chance to learn them in any kind of organized way—which is exactly what we're going to do.

Here's your first lesson: before you listen to anyone explain anything about personal finance, you should first understand what their agenda is. That's just what this preface is for—but in order to explain my objective in writing the book, I'll need to tell you the story that led up to it.

I'm a dad, and I have two college-age sons. Like most parents, I wanted to make sure that my sons got at least some exposure to the subject of how to manage their money. Since they weren't likely to get this kind of training in school, and since I have a financial background, I knew that I was the likely candidate to teach them. Besides, I knew just how I wanted to approach it. My own dad had been a finance professional too, and that's how I had first learned about the subject—friendly fatherly lectures spontaneously delivered as teachable moments arose. If that sounds a little boring, it really wasn't; my dad had a great way of making it fun as well as educational. And since that approach had worked well enough with me, why not make it a family tradition?

But had it really worked for me? After some reflection, I had to admit that the answer wasn't quite as clear-cut as I'd been imagining. Even though I've ended up in a position of financial independence, I took a very roundabout way of getting there—because I didn't really take the whole topic very seriously at first. I made a lot of mistakes, especially when I was just starting out. I eventually began doing a lot of the things that I'd been taught, but sometimes only after a little experimenting on my own—with predictably bad results. Other times I did the right things, but in the wrong order, or without the appropriate safeguards.

I'd enjoyed my dad's early lessons and understood them at the time, but more as an opportunity to match wits with him than to really try to master the topic. My thinking was that I had my whole financial life in front of me, and there was plenty of time to get serious about money management later. In the end, that's just about how it turned out—an informal explanation of the basics, then plenty of mistakes and experimentation, followed by renewed determination and recovery from the mistakes, and finally a relatively happy ending. Good enough for me, so it would be enough for my sons, right?

Wrong.

Here's why: the financial world has changed, and in some very significant ways. I didn't realize it at first, because the changes had occurred incrementally, bit by bit. But once I began doing some research to refresh my memory on the basics, I came to realize that over the course of an entire generation, the cumulative effect has been dramatic. The problem isn't that what my dad taught me has gotten out of date—on the contrary, these timeless principles have become more important than ever. But what has changed is the financial *environment*. And it has changed in such a way that requires you to have a much more complete understanding of personal finance right from the start of your financial life. Spending a decade or more to finally get serious about a long-term financial plan—like I did—is a luxury that today's young people can no longer afford.

The financial world that I grew up in was quite forgiving, although I didn't appreciate it at the time. In those days, the whole key was finding and maintaining a good steady income. Once you'd done that, turning that income into long-term financial security didn't require too much heavy-duty planning or decision making. Of course, there were some choices to make, but they didn't tend to be of the make-or-break variety. I was lucky to have gotten some sound, early training in money management, but in those financially friendly times, it wasn't really essential—it was more like icing on the cake.

Back then, the employment landscape was more stable. It wasn't unusual to work for the same employer for many years at a stretch, even decades. And once you had a job (and/or joined a union), lots of things were taken care of on your behalf. Medical insurance was heavily subsidized (which prevented many of us from noticing just how fast health-care costs were steadily increasing). More important, years of service were typically rewarded with a wonderful retirement benefit called a *pension*: the employer continued to pay the employee a fixed monthly amount, after retirement, *for life*. This meant that behind the scenes, employers and unions were making most of the important long-term investment decisions on behalf of their employees; the employees just had to concentrate on their jobs. On top of that, Social Security could be counted on to supplement pension income with monthly payments after age 65. If you also owned a house, then you had a chance for even more security; the increases in housing prices were so dependable that a big equity was almost a guarantee. Of course, all those advantages could be reversed by getting into significant debt, but that wasn't too common, because credit was pretty tough to get—especially for young people.

But the foundations of that simple world have been crumbling for some time. If there was any remaining doubt that the old days are gone forever, it was dramatically erased by the recent subprime lending crisis and widespread financial meltdown. Today's employment landscape is far more fragmented, and long stretches with a single employer are the exception instead of the rule. Self-employment and short-term contract work are now much more common. Medical insurance is often still subsidized, but the subsidies are shrinking while the costs continue to balloon. The days of employer pensions are just about completely gone, replaced by investment plans like 401(k)'s; employees must now make their own decisions about how much to save, which investments to choose, how to adjust them over time, and how to manage the intricacies of the available retirement tax shelters. At the same time, the range and complexity of available investment products has increased tremendously. There is serious and growing doubt about the long-term viability of Social Security as we've historically known it. Young people today often *begin* their financial lives in debt, in the form of student loans. On top of that, credit cards are aggressively advertised and readily available, despite recent reforms. Confidence in home-equity growth as a staple of retirement planning has been deeply shaken—and for good reason.

So is there any hope? Is it still possible for today's young adults to achieve any kind of long-term financial security? The answer is a resounding *yes!* The fundamental principles of personal finance are just as valid today as they ever were. You can still achieve a very strong financial future from almost any income level—but *you'll* need to do the right things to make it happen. You can no longer rely on the institutions of the past to handle things on your behalf.

But how are you supposed to know what these right things are? That is precisely what this book is about. We'll cover all the decisions, actions, and habits that will be most important for you to know, exactly how and when to apply them, and how to avoid the most common mistakes. You'll be glad to know that these right things aren't particularly hard to understand or to do; but it is vitally important to do them right, to do them consistently, and to do them in the right order. Most importantly, if you get an early start, the risks are minimal and the payoff is substantial. But each year that you wait to begin doing these things, the risks go up and the payoff goes down. That means that you'll need to hit the ground running.

Back to the story: everything that I learned about this much-less-forgiving financial world meant that I was going to have to take a much different approach to teaching my sons than what I'd been planning. Because they were going to have to know the ropes right from the start, the lessons were going to have to be comprehensive as well as practical. Most of the main ideas were the same ones that I had learned, but they needed to be organized into a logical, properly sequenced, and easy-to-remember structure. I realized that it was going to have to be well planned in advance, and that I was going to have to put some careful thought and research into it.

When I casually mentioned to friends and colleagues what I was up to, I was surprised by the intensity of their interest. Almost everyone had a comment about the lack of that kind of information; most asked if they could get a copy of my outline when I was finished. I was even more surprised when my sons told me that some of *their* friends said that they wanted copies too. It became clear to me that lots of young adults and their parents recognize that a strong early education in personal finance is now a necessity but aren't sure how to go about finding it. I realized that if the key lessons could be collected and clearly explained, a lot of young people could benefit from them, not just my sons. That meant that I had to write more than just an informal outline that I could use when teaching my sons; it had to be useful and understandable to any young person, whether I was there to explain it or not. That's how a loosely defined plan to deliver a few fatherly lectures eventually grew into this book.

Throughout this evolution, there was one element of my dad's approach that I was determined to keep: *analogies*. I remembered from my own experiences in young adulthood that when an older person tried to teach me something by dumbing down the material for my benefit—or worse, by trying to mimic my generation's language—the effect was condescending and ineffective. But my dad never did that; instead, he used analogies to connect new ideas to ones that I already understood. It seemed like a more respectful approach, as if he were saying, "You're intelligent, just inexperienced." Simply put, analogies can make abstract concepts more understandable, and sometimes more memorable, too. My dad once explained that trying to get ahead financially while owing money was like trying to run up a down escalator; to this day, I remember that lesson every time I see one! When I'd used the same approach in explaining things to my own sons, it was clear to me that the effectiveness of analogies was still in full effect. So you'll find *lots* of them in this book, along with case studies (ranging from one sentence to chapter length), impromptu quizzes, and other devices designed to keep things interesting. Some of the analogies may seem hopelessly unrealistic, but I hope you'll play along with them long enough to get the main points.

You might think that teaching young people the basics of personal finance would be something our educational system would cover, but it is virtually nowhere to be found. If there was ever a subject that would benefit just about *all* of us, individually and collectively, isn't it the basics of managing personal finances? Many of our country's economic problems wouldn't be nearly as pressing if our overall financial literacy were higher; our average personal savings rate would be better, our retirements wouldn't be so woefully underfunded, those outside of working years or otherwise unable to provide for themselves would be better cared for, and so on. Why not tackle this head-on via our educational institutions? Why not a "driver's ed" equivalent for personal finance fundamentals at schools across the country?

There is some encouraging momentum building in that direction, but you're ready to begin your education *now*. Besides, maybe it's a blessing in disguise that you're learning about personal finance from this book rather than in school. Before something can go into a broadly distributed textbook, it has to satisfy the concerns and viewpoints of a very wide range of interested parties. This means that a formal academic treatment of personal finance might have a tendency to be *descriptive* rather than *prescriptive*. But not me; I'm going to be about as prescriptive as it gets! My objective from the beginning is to teach and advise my own sons, not satisfy school boards, government bodies, or influential alumni. So what you'll find in this book are specific, strongly worded, personal *recommendations*. If you're anything like my sons, when it comes to personal finance, you're not particularly interested in reading a thorough survey of all possible points of view. Instead, you want someone who already understands all that, and who has your best interests at heart, to simply advise you exactly what to do and how to do it. That's just what you'll find here.

You might be wondering what my qualifications for writing this book are. I have extensive academic and professional experience in the field of finance. I earned an undergraduate degree in economics (along with a minor in mathematics) and then a graduate degree in corporate finance. Later, I worked for nearly three decades as a finance professional at Hewlett-Packard, a large, well-known, and highly regarded Silicon Valley technology company. At the time of my retirement, I was vice president of finance for two of HP's global business units. It is true that personal finance and corporate finance are different fields, but they aren't exactly *unrelated*, either. The jargon, tools, and levels of complexity are very different (so are the staff meetings!), but personal and corporate financial management are, at the core, both about establishing sound habits and practices aimed at making sure that the ins are consistently bigger than the outs and that they stay that way. If anyone tries to tell you that there is some other mysterious "secret" to it—beware.

So if you're the type who gets put off by the complicated jargon, graphs, and equations that sometimes appear in books or articles about personal finance, and if you've always wished that somebody who "spoke geek" would just summarize the main points for you in everyday English—your wish has come true, and I'm your geek.

A great deal is written on the subject of personal finance, and I've studied a lot of it in researching this book. What I found was that it is indeed a jungle out there, and the quality is all over the map. However, *some* of the information is outstanding; I've drawn heavily from a lot of this good work and have cited it where appropriate. But even though excellent information is available, most of it is intended for those who are much further along in their financial lives than you are. Relatively little of what is written about personal finance is squarely and directly aimed at young people, *just starting out* in their financial lives. You really seem to be something of an ignored audience.

Well, you are ignored no longer! If you are just starting out in your financial life—or are about to do so shortly—then this book is designed specifically for you. The introduction that follows will outline how the book is structured and give you a preview of the topics that we'll cover. I hope you'll find this book useful for years to come and that you'll share what you learn with others. Most of all, I hope that what you're about to learn contributes to a bright financial future for you.

Introduction

$\mathcal{H}$ere is what this book emphatically is *not*: it is not about how to get rich quick, with little effort. It is not about how to exploit the specific circumstances of "today's historically unique economic conditions." It is not about new, revolutionary, never-before-told secrets being revealed. It definitely doesn't have a subtitle that suggests that you're about to learn something that somebody else "doesn't want you to know." And it certainly isn't about how to profit at the expense of others.

In fact, it is just about the complete opposite of those things.

What we'll talk about *will* require effort on your part, and that effort will need to be sustained. None of it is particularly difficult, though, and some of it even becomes surprisingly effortless—eventually. The approaches that we'll cover are based on solid, commonsense principles, many of which have been around for centuries. They aren't dependent on any one particular set of economic conditions—they'll work just as well for your children and grandchildren as they will for you. None of what we'll cover is a secret, but it is amazing how few people really understand some of the most important points. Finally, once you master these concepts, you can share them with others. If you do, the result won't be less for you. Instead, the result will be that you'll spend your life surrounded by people who are *also* on a path to long-term financial security—and who will be very grateful to you for the helpful role that you played. Now, those are good people to be surrounded by.

By following the principles that we cover in this book, you won't get rich quick. Instead of a big, immediate payday, the idea is to improve your position a little bit at a time—carefully, methodically, and dependably. Most importantly, we'll emphasize how very much easier it is to achieve a strong financial position *if you get an early start*, even if your initial steps seem tiny.

1

Doing the right things, making the right financial decisions, over and over, right from the start, is the key. The purpose of this book is to explain—exactly—what those right things are, in such a way that you can easily apply them in your financial life.

Even though your financial rewards will accumulate slowly, a different kind of reward does show up quickly and will stay with you throughout your financial life: *confidence*. It can't be overstated—when you know with complete certainty that the path you're on is leading you toward an ever-improving financial condition, the journey becomes much more enjoyable! To appreciate how important this is, consider the alternative. Everyday life is filled with constant reminders of your personal financial condition and prospects. Every time an unexpected expense comes along, or you are tempted by an appealing purchase, or you hear about someone you know in financial difficulty serves as a prompt for you to consider your own financial situation. For most people, this steady stream of reminders can result in stress, uncertainty, and frustration—or maybe in very bad decisions. In contrast, if you have a solid understanding of your financial path, you can greet each of these reminders with calm assurance. The difference that this will make in your daily life is huge—and permanent.

YOUR FINANCIAL LIFE

Throughout this book, a term that you will hear a lot is *your financial life*. Let me explain exactly what I mean by that. Your financial life begins once you have established a steady income and have become completely responsible for your own financial affairs. It can begin abruptly, gradually, or somewhere in between. For most people, financial life begins somewhere in their late teens or twenties. (When you are handed a diploma, if you notice your parents seeming even more overjoyed and relieved than you might have expected, that might be a signal that your financial life has just *abruptly* begun!) Likewise, your financial life ends when you are no longer responsible for your own financial condition, and this too can be abrupt or gradual.

I want you to think of your financial life as having three roughly equal phases. To help you begin thinking this way, a typical breakdown might look like this:

1st third: age 20s and 30s
2nd third: age 40s and 50s
3rd third: age 60s and beyond

The exact ages don't matter; your beginning and ending points may be sooner or later, the length of your thirds may be shorter or longer, and what we're about to cover is not dependent upon you having a precise estimate of your life span. What *is* important is for you to adopt a rough mental picture of your financial life as being separated into thirds.

This book is aimed directly at those who have just begun—or are just about to begin—the 1st third of their financial life. Nearly everything written here is going to be about what to do, how to do it, and why it is important— *during the 1st third* of your financial life.

If you are already well into your 1st third, I'd encourage you to keep reading anyway. Most of what is covered here will still be applicable to you. If you've made some missteps, reading this ought to make it clear to you what those were; you still have some time to correct them and get back on track. However, if you're already into your 2nd third, or even later, you would probably be better off seeking education elsewhere. Don't worry—a great deal of what is written on personal finance is aimed at those who are already under way, so you're sure to find something helpful. Our focus here, though, is on the often-neglected newcomer.

Now, stand by for an extremely important concept. It is one that you've probably never been taught, and it isn't well known. Lots of people eventually understand this concept, but only when it is too late to do them much good. It isn't particularly intuitive, but once people thoroughly understand it, its implications immediately change their perspective and priorities. The concept isn't new or revolutionary, but somehow it always seems to avoid the spotlight. And it isn't controversial: I'd be willing to bet that the vast majority of respected personal finance experts would readily and wholeheartedly agree with it. Are you ready?

When it comes to personal financial management, the 1st third is vital. It is immensely easier to achieve a strong financial position by taking the right steps during the 1st third than it is by taking similar steps later in your financial life.

Take a minute to let that sink in—because if you're like most people, this is not how you've been thinking about it up until now. Most people think that the 1st third is a time for getting their feet wet in the financial world, so that they'll be ready for the real action that comes later on. Worse, maybe they think that the 1st third is all about rewarding themselves for all the hard work that it took to achieve the paycheck-earning status, before they settle down and become more financially responsible later in life. Still other people decide to just "go with the flow" and just do what everyone else seems to be doing financially. Worst of all, some people might not think about their financial futures at all.

One of three things will be true at the end of the 1st third of your financial life:

1. You will have dug yourself into a hole that you'll spend much of the rest of your financial life digging out of, which you may or may not ever fully succeed in doing.
2. You will have avoided digging a hole, but you won't have much to show for roughly 20 years of work. And you will have wasted the very *best* opportunities to invest that you will ever have.
3. You will be on a safe and secure track to a very bright financial future. You will have avoided the many pitfalls, established the indispensable habits, and planted the right financial seeds that make such a future a virtual certainty.

The entire purpose of this book is to give you the education necessary for you to put yourself in the *third* category. Some of it will just sound like good common sense, some of it will involve things you've never even thought about before, but none of it will be very difficult to understand or to put into practice in your financial life.

If you think it all depends on income, which is a message that seems to be endlessly repeated in our culture—it doesn't. Income plays a role in determining how long it might take and what kind of lifestyle awaits you when you arrive, but the fact is that a solid and secure financial future can be built from virtually any level of steady income. In fact, the lower your income, the *more* important it is to practice sound financial management principles. (By the way, a high income is no guarantee of financial success—more on that later.)

If you think it all depends on luck, educational level, a big inheritance, willingness to take big risks, or who you know—it doesn't. All of those things can help (sometimes, at least), but you don't have to depend on them. The strategy that we're going to outline puts you in a position to capitalize on any advantages that you might have, or good fortune that may come your way, but it doesn't rely on them.

The approach that we're going to take is probably the most common one that people who have achieved financial success have used, but it is far from the most famous. The consistent practice of sound, commonsense principles wouldn't make a particularly good movie plot. But when you think about it, is your financial life the part of your life where you want danger, excitement, and thrills? Or worst of all—suspense?

The path that we'll carefully describe has none of those. You might even describe it as boring. It is safe, utterly dependable, and emphasizes discipline and responsibility over risk taking. Best of all, it is available for absolutely anyone to use.

WHY THE 1ST THIRD IS SO IMPORTANT

Have you ever tried swimming in a river? If you have, then you know that there is a huge difference between swimming *with* the flow of the water (downstream) and swimming *against* it (upstream). When you're swimming upstream, every stroke is a battle. You're trying to advance yourself, as well as steer in the right direction, simultaneously. If you relax or slow down, even briefly, you immediately start going backward and end up pointing in a different direction. But swimming downstream is a smooth and care-free glide! Your strokes are deliberate and leisurely. You can even relax from time to time, just making an occasional stroke to fine-tune your steering, while you let the water do the work.

Unlike real rivers, financial rivers can flow in either direction—and what you do or don't do in the 1st third of your financial life determines which direction your financial river will start flowing. The strategy that we'll describe in the coming pages is specifically designed to get the river flowing in the direction that you want, as early in your financial life as possible. At first, the water will move very slowly; but if you persist, your financial river will pick up speed and force. Once that is accomplished, the 2nd third and the 3rd third can be a breeze; your main financial decisions will be about fine-tuning your steering.

But if the river starts flowing in the wrong direction during the 1st third, your financial life won't be an easy glide. Once the river starts picking up momentum, reversing its direction requires considerable time and energy. You can still reverse its course in the 2nd third of your financial life, but it will be very difficult to make up for all the time that you could have been gliding along in your desired direction.

But *why* is this true? What is it about the 1st third of your financial life that makes it so special? Two very important things, actually—and not ones that sound very exciting. What are they? Habits and math. (See, I told you they wouldn't sound exciting.) Let's give each of them a closer look.

The word *habits* conjures up an image of something like flossing your teeth: yes, it's important, and yes, you probably understand that you need to do it, but it's not particularly likely that flossing your teeth daily will result in a life-changing view of the world. The best you can hope for is to work it into a daily routine in such a way that you barely notice that you're doing it and that it somehow results in better dental health—and that's it. Make no mistake, *some* of the habits that we'll be talking about fall into this tooth-flossing category, and the best that I will be able to say is, "Do it because it's important, not because it will be the highlight of your week."

But not all habits are like tooth flossing. Some experiences really do change the way that you look at the world, and specifically your financial world. These kinds of habits are called *transformational* habits, and we'll be recommending some of those, too.

When an appropriately composed ball of dough spends the right amount of time in a hot oven, it comes out as a loaf of bread—and it will never be a ball of dough again. Once a cucumber becomes a pickle, it can't reverse course and go back to being a cucumber. Likewise, once you've gone through the process of mastering a truly transformational habit, you are permanently and fundamentally different from how you used to be.

How does this work? Once you've summoned up the nerve and conviction to forgo some tempting and major form of immediate gratification in order to put yourself on sounder long-term financial footing, you'll like the feeling that this gives you. You'll cross over into having a new perspective; not all at once, but gradually. You will begin finding that the peace of mind and security that comes from making these kinds decisions is becoming stronger than the fleeting sense of disappointment and sacrifice. The more you do this, the stronger that perspective will become. It doesn't matter that the first few times involve relatively small amounts of money; once you experience this powerful change in perspective, it will be second nature to you when the amounts become much larger. You will automatically and consistently make decisions that will improve your financial future, without feeling anything like sacrifice. Instead of thinking of these events as depriving yourself, you will begin seeing them as gifts—to your *future* self. As time goes by, the amounts of money involved will increase—and eventually the cumulative effect of all of these decisions will become very considerable.

But don't try postponing these kinds of transformational habits too long, because they work in both directions. If you decide to give in to immediate financial gratification during the 1st third of your financial life, with the idea of taking a more responsible approach later on, it won't work. You'll be like the loaf of bread trying to turn back into a ball of dough. Your financial habits will already be baked in, and your financial future is likely to remain . . . pickled. (Sorry.)

Instead, if you use the 1st third of your financial life to deeply ingrain all of the tooth-flossing-type habits, and to fully embrace all of the transformational habits, you can get the river flowing in the direction that you want right from the start and keep it flowing that way—*for life*. This book will show you exactly what those habits are and how to go about mastering them.

What about the other aspect: math? The building of wealth has a purely mathematical element that gives you a huge advantage while you are in the 1st third of your financial life, no matter who you are and no matter what your starting point is. Two investors can approach an identical investment opportunity—one, a person in the 1st third of their financial life, and the other, much later in theirs. The younger person has an automatic, built-in advantage that is nothing short of enormous. The results available to the younger investor are overwhelmingly greater, despite the older investor's advantage of experience, market knowledge, or Wall Street connections as long as the investment is made in the way that we'll describe.

How does this overwhelming math advantage work? I can't tell you, I have to show you. (Hint: you won't have to wait very long. It's the entire subject of the very first chapter.)

THE ROLE OF MONEY IN YOUR LIFE

Your financial life is not your whole life. Your whole life has many elements; you have a family life, a work life, a social life, a personal health life, a love life, an intellectual life, perhaps a spiritual life, and so on. Which one is more important? I hope you didn't try to answer seriously, because that was a trick question! *All* the elements of your life are vitally important, each in its own way, and at various times and in various ways they are all dependent upon one another. A serious problem in any one element of your life can disrupt some or all of the other ones. It is far easier said than done, but most people agree that the key to a rich and fulfilling life is to find a harmonious balance among all of these elements.

So don't think that financial success alone can automatically result in a rich and fulfilling life. You don't need me to tell you that when financial success becomes an end in itself for someone, the result is rarely a pretty picture. Financial success is not a competition, and there is no prize for finishing first in your peer group or family. A far healthier ideal is to think of personal financial success as a tremendously useful advantage in seeking value and fulfillment in the *other* areas of your life, including contributing to the security and well-being of others. That's the prize!

On the other hand, some people regard any pursuit of personal financial success as distasteful, or even immoral. Whether this dislike is sincere or just a rationalization for not understanding how to achieve success, such an attitude can have profoundly disruptive implications in the other areas of your life. A reluctance to master at least the basics of personal financial management will likely result in a series of financial crises; whatever your higher values are, you probably won't be able to pursue them very well in such a situation. These crises aren't just numbers in a bank account. These are the kinds of situations that can suddenly leave you without a car or a place to live; the paycheck that you've been counting on can be seized by creditors. These financial crises have the potential to destroy everything from family relationships to your own health. If you find being concerned with money distasteful . . . well, being completely unconcerned with it can turn out to be pretty distasteful, too. And not just for you, but for those around you. The truth is that you either master the basics of personal finance or your personal financial situation will eventually master you.

Different people have all different types of attitudes, assumptions, and philosophies about money and the role that it can and should play in their lives. The philosophy that we will take in this book is based on a single, over-riding premise. Learning how to responsibly and safely manage your personal finances is a completely different thing from deciding how you will ultimately use your financial resources—and these two very different subjects shouldn't be confused or mixed together. You and I might have completely different ideas about the best way to use financial resources to improve your life and the lives of others. That's fine, because such a question is a matter of personal val-ues, and we're all fully entitled to our own. But no matter what your personal values are, can we agree that *learning how* to responsibly and safely manage your personal finances is a completely worthwhile endeavor? And that doing so will enable you to better find fulfillment in the other areas of your life, whatever that might mean for you? If so, you've come to the right place, and welcome!

A related point to make is that you'll find this book to be a politics-free zone. That seems to be a little rare these days; the expression of political views of all types is commonplace in our culture, and on the whole, that is a decidedly better state of affairs than the opposite. When it comes to personal finance, it is not unusual for writers or speakers to include their political views, either as side comments or fully integrated into their main points. After all, a discussion of finances can naturally lead to a discussion of overall financial con-ditions, which leads to economics, which leads to economic policy, and before you know it, there we are in a full-blown political discussion. But that is not at all where we are headed in the coming pages. Sound personal-finance prin-ciples are equally available and advantageous to everyone, regardless of politi-cal persuasion or lack of one. Differences in political or social ideology quickly emerge when it comes to deciding *how* financial resources should or shouldn't be used, but our focus is going to be on the *generation* of those resources, not their ultimate use. I believe that it is unnecessarily difficult to learn and master new concepts while simultaneously engaging in an ideological debate, so my intent throughout is to avoid the distraction of such discussions altogether.

A LOOK AHEAD

As I've mentioned, none of the fundamentals of personal finance are particu-larly difficult to understand, but there are a quite a few of them, and they are interrelated. Because of that, personal finance is much easier to learn if the individual ideas are presented and mastered in a logical sequence. The topics in this book are ordered so that it is easy to see the interrelationships; each idea builds on the previous ones.

The main body of this book is organized into four parts, and there are five chapters in each part. As you progress through the sections, you'll notice that what you're learning gets deeper—and narrower. In part I, for example, you get a relatively short exposure to lots and lots of different ideas. Some call this "a mile wide and an inch deep." By the time you arrive at part I, all your learning will be in one single area, but we'll cover it in considerable depth. In other words, the final section will be "an inch wide and a mile deep." Let's take a closer look at each of the parts, one by one.

Part I is designed to set the stage for your financial success by exposing you to the most important concepts first. These are concepts that are so fundamental, they will reappear continuously throughout the rest of the book; most of the more advanced topics that we'll cover later are based on these fundamentals. The better you familiarize yourself with these, the more readily you'll be able to understand and apply the ideas that appear later in the book.

In **part II**, the theme becomes much more operational. Here, we'll take a very pragmatic look at the most common financial decisions, processes, and practices—the kind that you'll face every day, or at least every month, throughout your financial life. We'll cover budgeting, spending, saving, borrowing, credit scores, taxes, and risk management—in other words, the very foundation of your financial position. You'll learn how to set up each of these processes so that they all provide *solid, dependable support* for your financial condition while you work to improve it.

We narrow the focus in **part III**, where we talk about the two truly big-ticket items that most people face: cars and houses. Even though you don't make these kinds of purchases very often, they are big enough to cause you substantial problems if you don't get them right. As you are probably aware, lots of people *don't* get them right—or don't get them as right as they could have. Our goal is to provide you with practical, useful approaches to these major purchases so that you'll be among those who *do* get them right.

The focus of **part IV** will be narrower still. We're going to devote that entire part to just one single subject—long-term investing. We'll provide some overall education on investing in general, but most of the time will be spent detailing exactly what to buy, when to buy it, from whom to buy it, where to hold it, and how long to keep it. We can get that specific because of a remarkable, overwhelming investment advantage that each of you has. Oh, weren't you aware that you had a remarkable, overwhelming investment advantage? Well, you do! And you'll learn all about it in part IV. Once you understand our approach to long-term investing, you'll be amazed by how simple—and how powerful—it is.

As described earlier, the topics have been sequenced in the way that makes them easiest to learn and understand comprehensively. But that may or may not have anything to do with the order that you'll actually encounter them in your real financial life. I know it will be tempting not to, but please, please read through these topics in the order that they are presented. If you immediately jump to the house-buying chapters before learning about budgeting, borrowing, and credit scores, the approach that is presented *probably won't work*. In fact, you might end up making the kind of mistake from which it would take years to recover. If you jump ahead to the long-term investing chapters before learning about taxes, saving, and cash buckets, the investment strategy that is presented *probably won't work*. The book can be a valuable reference guide for you for years to come, but I urge you not to use it as a reference book until you have gone through it carefully, *in sequence*, at least once.

FISH

There is a wonderful, well-known Chinese proverb that goes like this: "Give a man a fish, and you feed him for a day. Teach a man to fish, and you feed him for a lifetime." This proverb has stood the test of time because of the beautifully powerful truth behind it. The way that it is worded puts your attention on the big difference between being a *fish recipient* and a *fishing student*.

What if we reworded it, though, to put the emphasis on the teacher instead of the student? "Give a man a fish, and you don't have that fish anymore. Teach a man to fish, and you still know everything that you ever did about fishing." That's just as true as the original, and also quite a powerful thing to understand. In a very fundamental way, knowledge is different from a fish, or a car, or a dollar, or any "thing": when you give it away, you still have it!

What if we took it even a step further? What if *everyone* were taught to fish? If we just passed a fish around from one person to the next, we'd still just have one fish. But if everyone were *taught* to fish, the knowledge of fishing would simply grow, and keep growing with every lesson. You might be thinking that if that happened, sooner or later we'd run into an overfishing problem, and you'd probably be right. But finances don't work like fish! If *everyone* knew how to manage their personal finances toward a safe and secure financial future—if our collective financial IQ were significantly increased—we would *all* be better off. And we'd be better off in so many ways, on so many levels, that it gets hard to even imagine just how marvelous that would be. (If you're thinking that if everyone practiced these concepts, the economy would just eventually run out of money—not so. On the contrary, the economy would be in fantastic shape. But that's a topic we'll leave for an economics class, not this book.)

The point is, this kind of knowledge is for sharing. Once you've mastered the lessons presented here, you'll be well on your way toward a bright financial future. Don't stop there! Share what you've learned with others. You'll be better off, they'll be better off, and all of us will be, too.

Ready? Let's go fishing!

Part I

THE ESSENTIAL CONCEPTS

• 1 •

The Truly Amazing Power of . . .

In the world of personal finance, there is a power so great, so completely dominant, and so incomparably mighty, that any serious book about personal finance simply must start with it. But I'll warn you ahead of time that when I tell you what it is, you probably won't be too impressed. You see, as truly amazing powers go, this one doesn't make that great of a first impression. It's a little bit like meeting Clark Kent for the first time, with his thick glasses and baggy suit in his office at *The Daily Planet*. "*This* is the Man of Steel?"

Part of the reason for this is that the power we're talking about is . . . well, sneaky. When it first makes its appearance, its effect is so small as to barely be noticed at all. Only when given enough time to pick up steam does its real power begin to become apparent. Eventually, it snowballs into a force that is completely unstoppable. But when I tell you what it is, you'll say "What, *that?*"

And before we go any further, it is vital that you understand something else about this power: *it can either work for you or against you*. It isn't neutral. It picks one side, friend or foe, and gets right to work.

I am starting with this subject for two reasons: first, because it is the single most powerful idea in the whole field of personal financial management. The majority of people who are in great shape financially are in that position because they understood this power and have had the patience and discipline required to use it to their advantage. On the other side of the coin, it is even more common for people to be completely and utterly wiped out because they didn't understand that this power was working against them; or, more likely, they knew it was working against them but deeply underestimated by how much. The second reason that I'm starting with this power is that we will come back to it again and again when discussing other topics, so it is good to have a solid understanding of it right from the start.

Okay, so what is it? What is this overwhelmingly powerful force? Are you ready?

It's compounding.

Yes, compounding. If you were first introduced to it in a math class, it might have been called powers or exponents. Later on in math, or in a science class like biology, you might have covered the idea of exponential growth. Well, compounding is really the same thing, but applied to your personal finances, where it is usually referred to as *compound interest*. You can either earn compound interest or be charged compound interest. You *earn* compound interest when you save and invest; you are *charged* compound interest when you borrow.

If you think you already pretty much know about compounding, and that this chapter is just a repeat of something you've already learned elsewhere, you're not alone. Most people believe they already understand this, and maybe you're one of those who really do. But just in case, I'd like to ask you to read through the next part carefully, anyway.

You see, I am already assuming that you know the basics of how the math works, and that you already know, at some level, that the effect is really big. The main point I want you to get from this explanation is just *how* big the effect is. In fact, I want you to learn this with such a jolt that you come away thinking, "Wow! If I don't learn anything else from this book, I want to figure out how to get this power working for me and not against me." So I ask you to read on, remembering what you know about the math, but with a completely open mind about how powerful the effect is.

THE CHECKERBOARD

So here we go—time for a simple multiple-choice question. No calculator, no pen or pencil, just from what you see below: What would you rather have, A or B?

A. One million dollars, valid U.S. currency, cold hard cash, tax free, right now.

B. Picture an ordinary checkerboard, 8 rows of 8 squares each. That makes 64 squares in total. Let's say I start with the first square, in the lower left-hand corner, closest to you. I will put a penny in that square, then two pennies in the next one, four pennies in the one after that. By the time we get to the end of the first row, there are $1 + 2 + 4 + 8 + 16 + 32 + 64 + 128 = 255$ pennies, or \$2.55. Now I will go on, square by square, doubling the number of pennies each time, until I have the whole board completed. When I am finished, you get *all* the pennies on the checkerboard. Got it?

All right, I know what you're thinking—I just spent several paragraphs telling you how amazingly powerful compounding is and now throw this obvious trick question at you? Good test taker that you are, you spent 2 seconds thinking about it, then said, "Easy! B's gotta be the right answer!" Well, you're right—*of course,* it's B! But now comes the real point: again, without calculating anything directly, take a stab at just how much better B is than A. Is it twice as much? More like 100 times? Remember, I've already told you that I am trying to completely blow you away with how powerful compounding is, so go ahead and guess really high—just remember your guess.

Okay, so what's the answer? Let's start by considering how many pennies are only on the 64th and final square. The answer? Well, there are *this* many pennies: about 9,200,000,000,000,000,000, which is otherwise known as 9.2 quintillion. Oh, you want that in dollars? About $92 quadrillion. Also known as $92 million, a *billion* times.

But that is only the amount on the 64th and final square. Don't forget that there is half that amount, $46 quadrillion, on the 63rd square, and $23 quadrillion on the 62nd square, and so on. By the time you add up all the squares on the *whole* checkerboard, you've got something like $184 quadrillion.

That amount is a little hard to think about, isn't it? What does $184 quadrillion even mean? Here's one way to think of it: picture yourself living in the year 3800 B.C. The Roman Empire, the Greeks, the Egyptians—these civilizations did not yet even exist. Ancient people like King Tut, Moses, and Alexander the Great were thousands of years in the future. Emperor Qin Shi Huang wouldn't unify China and begin construction of the Great Wall for another 3,000 years. Even the prehistoric structure of Stonehenge was not yet imagined.

So what *was* going on then? One notable culture at the time was centered in Mesopotamia, and most scholars agree that there was a revolutionary new technology just breaking through there called (get ready . . .) "the wheel"! (First used in pottery making, then mill grinding. Using wheels for transportation was still a long way off.) So imagine that you're that bright Mesopotamian who came up with the first actual wheel. In your glee, you decide to celebrate by going out and spending a little money. If you walked out of your wheel-hut that afternoon and immediately began spending *1 million dollars per second,* around the clock, without stopping to eat or sleep, day after day, year after year, you'd be just getting close to $184 quadrillion—today!

Remember our A vs. B multiple-choice question? Now you know—B isn't twice as big as A, or 100 times. It is *184 billion* times bigger than A. How does that compare to your guess?

I hope I have your attention and that you don't think that I was exaggerating when I called the power of compounding truly amazing. Compounding has been called the eighth wonder of the world, and now you have an understanding of why.

MORE ABOUT COMPOUNDING

Some of you more math-friendly types probably want to see how the staggering checkerboard result was reached. Fair enough; I'll take you through it in the next paragraph. But if you're not that interested in the math and prefer just to take my word for it, that's okay too. It is much more important to appreciate fully what compounding can do than it is to understand the mathematical mechanics. So, mathletes, read on; everybody else, just feel free to skip the next paragraph.

Optional checkerboard math explanation: The number of pennies in any square is $2^{(N-1)}$, where N is whatever square you're on. Since there are 64 squares on our checkerboard, the number of pennies on the last square is 2^{63}, which just about any calculator or spreadsheet program can tell you is about 9.2 quintillion, or \$92 quadrillion. And since each square is double the preceding one, the total number of pennies on the entire checkerboard is one penny less than double what is on the last square. (You can either add up all 64 squares on a spreadsheet to get this, or use some fancy summation rules math to deduce that the total equals $2 \times N^{64}$—N^0, or \$184 quadrillion minus a penny.)

Let me assure you that you don't need any high-level math skills beyond basic arithmetic to understand fully what compounding is all about. Here's a much simpler explanation of the math involved: compounding just means taking an amount and then continually increasing it, over and over again, by the same fixed *percentage*. Since each increase is constantly proportional to each beginning amount, the increase *amounts* get bigger and bigger with each cycle.

There is a very important aspect to the way compounding works that I want to make sure you notice. Even though the math guarantees that the rate of increase will be smooth, our *perception* of it doesn't tend to work that way. Instead, unless we're paying exceptionally close attention to each and every increase, we tend to notice it in distinct phases. In the first phase, the increases are tiny. If we notice them at all, it is simply to conclude that they're too small to ever amount to much, so we dismiss them as barely worthy of attention. After enough time, though, the amounts get big enough to mildly surprise us. In this phase, the compounding has really begun to "pick up steam," and we begin to conclude that it really might add up to something significant after all. After even more time, we enter the third phase: this time, we aren't just surprised by the size of the increases—we are *astonished*! An easy way to think of these three perceptual phases is this: the "snoring" phase, the "eyebrow-raising" phase, and the "jaw-dropping" phase.

In our checkerboard example, by the time we get to the end of the first row, we have only \$2.55; the very idea that this little scheme could ever compete with $1 million in cash seems laughable. Watching the tiny increases is enough to put anyone straight to sleep. At the end of the second row the total amount has grown to $655.35. This is still far short of our $1 million alternative, but it is enough to make us raise our eyebrows, as we begin to realize that this checkerboard scheme might have a chance to really add up to something. The pennies reach the $1 million mark during the fourth row—less than half-way through—and our jaws drop with the realization that we are witnessing something astounding. With the completion of each successive row, our jaws drop further and further. We are now well into the third phase.

This is why it is really important to learn about compounding when you are young. The earlier you begin letting the power of compounding work for you, the more time you have to let compounding build up momentum and get into its most powerful stages. Someone who starts at age 20 and utilizes positive compounding until they are 60 has 40 years of compounding working to their benefit. Someone who waits until they are 40 to put compounding into place has only 20 periods of compounding to work with. Before you read this chapter, you might have thought that 40 periods would be twice as good 20. But now that you know about the checkerboard, you know the truth—40 years of compounding is *immensely* better than twice as good as 20 years.

By now, it is probably becoming quite apparent to you why compounding is such a huge concept in personal finance—because the effect is so unbelievably powerful. How powerful it is depends, as we've seen, on *how long* the compounding goes on. But it also depends on *how fast* we compound. In our example, we doubled the number of pennies with each successive square. We would have gotten a different answer if we had tripled or used some other compounding factor. In finance, the fixed percentage at which amounts are compounded is called the *interest rate*. That's why financially smart people pay very careful attention to what might seem like very small changes or differences in interest rates.

Of course, the checkerboard example isn't too realistic; doubling your money with every time period is equivalent to an interest rate of 100%. (In fact, if you find a "checkerboard" investment opportunity that promises to double your money every year, *contact me immediately*. Better still, keep your money in your pocket and contact the authorities, because it is almost certainly a scam.) We chose the checkerboard for its dramatic value, not for its realism. But that's okay, because you don't really need $184 quadrillion to be considered a financial success. I'll bet you'd settle for a measly trillion or two.

In real life, safe and legitimate investment opportunities that can consistently deliver a 10% interest rate per year are rare but not unheard of. On the other hand, it is quite easy to find real-life examples of compounding working against you at interest rates higher than 10%; almost any credit card will do it. That brings us to another important truth about compounding: as amazingly powerful as this force is when you save and invest, it will usually work even harder against you when you borrow. Why is this? It doesn't seem quite fair, does it? We could enter into a long discussion about why this is, but that is beyond the scope of what we need to cover here. For now, just realize that nearly always, the interest rates that you'll pay for borrowing are usually *higher* than those that you'll earn from saving and investing— sometimes by a little and sometimes by a lot.

CASE STUDY: COMPOUND UNIVERSITY REUNION

Xena, Yolanda, and Zelda were friends and college classmates at Compound University, and they attended their graduation ceremony together. The commencement speaker was very interesting. He spoke about the importance of saving and investing, and he stressed that making it a lifelong habit could really pay off in the long run. Further, he explained how one could invest in such a way as to consistently earn an average return of 6% per year over a long period of time, without taking any unreasonable risks.

Note: Compound University is located in a mythical land without taxes or inflation. That doesn't mean that those aren't important; they are, and we'll talk about them both later on. It just means they have nothing to do with the point of this particular case study.

After the ceremony, the trio sat down for one last cup of coffee together at their favorite hangout. Xena was the most impressed. "Wow! That guy was absolutely right, and I'm following his advice. Here's what I'm going to do: I'm going to put away $1,000 a year, every year, no matter what, for the next 40 years. Some years will be easy, some will be harder, but I won't skip a year. I'm going to invest it just like he said and earn 6% a year on it. What do you say? Let's all do it!"

Yolanda was also pretty impressed, but she had a slightly different take. "I'm with you, Xena, but I want to be realistic. I think I could manage to save $1,000 a year for quite a while, especially when I'm young. After all, we've been starving students these past few years, so I'm already pretty used to living on a tight budget. But after a while, life will get more complicated. There will be houses, kids, cars . . . kids with cars . . . and then kids in college. I just don't think it will be realistic to be planning on saving any money during those 'high-expense' times in my life. But I'll meet you halfway: I'll save $1,000 a year for the next 20 years, invest it just like you will, but then I'll stop. I won't dip into the investment during the following 20 years; I will let it continue to earn interest. But I'm just not going to add any more to it after the 20th year."

"Yolanda, you've got it completely backward," said Zelda. "Think about it. We're just graduating now, and our pay over the next few years is going to be the lowest that it will ever be. I think that $1,000 a year is out of the question when we're just starting out. Plus, we barely own *anything* now. We each have to buy a first car, a first TV, a first set of furniture, probably a first house—all out of our low starting pay. But the odds are, our pay will keep going up throughout our careers, and after enough time, $1,000 will be pocket change. So I'm doing the opposite of your plan, Yolanda. I'm going to save $1,000 a year, just like you, and for 20 years, just like you, but I am going to start in year 21, just when you're stopping. I think that is much more realistic."

After a little more discussion, they agreed to meet in exactly 40 years, at the very same spot, to compare their experiences. As an incentive, they decided that whoever was most disappointed in her strategy would be the one who had learned the most valuable lessons, and therefore should be the commencement speaker for that year's graduates. Since none of them relished the idea of publicly sharing why their strategy was so disappointing, they all left that day firmly resolved to follow their respective plans to the letter.

Forty years later—exactly—they arrived simultaneously at the coffee shop, which was still in business at the very same location. And they each came with reports in their hands, showing the current balance in their investment accounts. In remarkable displays of determination and persistence, each had followed through—exactly—on the plans that they'd outlined 40 years earlier. And the commencement speaker had been right about his investment recommendations; Xena, Yolanda, and Zelda each earned an average of 6%—exactly—on the amounts that they'd invested.

Now, before the three friends reveal their investment balances, what do you think the outcome is going to be? I'm betting that you have a pretty good idea of who will finish first, second, and third. But I am also betting that unless you couldn't restrain yourself from doing the math, you'll find the answer pretty eye-opening. So, back to the coffee shop . . .

The three friends each laid their investment reports on the table. And the outcome was:

Xena:	$164,000
Yolanda:	$125,000
Zelda:	$39,000

Zelda was flabbergasted, and her jaw literally dropped. "Xena, I guess I knew all along that you'd win, since you invested more than either Yolanda or me. But Yolanda, how did *you* beat me? And by *so much?* I mean, we invested the exact same amount, but you have over three times as much as I do. What can possibly explain that big of a difference?"

"Compounding," replied Yolanda. "You see, in the last 40 years, I've learned that it is unbelievably powerful. You might even say that it's truly amazing."

Xena added, "Compounding starts out slowly, Zelda, but then it picks up steam. Even though you invested the same amount as Yolanda, she had the power of 20 *more* years of compounding working for her, around the clock. But don't feel bad—you must be very happy that you spent $1,000 extra every year for the first 20 years on indispensable necessities, aren't you?"

Zelda was beginning to get a little defensive. "Well, I still think I had the right idea by not starting until year 21. But now I realize that I made just one small mistake. I should have invested a little more than $1,000 per year to make up for Yolanda's head start. I bet it wouldn't have taken that much, either. I wonder how much?"

Xena clicked a few buttons on a calculator and said, "Not just *a little* more than $1,000, Zelda. You'd have had to save and invest well over $3,200 a year to have gotten the same result as Yolanda. By waiting to start your savings as long as you did, you made it much, much more difficult to catch up."

By this time, Zelda was starting to see the light. Inspired, she grabbed Xena's calculator, which had a convenient graphing function. After a few minutes, she turned the display toward her friends and showed them a graph (see figure 1.1).

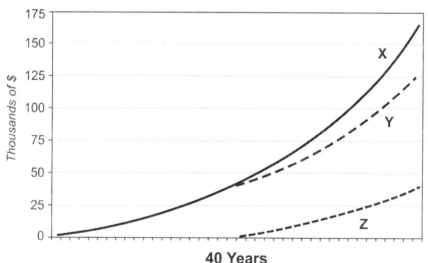

40 Years

Figure 1.1.   Investment balances for Xena, Yolanda, and Zelda.

"Wow! Now I see what happened. Look, Yolanda: after 20 years of investing, I was at exactly the same place that you were after 20—$39,000. But you let that amount keep compounding for 20 additional years. And that allowed your investment to go from $39,000 to $125,000, while you didn't have to do anything but sit there and watch it grow. I had the same amount of time, but I used my extra 20 years of delaying to . . . buy 'stuff.' Well, all that 'stuff' is gone now, but you still have your $125,000. How could I have been so shortsighted?"

"Cheer up, Zelda," said Xena. "At least you've got the $39,000 to build from. I know lots of our classmates who started borrowing what seemed like small amounts right after graduating. I guess they wanted to buy even more 'stuff' than you. They've learned all about compounding too, but in a much more painful way than you did. In fact, most of them would be glad to trade places with you. Maybe one of *them* should give the commencement address."

"Commencement address!" exclaimed Zelda. "I forgot all about that. Well, I know exactly what I'm going to say, and it's *not* going to be 'spend now, save later.'"

SUMMARY

1. Compounding is the mightiest force in the personal finance universe!
2. The effect of compounding starts out small and slow, which is one reason why so many people fail to appreciate its power. But eventually it picks up steam, and then the growth *really* accelerates, and the numbers can get very big very fast.
3. How much power compounding has depends on the amount that you start with, how long the compounding goes on (the number of compounding periods), and the fixed-percentage increase that occurs after each period (the interest rate).
4. Compounding works *for* you when saving and investing, but *against* you when borrowing.
5. Interest rates when borrowing are usually higher than interest rates when saving and investing.
6. Compounding hugely rewards early investments, compared to later ones. The rewards for investing when young are disproportionally very high, and so are the penalties for waiting. It can't be emphasized too much or too often—*start saving as early as you possibly can.*
7. We will discuss long-term investing much more thoroughly later; for now just remember that your long-term savings will grow the most

the earlier you start, and the higher the average rate of compounding. But . . .

8. Caution! It is a big mistake to begin investing before you know exactly what you're doing. So begin saving as soon as you possibly can, but keep these savings in a nice safe savings account until after we cover long-term investing in part IV. In the meantime, you'll still be getting *some* of the power of compounding working for you.

• 2 •

Your Financial Health

If you want to know how tall someone is, you have them stand on a level surface, back against a wall, then make a mark on the wall and get out a tape measure. If you want to know how much someone weighs, you have them stand on a properly calibrated scale. Simple, right?

But what if you wanted to measure someone's financial condition? When I said earlier that our goal is to achieve a strong financial position, what did I mean by that? How is personal financial strength measured? What is the equivalent of inches or pounds when it comes to personal financial health?

It's an important question, because you won't be able to tell if you're succeeding unless you've got a way to measure your progress. To find your way using a map, the first step is identifying the you-are-here point—and knowing where you are requires a measurement.

The way we measure personal financial health is called *net worth*. Net worth isn't an opinion or an impression; it is a very well-defined measure with a specific definition that is widely accepted. We'll describe how to calculate it shortly, but before we do, most people find it helpful to understand it conceptually first—and for that, we need an analogy.

THE NET WORTH BATHTUB

Think of an ordinary bathtub. When you turn on the faucet, water runs into the bathtub. The water will stay in the tub until the drain is opened. This tub has a really big drain, and it is adjustable. So it is possible to drain the water out more slowly than it is coming in, faster than it is coming in, or at exactly the same rate. Got it?

You've probably already figured out that the faucet represents money coming in. This is income from all sources: the paycheck from your job or jobs, your lottery winnings, gift checks from your grandparents, whatever. The drain, of course, is money going out: paying your bills, buying airplane tickets, money in wallets that you lose, and so on. Obviously, when water is coming into the tub faster than it is draining out, the water level in the bathtub will rise; when water is draining out faster than it is coming in from the faucet, the water level will fall.

Now here is the point: when it comes to personal financial management, what we care about most is the water level in the bathtub. The water level in an individual's bathtub represents that person's net worth. Other terms for a high water level are *rich* or *wealthy*. So the object of the game is to increase your net worth. Fill up that bathtub! All that we have talked about, and will talk about, are strategies to increase your net worth. Any financial decision that you make should be made with net worth in mind.

Some very important realizations are apparent from the bathtub analogy; in fact, they're so obvious that they hardly need to be pointed out. If you want the water level in the bathtub to rise, then the drain has to be adjusted to a rate that is slower than the faucet is running. And the longer the drain is running slower than the faucet, the higher the water will rise. Stated a different way, it isn't the *absolute* rate that the drain and faucet are running that is important—it is the *relationship* between the two.

COMMON MISCONCEPTIONS

Even though these implications are quite readily apparent when it comes to bathtubs, it is amazing how murky people's thinking can get when applying the same ideas to personal finance. The two most common misconceptions are to confuse either the faucet or the drain with the water level. Let's look at them one at a time:

Misconception #1: The faucet is all that matters. A fast-running faucet means a really high income, right? In many different ways, the faucet gets so much publicity that it is easy to see how some people get the idea that this is really the only important goal. In our culture, a high income is regarded as prestigious or even glamorous. Controlling expenses and being thrifty (or watching the drain closely) are often regarded as the opposite—only for those with very low incomes.

Anytime income tax rates are in the news, the news media like to refer to people in the higher income tax brackets as "the rich." This serves to further the misconception that high income automatically means high net worth.

High earners in the upper tax brackets may or may not have parlayed that high income into substantial wealth; it depends on how well—or not—they have managed their drain.

Misconception #2: The drain is all that matters. A fast-running drain means lots and lots of spending. If we see someone who is driving a luxury car, maybe even has a few extra cars, lives in an expensive home, and takes a lot of extravagant vacations, it is not uncommon to hear their neighbors conclude, "Oh, that person is really rich!" (In fact, one of the main reasons that this person buys all those things may be precisely because he or she *wants* the neighbors to say that.)

The idea that a wide-open drain is proof of a full bathtub is regularly reinforced culturally, too. It is a favorite theme of advertisers; after all, it doesn't do the advertiser any good when you tighten your drain controls. Their job is to get you into a "spend spend spend" frame of mind. It's also a favorite theme in most popular entertainment. A rich-looking hero speeding away from his or her mansion in an ultra-hot sports car probably captures your attention a little better than one who is huddled over a spreadsheet, intently preparing next month's budget. Just remember: *your financial life is not fictional.* Advertisers and media have their agendas, and that's fine—you have your own.

Despite these misconceptions, the truth is pretty easy to understand when you think about the bathtub analogy. Neither the faucet, nor the drain, is the be-all and end-all when it comes to increasing net worth; it is the relationship between the two. A fast-running faucet provides a better opportunity to increase net worth, but it won't happen without proportionate drain control. Watching expenses carefully may not be portrayed as something that wealthy people need to be concerned with, but controlling spending is essential to building a high net worth.

A famous book titled *The Millionaire Next Door* by Thomas J. Stanley featured detailed, survey-based descriptions of the lifestyles of the wealthiest people in the United States. In fact, the subtitle of the book is *The Surprising Secrets of America's Wealthy.* By now, you might be able to guess what the surprise is: the most common profile of America's wealthy does *not* conform to either the big faucet or the big drain stereotype. In fact, it is surprisingly common for those with big faucets to fall into a big-drain habit that leaves them with only modest water levels. Instead, it is quite a bit more common for wealth to be built by consistent drain control. Most of America's wealthy turn out to live in much less expensive homes than they could afford, to buy used cars, and to generally avoid any spending that could be considered extravagant.

Does this surprise you? It is certainly a very different picture than the way that "wealthy" is usually portrayed in the popular culture. But it makes sense when you think about it, using the bathtub analogy. In a way, it is a classic illustration of the old saying "You can't have your cake and eat it, too." America's wealthy *have* their cake. America's biggest spenders have *eaten* most of theirs, and now it's gone.

Take a minute to think about this . . . it is really important for this point to sink in. Once it does sink in, you'll never think about spending money in the same way again. You'll stop associating spending with what it can buy you today; instead, you'll view spending as lost opportunities to save, invest, and grow your net worth. This way of thinking will then become a power-ful *transformational habit* for you. If you want the freedom to retire early, or to weather any kind of unanticipated financial storm, or to be in a position to help those close to you if needed, you'll want to have most of your cake left. That means that you'll have to keep a careful eye on how much of it you eat—plain and simple.

MORE ABOUT NET WORTH

How do you measure your own or someone else's net worth? How is it cal-culated? A really complete, accurate, and technically correct answer to that question would require a stack of books and months of study—way beyond the scope of what we need to do here. The simpler answer is that net worth is *assets minus liabilities*. Your assets are the financial value of everything you own, valued at today's fair market value—what you could sell them for today, *not* what you originally paid for them. Here are some typical assets: all the money you have in the bank today (checking and savings accounts), plus all of the investments you have (valued at today's price, not the price when you bought them), plus all of the things that you own, like houses, cars, property, com-puters, furniture, and clothes (valued at what you could sell them for today, not what you bought them for), plus all the money that anyone else owes you (assuming that there is a high chance of it actually being repaid). If you add all of that up, that is the value of your assets.

Liabilities are simpler: this is the money that you owe others. For many people, their biggest liability is the unpaid mortgage balance on their house. Any credit card or student debt you may have goes here too, as do the unpaid balances on any other loans, for things like cars, giant TVs. (More on credit card debt and car loans later. Hint: credit cards and cars can be good, but credit card *debt* and car *loans* are bad.) Now, take the value of all of your assets and subtract the value of all of your liabilities, and what you're left with is your net worth. This is what we're trying to maximize.

Is it possible to have liabilities greater than assets—a *negative* net worth? You bet, and it's no fun: it's called being in debt. And if your net worth gets negative enough, it's called bankruptcy.

It is important to emphasize that assets are measured at their *current resale value*. Here are three examples.

1. You just went out today and bought a brand new car from a dealer for $25,000 in cash. You've reduced your cash by $25,000, but now you have a $25,000 car, so there's no change to your net worth—right? Wrong. As soon as you drive the car off the dealer's lot, it isn't a new car anymore; it has just become a *used* car. Because of that, you can't resell it for $25,000; you might get something more like $18,000. As a result of your purchase, your net worth has just *declined* by $7,000.

2. Imagine that you've taken an around-the-world cruise, which cost you $7,000. Yes, I know—the memories are priceless. But from a net worth point of view, you can't actually resell *any* of that experience—so again your net worth has declined by $7,000.

3. Now suppose that you've spent $7,000 on an investment like a very low-cost equity index fund. (If you don't know what that means, relax: we'll cover this thoroughly during part IV.) In this case, not only *can* you resell this investment someday, *you fully intend to*. In fact, your explicit goal is to resell it someday for much more than you originally paid for it. So what is the net-worth effect of this $7,000 investment? As the value of this investment goes up and down, so does your net worth. If you later check the market price of the fund and you find out that you can resell it for $10,000, then your net worth has just *increased* by $3,000. Instead, if it has fallen to $4,000, then your net worth has just *declined* by $3,000.

These examples make it clear that our simple bathtub analogy needs a little refinement. There is a fundamental difference between a pure expense (like the cruise) and a pure investment (like the index fund). Only pure expenses go immediately down the drain. In contrast, investment values can go up or down, causing the water level to either rise or fall.

The car is an example of something that is partly expense and partly investment. Cars aren't the only example of expense/investment combinations; lots of big-ticket purchases fall into this category, most famously houses. We'll spend all of part III talking about expense/investment purchases like these. Now that you understand much more about net worth and the fundamental difference between expenses and investments, it will come as no surprise to you what our part III strategy is going to be: how to minimize the effect of the expense portion of your purchase while improving the performance of the investment portion.

THE FIRST RULE

Most of part I is devoted to explaining some fundamental concepts to you; more specific guidance about what to do, and how and when to do it will come later. But here is an exception. That's right: now that you've got a solid understanding of the relationship between net worth, income, and spending—here comes your First Rule.

We're calling this the First Rule because it is the first one you'll be given—but that's not the only reason for the name. The rule you're about to learn is also first in importance. This rule stands before all others as "the prime directive" of personal financial management. If you always follow it, your chances of overall financial success are extremely good. The First Rule gets your financial river that we talked about earlier flowing in the direction that you want it to, so you can start swimming downstream instead of upstream. Following it will enable you to do everything else that will be covered in the rest of the book. But if you don't follow it, it is not likely you'll even be in a position to follow most of the rest of the upcoming advice. Are you ready?

Save at least 10% of everything you ever earn.

This isn't a some-of-the-time rule or even a most-of-the-time rule—it is an *all-the-time* rule. You do this month after month and year after year, starting now. You become so consistent about this that it becomes more like a year-round habit than a conscious decision.

By the way, that's 10% of the *gross* amount that you earn. If the top line on your paycheck says $2,000, and then various deductions whittle it down to $1,300 before it actually gets deposited into your account, then your goal is to save at least $200—not $130.

Where do you save it? We'll elaborate more in part II, but for now just put it into a savings account. Make sure that this account is separate from any other accounts you have; you will want to see this account growing *only* from your consistent savings, not mixed in along with any other funds.

Don't withdraw from this account unless you are experiencing a true financial emergency. If you have an urgent need, save up for it separately.

Remember that 10% is the bare minimum. It is your *starting* point for considering how much to save, and you go upward from there. If you want your financial river to flow faster, and to achieve financial success sooner, then save more than 10%. If you want your post-income-producing years to be at a higher rather than a lower lifestyle, then save more than 10%. But save at least 10%, minimum, always.

Just in case it isn't obvious, following the First Rule automatically means that you don't borrow money—*ever*. Borrowing is the opposite of saving, so if you are consistently saving at least 10% of everything you ever earn, month after month and year after year, then that rules out borrowing of all kinds. A loan from the bank? Never. Buying a car with "unbelievable financing"? Nope. An infomercial special with "six easy installments"? Not for you. Unpaid credit card balances? Definitely not! The *only* possible exception that you will ever consider to the never-borrow-any-money rule is a mortgage on a house, which we'll cover in part III.

In most areas of financial life, maturity and experience are an advantage. But when it comes to the First Rule, youth and inexperience actually give you the edge. The sooner in your financial life you start applying the power of compounding to your savings, the bigger this advantage is. And if you make a habit of this right from the start, it won't even seem like a sacrifice; you will never miss that 10% plus because you never got in the habit of spending it in the first place. The longer you wait until you adopt this habit, the more painful it will feel when you do, and the less likely you are to stick with it. So why not establish this habit right away? Along with the rest of the advice that you'll get in this book, adopting this habit right now is the surest path to a strong financial future.

SUMMARY

1. In any endeavor, it is critical to understand what the objective is and how to measure it. In personal financial management, the objective is a strong net worth. *Rich, wealthy,* and *high net worth* all mean the same thing.
2. A bathtub can be used as an analogy to understand the relationship among income, spending, and wealth; income is water coming in through the faucet, expenses are represented by water leaving through the drain, and wealth is the resulting water level in the bathtub.
3. Net worth is calculated as assets (things of financial value that you own, measured at today's fair market value) minus liabilities (debts that you owe to others).
4. Having a high income doesn't necessarily ensure high net worth. Neither does a high level of spending. Yet these are often mistakenly assumed to be the objectives.

5. The key to increasing net worth is to ensure that spending (water leaving the bathtub through the drain) is consistently less than income (water coming in from the faucet).

6. According to the book *The Millionaire Next Door*, the most common profile of wealthy people in the United States comes as a surprise to most people; it is various levels of income paired with proportionately modest levels of spending. Evidently the relatively unglamorous aspect of drain control is actually highly useful in achieving financial success.

7. The First Rule of personal financial management is this: *Save at least 10% of everything you ever earn.*

8. The 10% savings is 10% of *gross* income (before any withholding or deductions).

9. Following the First Rule automatically rules out borrowing of any kind, because borrowing is the opposite of saving.

10. The earlier in your financial life you can begin practicing the First Rule, the better. Saving at least 10% becomes a near-automatic habit and therefore isn't viewed as a sacrifice or an imposition.

• *3* •

The Big Picture

The bathtub analogy helped you get a solid understanding of the relationship among income, spending, and saving. You have also now learned what net worth is and how to calculate it in simple terms. Now it is time to extend your understanding even further. To do that, we need to add a new dimension: *time*. The millionaires next door that we discussed in the last chapter built high net worth by consistently and methodically spending less than their income over a *long* period of time. For them, this didn't happen by accident—it happened because they adopted a habit of long-term thinking when it comes to personal finances.

Many people fail to develop a habit of long-term thinking because of the urgency of the current month's financial realities. Most of your regularly occurring bills will require monthly payments, and you'll be constantly and visibly reminded of their due dates. If you are late in meeting these obligations, the reminders will multiply almost instantly. Unless you develop a habit of paying everything on time, financial trouble will start piling up quickly. Most people realize that and make every effort to stay ahead of their monthly financial deadlines.

But here are some facts of financial life that you may not be aware of: paying attention to the current month is required, but it is the bare minimum. People who pay attention *only* to the current month are probably headed to a low long-term net worth. People who pay attention to the current month and the next several are probably headed to moderate long-term net worth. But the people who are headed to a high net worth have developed the habit of very long-term thinking—months, years, and even decades. They see the big picture of how seemingly small monthly gains can accumulate over the course of their financial life.

This doesn't mean that an ultra-detailed multiyear financial plan is necessary. A long-term outlook is a *way of thinking* rather than some specific planning technique. We want to get *you* in the habit of long-term financial thinking; this is a *transformational habit* with the power to deeply alter your financial perspective for the rest of your life. Helping you understand and develop this way of thinking is the purpose of this chapter.

To accomplish this, we're going to use a tool—an income, spending, and net worth graph. The main advantage that it has over the bathtub is that it emphasizes the effect of income and spending habits over a long period of time. Our graph can be thought of as a historical record of the faucet and the drain for any given household. Because of the long time scale, each graph is like seeing a summary of that household's entire financial life at a single glance. We'll call this view the big-picture graph.

In this chapter, we'll take a look at big-picture graphs for several hypothetical households. One purpose of doing that is to get you thinking in much longer time frames than you are probably used to. But there is another purpose, too: as you look through the various big-picture graphs, you will begin to develop some very useful insights about how various financial habits play out over the course of an entire financial life. In turn, I'm hoping that these insights develop into a few definite conclusions—the kind of conclusions that are particularly valuable for *you* to have in place right from the start of your financial life. (Just to make sure, though, I'll spell out the hoped-for conclusions in the chapter summary.) Are you ready? Let's take a look at our first example, for household #1, shown in figure 3.1.

Before trying to interpret exactly what this graph is showing, let's first go through each of its parts to make sure that you understand what you're seeing.

The lighter-shaded line. The lighter line represents income from all sources—your primary job, any part-time or supplemental income you earn, rent that you are paid, inheritances, casino winnings—everything coming in is included.

The darker-shaded line. The dark line represents expenses. As in the analogy of the bathtub drain, we're considering this to be money going out for expenses only—not for investments. Especially when it's viewed over multiple years, you can think of the dark line as representing lifestyle. An extravagant, luxurious lifestyle requires an extended *high* dark line, and a very basic, subsistence-only type of lifestyle would be shown as an extended, very *low* dark line.

The space *between* the lines. The gap between the lines represents the effect on net worth. When the light line is above the dark line, all is well, because net worth is increasing—the bathtub is filling up. We'll show this by shading in the space between the lines in a light tone. The bigger the favorable gap between the lines, and the longer it is sustained, the bigger the lighter-

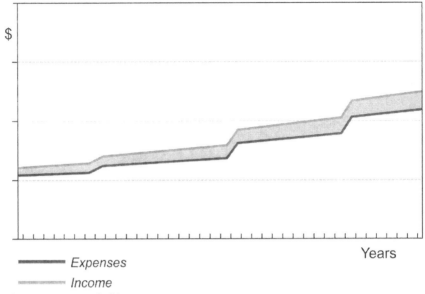

Expenses

Income

Figure 3.1. Household #1.

shaded area. When the opposite is true—when expenses exceed income, and the water level is going down—we'll indicate that by coloring in the space in a dark tone.

An easy way to help remember: lighter tones means the financial sun is shining. The income line is lighter, and lighter fill-ins are used when the household is saving. But when the financial clouds appear, everything darkens. The darker line represents expenses going out, and the darker fill-in represents a declining water level in the financial bathtub.

Economists have some special words for the lighter- and darker-shaded areas: *saving* and *dissaving*, respectively. To an economist—and in our graphs— the lighter-shaded savings area could mean literally saving money and depositing it in some kind of account, or it could mean reducing debt, if there is any. Likewise, the darker-shaded dissaving area could either mean borrowing money or it could mean drawing down savings, if there are any.

The time frame. The period of time that we are focusing on is the 1st and 2nd thirds of the primary earner's (or earners') financial life, so you can think of the horizontal axis as showing about 40 years' worth of earning and spending, spanning roughly the ages early 20s through early 60s. In other words, for most people, these would represent all the incoming earning years, prior to retirement.

The dollar scale. It isn't labeled, because the *absolute* dollar levels don't matter. What matters is the *relationship* between the lines. So you can just think of the dollar scale as being low, medium, and high as you go from bottom to top.

Now that you understand the graph, what is it telling us about household #1? First notice the lighter-shaded line: money coming in. In this example, the line is continually going upward—usually gradually, but there are a few abrupt upward movements, too. The earner in graph #1 has managed to find a career that rewards continual growth in skills and experience; that's what the gradual upward slope represents. The more abrupt jumps could be promotions (to a higher pay scale), shifts to a higher-paying employer, or even a move to a higher-paying type of job. Continual upward growth in income is certainly the goal, but of course, it is dangerous to count on it.

What about the darker-shaded line—spending? The graph shows that household #1 has taken a very responsible and disciplined approach to spending. There isn't a single year where spending has exceeded income, and therefore borrowing has never been necessary. If this household were a government, you would say that they consistently ran a small surplus, always "living within their means." (I'd vote for them on that basis alone!) Because of this responsible approach to spending, the gap between the lines is all shaded in the lighter tone, indicating consistently growing net worth. By the end of the time period shown here, this household has accumulated a nicely positive net worth. Household #1 gets at least a "B" in personal financial management.

Notice that household #1's dark (expense) line never goes downward. Why is this worth noticing? In addition to the purely financial effect, changes in spending level have an important psychological impact, too. The spending line is correlated with lifestyle—so when the dark line moves downward, lifestyle takes a step backward. Downward lifestyle adjustments aren't the end of the world and needn't be viewed as such. For example, a lifestyle reduction caused by forces outside your own control isn't too objectionable, because everyone in the household understands the reasons behind it. Likewise, a lifestyle reduction that you consciously decide to make in order to improve your financial condition can actually be seen in a positive light. But if a household is *forced* into a lifestyle reduction as a direct result of previous overly high spending levels—that is no fun at all.

The psychological effects of spending changes are usually temporary. When the dark line goes up—even a little—everybody in the household is happy about it. The earners are the household heroes, and life is good. Before long, though, everyone in the household adjusts to this new, spendier lifestyle, and it becomes the new normal. On the other hand, when the dark line goes down—even a little—for reasons that could have been avoided, *nobody* is happy. Even if the new, lower expense level is no lower than a level experienced in the recent past—a lifestyle that was perfectly satisfactory then—

moving back to it will *feel* like a setback. Household members will feel entitled to the previously higher spending level and will grumble when forced backward, at least for a while.

The point is to try to avoid the *need* to reduce spending, by being very careful about ever increasing it in the first place. That's why household #1 gets a "B" instead of an "A." Even though spending is always less than income, notice that spending jumps—immediately—every time that income does. It would have been wiser to postpone those spending increases until there was more breathing room between the income and expense lines.

Now that you've got the hang of looking at big-picture graphs, let's take a look at another household (see figure 3.2).

Household #2 is a mess, isn't it? It looks like this household has been "kinda sorta" trying to keep spending from getting too far out of hand, but they're not very good at it. The income line is consistently going upward—in fact, it is the exact same income line as household #1. But household #2 just can't seem to contain its spending appetite. Even though the income line is going up, the darker (expense) line exceeds it during several of the years. It's easy to spot those years, because the gap between the lines is shaded in a darker tone. You know what that means: household #2 has borrowed money at those times, which is the *last* thing that anyone wanting to build net worth should ever do. Household #2 is learning firsthand about high rates of compound interest working against them.

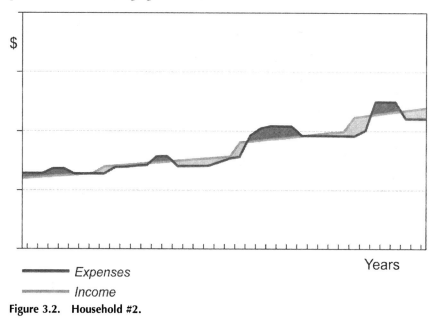

Figure 3.2. Household #2.

The jumps in the expense line probably represent some large purchases that they really wanted but hadn't saved up for; so they bought anyway and financed the purchase. (Financing is just another word for borrowing—plain and simple.) The expense-line jumps may also have been financial emergencies (uninsured damages or medical issues, for example) that they were not prepared for and that also could have led to a need to borrow money. No matter what caused the borrowing, you can see that it got them into trouble from time to time, and the only way for them to recover was to reduce spending. In fact, you can see that they had to use the dreaded "expense-line reduction strategy" not just once, but several times. Ouch! By the end of the time shown, household #2 has paid off a good amount of its debt but still probably has a negative net worth.

Now here is the kicker: as messy and uneven as the picture looks, the sad truth is that household #2 is a pretty typical U.S. household. Little emphasis is placed on saving and accumulating net worth. As a result, there is virtually no reserve for any unexpected negative surprises. The earners in household #2 will have to keep earning for as long as they can, because little has been put aside for retirement. The motto seems to be "I'm going to spend every bit that I possibly can—and maybe even a little more." Grade: C-. (And that's probably generous.)

As long as we're showing examples of what *not* to do, look at household #3 (see figure 3.3). This household can't be given any grade other than "F."

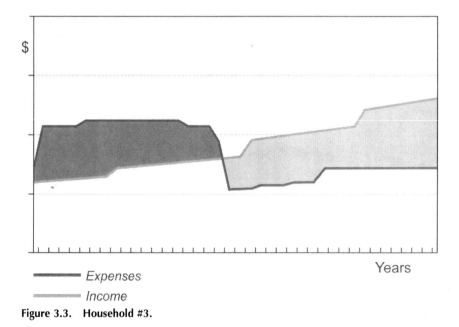

Figure 3.3. Household #3.

Here is a household that discovered just how easy it is to get credit as long as they have a respectable income line. Household #3 looks like they fell in love with credit cards. What happened when they reached their credit limits? Easy—they just got *new* credit cards to pay off their *old* ones. It's a nice lifestyle, too—while it lasts. But obviously, this approach will implode sooner or later; it is easy to see on the graph exactly where this happens.

If you look at the entire time period shown, the total amount of dark ink and light ink is about the same. So that must mean that by the end of the graph, household #3 has finally dug their way out of debt, right? Wrong!

Don't forget the most powerful force in the world of personal finance—compounding. Because of compounding, "early" ink is more powerful than "later" ink. Surpluses or deficits early in your financial life have a disproportionally strong effect. In terms of the graph, this means that the further to the left any given ink tone appears, the stronger its effect. Since the entire left side of household #3's graph is covered in dark ink, it will take much, much more light ink on the right side to balance it out. In other words, household #3 is still heavily in debt—and will be for years to come.

The next graph that we'll look at (see figure 3.4) shows the kind of household that many people aspire to. But let's see how well it holds up under closer scrutiny.

Household #4 is one that would certainly be portrayed in our popular culture as "very rich." This household enjoys an extremely high income and

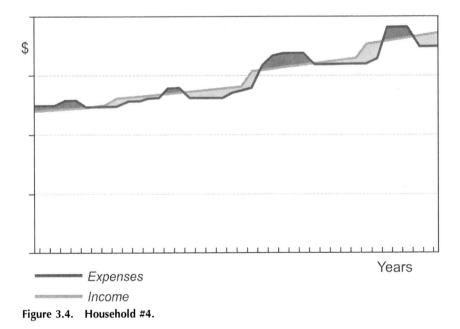

Expenses

Income

Figure 3.4. Household #4.

all of the prestige and status that goes along with it. And we can see that the extremely high income is matched with extremely high spending—meaning an extravagant and luxurious lifestyle. Very big faucet, very big drain. But what about the water level in their bathtub?

There's not much there. They're not the millionaire next door; they're the household living in the nicest part of town who everyone *thinks* are millionaires—but *aren't*. Household #4's very high income has given them the opportunity to fill their bathtub very fast, but they've blown their chance by spending at rates just as high. As a result, this apparently very rich household isn't rich at all. Their net worth is minimal—probably slightly negative. No doubt they've enjoyed all the spending, but they've constructed a lifestyle that is utterly dependent on continued high income. If anything happens to the income levels, they face a very, very abrupt reduction in lifestyle. They are just like household #2, but with more zeroes after all the numbers. So household #4's grade is the same as household #2's: a "C-."

Take a close look at the next big picture in figure 3.5:

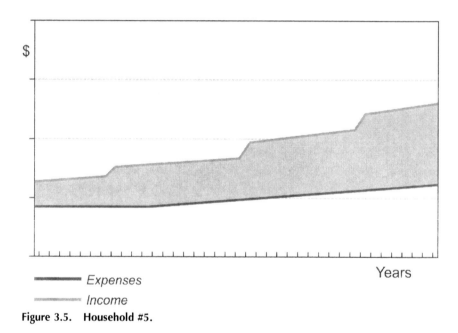

Figure 3.5.   Household #5.

If you've been waiting to see an "A+," you've found it. Even though the income is relatively modest, household #5 has managed to accumulate a very considerable net worth. How did they do it? They did it through very careful management of their spending. In particular, I'd like you to notice how this household adjusted their spending the first time that income took an abrupt jump: they didn't! They kept their spending—and lifestyle—exactly the same as before. This strategy allowed all of the new income to be saved. Only well after this higher level of income looks like it is going to be permanent does the spending line begin to increase—and even then, at a slower rate than income.

Let's look at another, quite different big-picture scenario. Have you ever wondered what your financial life would look like if you were a top-level rock star, supermodel, or pro athlete? Somebody who earns an extremely high income very early in their financial life, at least for a while? Of course, it is fun to imagine yourself in that kind of glamorous situation, but the real reason for taking a look at it is because it provides an opportunity to bring together several of the points that we've been discussing throughout the chapter. Take a look at our final two graphs, figures 3.6 and 3.7.

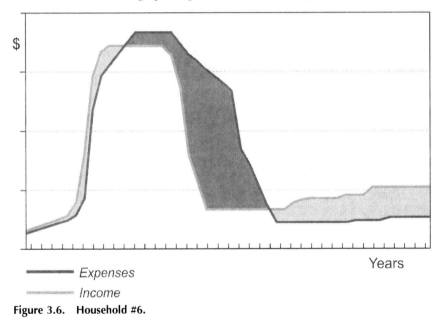

Expenses

Income

Years

Figure 3.6.   Household #6.

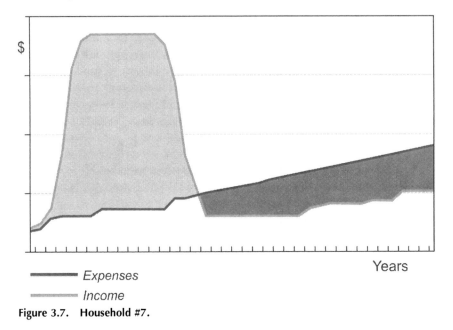

$

Years

━━━━━ *Expenses*

▭▭▭▭▭ *Income*

Figure 3.7.   Household #7.

Figure 3.6 shows a household that hasn't handled their newfound fortune and fame very well. While the earner's career is on the way up, so are
expenses. Early on, the big jumps in income are so unexpectedly large that it
is almost impossible to ramp spending up that fast, so a little bit of light ink
shows up. But it doesn't last long. Soon this household gets a taste of spending *really* big money—and likes it! Income inevitably levels off, but spending
doesn't. Finally the party is over, and income begins to fall rapidly. For a
household like #6, it is very difficult to give up the high-spending lifestyle,
and you can see that there is a sustained attempt to hold on to it even well after
the supporting income is gone. The result of these attempts is a huge accumulation of debt, and when debt limits are finally reached, the result is a painful,
and probably very humbling, expense-line reduction. They were probably
being told by others that they were "set for life" as new contracts were being
signed. But even though that opportunity was there, it didn't work out that
way. As a homework assignment, I will leave it to you to assign a letter grade
to this household's personal financial management performance.

In contrast, household #7 represents the financially *smart* rock star/su-
permodel/pro athlete. The income line is exactly the same as household #6,
but this household wisely refrained from getting caught up in the associated
high-spending lifestyle. As a result, when the high-income party is over, they
are able to walk away from it gracefully and still be in a position to gradually
but consistently improve their lifestyle over the course of their financial lives.

Because ink that is accumulated early in your financial life is relatively stronger than mid- or late-financial-life ink, the huge net worth accumulated early (the left part of the graph) can be put to work compounding for an exceptionally long time. Household #7 truly is "set for life." (Some of you may have noticed that I have ignored the effect of income taxes in this example, and you're right. We'll cover income taxes later; for now, they would just unnecessarily complicate the main point of the example.)

AN IMPORTANT DEBATE: IS IT WORTH IT?

At this point, you may be thinking, "Enough of this! I've read enough to understand what your message is, and I don't like it. You're saying that the best thing to do is to scrimp and save my way to a high net worth. But what's the point of having a high net worth in the first place if I don't get to spend any of it? I want to enjoy at least some of the money that I work so hard for."

Fair point, and it is a common objection—so common, in fact, that this is what keeps many people from using, or in some cases from even considering, a spending-management-oriented approach like the one that I am strongly recommending.

Because saving money by carefully controlling spending is such a fundamental part of building a strong net worth, I am going to respond to the objection thoroughly—and vigorously. Consider these four points.

1. The strategy works. This strategy isn't an untested theory, and it isn't limited to only unusual circumstances. Far from it. This is the *most common* profile of how people become wealthy in the United States, even though it comes as a surprise to most people. This is one of the most fundamental messages of *The Millionaire Next Door*, and it is especially relevant to those just starting out in their financial life.

2. Retirement. When you stop working, the income line will be reduced—probably by quite a bit. The days of employer-funded pensions are virtually gone, and there is a substantial amount of doubt about how much you can count on Social Security by the time *you* become eligible for it. Unless you want to keep working indefinitely—assuming that you are even able to—the money that you are earning now will have to cover your current expenses as well as future ones. If you've accumulated a sufficient net worth, you will be in a position to choose whether to keep working or not, and when. If you choose to stop, you can draw on your accumulated net worth to cover your expenses without having to experience an expense-line (and lifestyle) reduction. If you have opted for current gratification throughout your working years, though, you won't have any choice but to continue working.

3. Peace of mind. Imagine the financial stress level in household #2 compared with household #5. The people in household #5 know that if a recession occurs, or a major uninsured loss happens, or an unexpected temporary loss of income comes to pass, they have the reserves to withstand it. Instead of constantly worrying about their financial life, they are free to expand and enrich all the other areas of their life. In household #2, however, any one of those would result in a painful downward lifestyle adjustment. Which household would *you* rather live in?

4. Sacrifice. Household #5 achieved a very strong net worth without ever having to experience a downward-moving expense line. Their lifestyle has been very modest, but they've never actually had to scale it back. Clearly, their strategy has involved some significant sacrifices—but not all sacrifices "feel" the same. For household #5, financial sacrifice has meant "not spending money on things that we'd like to, even though we *could* afford to." But this kind of sacrifice doesn't feel nearly as bad as an expense-line reduction, which means "not spending money on the very same things that we used to spend money on, became quite accustomed to, and even felt entitled to."

In short, you have a choice to make, and it is an important one. Whatever you choose, I hope that you'll make it a conscious and deliberate choice, not just something that you drift into by default without ever realizing it—or go back and forth on while your financial clock is ticking and your opportunity to lock in some really powerful long-term compounding slips away.

Your choice is very, very basic, and just about the oldest one known to humankind. You have to choose between two fundamentally different approaches: *immediate* or *delayed* gratification. It really is as simple as choosing whether to have your cake for the future or to eat it now.

Money you spend is simply gone. Money you save will not only be there for the future, but it grows *exponentially* while it is patiently waiting for you to use it. If you spend it instead, you're giving up that amount of money *plus* its future growth. This is what Zelda from Compound University learned the hard way—the sooner you begin saving, the greater the compounded result. And thanks to the math of compounding, the difference isn't minor, it's *huge*.

If you're thinking, "I'm going to split the difference and do a little of each," be careful. While such a choice is possible, it requires quite a bit of discipline to pull off successfully. If you're choosing this middle ground simply to avoid having to make a decision, then the odds are very much against you, and you're very likely to slide into a habit of choosing immediate gratification by default. But if you're serious enough about it to commit yourself to the necessary discipline, you can choose a strategy somewhat like household #1. It is good enough for "B" results; you'll be able to enjoy some of your money as you earn it, while still accumulating at least a modest net worth.

But I'd much *rather* see you adopt a strategy like household #5 and go for a really superior net worth.

SUMMARY

This won't be a point-by-point summary, like you've seen in the previous chapters. Instead, it is a statement of the conclusions that I hope you have come to as a result of studying all of the "big pictures."

Those conclusions are these:

A high income level is helpful in building a high net worth, but it isn't a requirement. And contrary to popular belief, a high income level is no guarantee of building a high net worth; lots of high-income/high-spending households end up with a minimal, or even negative, net worth.

As long as you have a consistent income, even if it is modest, the most important factor in building a high net worth is how much you spend. The surest approach to building a high net worth, and the strategy that is available to virtually anyone, is to control spending consistently to a level that is less than income, year after year. The more of a positive difference you can maintain, the longer you can maintain it, and the earlier you can begin it, the bigger the accumulated net worth.

Spending is the real key. And *you* decide how much you spend—no one else. So no matter whether you call it wealthy, rich, or high net worth, the person who is clearly in control of whether you attain that status is *you*!

To be successful in doing so, you have to make a fundamental lifestyle choice of *delayed* gratification and consistently stick to it. That's how most wealthy Americans became wealthy.

The choice is yours because *you* are the one who determines how much you spend. *That's* the big picture!

• 4 •

The Human Factor

$\mathcal{H}$ave you ever heard the term *dead right*? Some people use it to describe a situation where you are definitely in the right, technically speaking, but in such a way that it isn't likely to do you much good. Imagine a small sailboat on a collision course with a huge ocean liner. The skipper of the sailboat happens to be an undisputed expert on every last detail of navigational rights of way in those waters. He is certain, beyond any doubt whatsoever, that in this particular case, his sailboat has the right of way, and that the ocean liner is required to change course in order to avoid a collision. Nobody on board the ocean liner can even see or hear the tiny sailboat. But that doesn't stop our sailboat skipper from shaking his copy of the navigational regulations at the ocean liner while shouting, "*You* have to change course, I tell you! I'm right!" What finally stopped him from shouting? The ocean liner—steaming right into his sailboat.

Was the sailboat skipper "right" about his interpretation of the navigation rules? Yes. He was *dead* right.

Navigating the waters of personal finance has its own hazards, but they are a little different from the sailboat skipper's. Managing your money is a pragmatic, rational, step-by-step endeavor. It is inherently quantitative, much more science than art. It requires the construction of plans and processes and the discipline to consistently follow them. But even if you get the plans, processes, and spreadsheets perfect, you can *still* end up being dead right if you forget about the human factor. All too often, real life unfolds in ways that you didn't take into account in your plan. The trick is to develop the right financial plan for yourself and to build and practice the right habits along the way—without drifting into dead-right territory.

RIGHT BRAIN, LEFT BRAIN

Speaking of "right," you've probably heard of the differences between your left brain and right brain. If you haven't, it's a model based on the premise that your brain is divided into two halves, or hemispheres, each one having a different function. According to this model, the left hemisphere of your brain specializes in rational, quantitative, and linear thinking, while the right is characterized by creative, intuitive, and spontaneous thought. I want to emphasize that most neuroscience experts today would tell us that this model represents a hopelessly outdated and oversimplified understanding of how our brains actually work. Even so, we'll use the left brain–right brain model anyway because it is so well known. Accurate or not, it is a very useful way to illustrate how different kinds of thinking can get you into financial trouble, sometimes without your even being aware of it.

Applying the model to personal financial management, it is the marvelous capabilities of your left brain that allow you to do all the math, learn all the steps, and generate all the rational analysis necessary to produce and follow a brilliant financial plan. But the equally marvelous—and very human—qualities of your right brain are very capable of completely and utterly sabotaging it along the way, leaving your plan in a dead-right condition.

To be clear, your right brain is not your enemy. That's where your creativity, resilience, intuition, and lots of other valuable qualities come from. In many *other* aspects of your life, your right brain really is the star of the show, while your left brain is in a supporting role. But when it comes to managing your money, your left brain needs to be in charge.

To change our analogy from boats to cars: your right brain is like a very talented but unpredictable friend who sometimes desperately wants to drive the car but is a terrible driver. Sometimes, while your left brain is calmly driving, the right brain will suddenly lean over from the passenger seat and simply try to grab the steering wheel. But the left brain catches on to this maneuver pretty quickly, so the right brain soon develops more indirect, deceptive tactics. It will wait until the driver is intently paying attention to something else and then try to slowly and gradually assume control of the wheel. Either way, you are headed for financial trouble if the right brain succeeds in gaining steering control. Fortunately, some of the right brain's more dangerous financial tactics have been studied well enough for us to understand, and hopefully to guard against. That's what this chapter is about.

Here's a warning: many newcomers to personal finance underestimate the danger of the right brain. They see the management of money as the kind of purely rational activity that the right brain would take no interest in. They discount the human factor in carrying out the plan, thinking that it is only other people who might be vulnerable to the right brain's bag of tricks. *That's a mistake.* We're people, not computers, and no matter how smart or how careful we believe ourselves to be, the right brain has ways of making its presence felt in every one of us. Your personal financial condition is closely intertwined with feelings of security, control, and self-esteem. Because these kinds of powerful emotional triggers are often associated with financial decisions, it should be no surprise that the right brain will want to get involved. The key is to expect it and to be prepared for it.

An entire field of study called behavioral economics is devoted to how we human beings make financial decisions. It is a rich and fascinating field, and we can't give it anything like a complete treatment in a single chapter. (A much more thorough—as well as very readable and practical—treatment of this topic can be found in *Why Smart People Make Big Money Mistakes* by Belsky and Gilovich.) But what we *can* do is summarize some of the key principles, focusing on those likely to be most important for someone just starting out in their financial life.

Here are six examples of how your right brain can cause you financial problems and what you can do about it in each case.

1. VERY LONG-TERM THINKING

In the previous chapter, we emphasized the importance of developing a long-term outlook in your financial thinking. After reviewing several hypothetical households, we concluded that controlling spending at levels less than income—consistently and over a very long period of time—is essential to reliably building a net worth. Naturally, that requires discipline, patience, and delayed gratification practiced over many decades. But now consider—how did your two brains process this message as you looked through the big-picture graphs in the last chapter?

Your left brain wasn't bothered a bit by the very long time frame on the big-picture graphs. It did what it does best—analyzing numbers, shapes, and patterns. Your left brain treated the analysis just the same for a 40-year graph as it would a 40-minute graph. The conclusion that was presented, which featured a commitment to consistent spending control over at least the first two-thirds of your financial life, was probably quickly judged by your left brain to be utterly logical. If your left brain had a display, it would have read "Analysis complete, next problem."

What about your right brain? Different story! At first, your right brain probably took a nap, because we were only discussing hypothetical households. But as soon as your right brain realized that you were in the process of considering a very long-term plan for *yourself*, based on patience, discipline, and delayed gratification, it awoke with a jolt. Your right brain deals with thoughts about your future on an *emotional* basis. Eventually your right brain will come around to appreciate the feelings of security that go along with being on a sure path toward a strong financial future, but that probably wasn't its first thought. Your right brain is a big fan of instant gratification, so you can expect the idea of a multidecade period of sacrifice and discipline to set off major fireworks. If your right brain had a display, it would have read *"I object!"*

Your right brain's first tactic is likely to get you to drop the whole idea altogether. It may tell you, "This will never work. There are way too many things that can go wrong over that much time. Give up now." An alternate line of attack is "Even if the plan would work, 40 years is way too long—it just isn't worth it." And if neither of these is successful, your right brain might resort to the famous stall tactic, which goes like this: "The whole approach looks brilliant, and I can't wait to get started on it. There's just one thing—this *particular* month isn't such a good month to begin it. Come to think of it, *next* month might not be so great either. Don't get me wrong, I'm all for it—just not right away . . . "

Right-brain danger: Your right brain doesn't like long-term plans requiring long-term commitment and delayed gratification at all and will try a variety of tactics to prevent you from starting.

What to do about it: Recognize the tactics for what they are and begin anyway, as soon as you can. Once you've begun, your habits will become obstacles too formidable for the right brain's objections to overcome, and it will turn its attention elsewhere. Eventually your right brain may even learn to like the feelings of certainty and security that your long-term financial outlook brings.

2. YOU ARE IN CHARGE

Since you are just starting out in your financial life, someone else has probably been making at least some of your major financial decisions up until now. In fact, you may have relatively little experience being completely in charge of anything, financially related or not. But whether you have or not, here is a financial fact of life that I urge you to take to heart:

*YOU are in charge of your financial destiny. YOU are in charge of
developing a financial plan and of taking all the steps required to bring it to
fruition. And no matter who else you choose to involve at various points,
YOU are the one who will gain or lose based on the decisions that you make.*

Your right brain may not be comfortable at all with this fact of financial life. Being in charge means that you have to accept the responsibility for making decisions and dealing with their consequences. Since you aren't financially used to this yet, it is natural to feel a little fear of the unknown, and fear of *any* kind gets your right brain working overtime. If someone else—just about anyone else—has an opinion or offers any advice, the right brain will say, "Take it! They probably know more than you do." And if the person offering advice happens to be a professional who is selling some kind of solution to a financial problem that you may be dealing with, then your right brain will loudly lobby for you to sign on the dotted line as soon as possible.

Of course, you will need financial advice and services from lots of different people in your financial life. Remember, though, that you don't have to accept and act on every piece of advice that you get until you are completely comfortable with it, and you don't have to do business with the first financial professional that you happen to talk to. Choose those people carefully, evaluate what they are telling you carefully, and decide whether or not to follow their guidance carefully. Ask lots of questions and try to learn as much as you can in the process. Remember that no matter who you deal with or how financially knowledgeable they may be (or seem to be), other people may have their own agendas. Even if they are just sincerely trying to be helpful, nobody cares more about your financial condition than you do.

Right-brain danger: Your right brain doesn't like the whole idea of making important financial decisions about unfamiliar topics and is fearful of making a wrong one. So it will try to convince you to let others take charge and make the decisions for you—the sooner the better.

What to do about it: Accept and embrace full responsibility for your own financial future. Choose whom to seek advice from carefully, and evaluate the advice that you're given carefully, to arrive at the soundest decisions.

3. ALL DOLLARS ARE GREEN, AND THEY ALL COUNT THE SAME

Your right brain can be downright sneaky. Sometimes it shows up disguised as your left brain.

Suppose you have your eye on a particular make and model of used car. You find two sellers, and the cars they are selling are identical in every way except color. The blue one costs $8,000, but the purple one—the color you *really* like—is $8,400. "Hm-m-m . . . " you say to yourself. "I really, really like the purple one. And it's only 5% more than the blue one. That's just a drop in the bucket compared to the whole price. I'll take it."

Repeat after me: all dollars are green, and they all count the same. In other words, $400 is still $400, no matter what you compare it to. The "drops in the bucket" all end up in—or come out of—the same net worth bathtub. If you were suddenly presented with a bill for $400 for something else, I'll bet you wouldn't say, "Just a drop in the bucket." In this case, your right brain is impersonating a left-brain type of calculation to get you to compare $400 with something much bigger. Its goal is to make you believe that $400 is somehow magically worth much less than $400. Now that's sneaky!

Here's another example of the same kind of sneakiness. A windfall is a significant amount of money that comes your way unexpectedly. If you received a $10,000 windfall, whether from a winning lottery ticket or an inheritance from an unknown relative, what would you do with it?

Your right brain would prefer to just spend it all right away, of course—the windfall is an absolutely ideal immediate-gratification opportunity. But it also knows that it can't just make that suggestion directly, because you are way too smart to fall for that. So instead, it concocts a little bit of an analysis. It goes like this: "I'm doing pretty well financially. All the bills are paid, and my savings are growing. If I spend all of this windfall money immediately, all of my bills will *still* be paid, and my savings will *still* be growing. So since my financial condition before spending the windfall and after spending it is exactly the same, the net effect of spending the windfall is *zero*. Therefore, it can't *possibly* be considered irresponsible to immediately spend this money. Let's go!"

Now that's not a bad piece of logic. You can see why so many people who haven't thought through this ahead of time would fall for it. And of course: this logic is dead right.

But you won't fall for this, because now you know the truth. All dollars are green and count the same. Spending $10,000 impulsively (on something like a cruise that can't be resold) will reduce your net worth by $10,000, compared to saving it. This is true no matter where the $10,000 came from and whether or not you had that $10,000 a year ago, a month ago, or a minute ago.

Because the right brain is so good at influencing you in windfall situations, it is a good idea to have a windfall strategy already established and ready to go, *before* any windfalls appear. Make this your rule: "100% of any windfall money will go straight into my savings account for a 6-month cooling-off period before I make any decisions about what to do with it." Your right brain is famous for its sneakiness but not for its endurance. Six months later, it will have forgotten all about the windfall and will have moved on to something else. Now you're in a position to make a much more rational decision about it. And you're likely to conclude that it looks pretty good right where it is.

Right-brain danger: Your right brain can use sneaky tactics that are disguised as sound logic, usually in an attempt to justify immediate gratification.

What to do about it: Remembering that all dollars are green and they all count the same usually exposes the right brain's dead-right logic for what it is. In the case of windfalls, commit to a plan of keeping them in your savings account for a 6-month cooling-off period before making any decision about what to do with them.

4. THE PATH OF LEAST RESISTANCE

Water flowing downhill will always follow the path of least resistance—and so will you, if you let your right brain have its way. Even if you're not conscious of it, your right brain will always insistently steer you in whatever direction requires the least effort, commitment, or attention—and it will do so even if the difference in resistance is tiny.

Here's an example. Let's say that you decide to join a gym where one of your friends is already a member. You like the convenient location, the extensive array of equipment, and especially the low monthly membership dues. Paying the dues has turned out to be a simple matter of preauthorizing an automatic monthly payment from your bank account. Several months later, you are surprised to hear your friend tell you that she has quit the gym because it has gotten too expensive. "I wish I would have read that contract more closely," she explains. "The low dues were only for the first 3 months—after that, they went way up. The contract I signed gave them permission to increase the automatic payment, but I didn't realize that. When I finally figured out what was happening, I terminated the contract, and now I go to a much less expensive gym. You should check your contract to see if that's going to happen to you, too." She's right—you *should* check your contract. But your right brain quickly sizes up the situation and finds all kinds of resistance— you'll have to dig out the contract, study its fine print, cancel it at the old gym, find a new gym, and change what had become a familiar routine. Then it will resort to another favorite right-brain trick—thinking of potential savings in monthly terms, not in terms of the entire contract. Soon your right brain proclaims, "All that work, just to save a few dollars per month? It's definitely not worth it." In reality, it *isn't* all that much work and the overall savings can be significant. But to realize those savings, you'll have to overcome your right brain's preference for the path of least resistance. (Fortunately, there is a simple left-brain tool called a monthly budget that will spot these kinds of increases with or without a warning from a friend, and we'll cover it right at the beginning of part II.)

Another famous example of the path of least resistance is rebates. You know how they work—the initial price is $100, but after a $20 rebate, you pay only $80. This allows the seller, perfectly legally, to feature the $80 price prominently in all of their advertising. When everything works according to plan, you give the seller an interest-free loan of $20, and then they eventually pay you back. But you have to do some work to get your $20 back. Your right brain is not happy at all about having to copy down serial numbers, cut out specific parts of packaging, fill out forms, and make trips to the mailbox—especially when you already have the item. In protest, your right brain will shout, "Forget about it! You already own it. What's a measly $20?" You see, advertisers know all about right brains and how resistant they are to the smallest of roadblocks. The sellers fully expect most consumers to give in to their right brains, and the sellers are usually right. There is nothing wrong with buying something with a rebate involved, as long as you have the discipline to overcome your right brain's objections and follow through on the rebate requirements.

By the way, we've just discussed how your right brain's preference for the path of least resistance can hurt you financially, but it can also be a powerful tool to help you. Early in part II, you'll learn a very effective technique called Pay Yourself First that actually tricks your right brain into becoming a powerful—but unknowing—teammate in your financial progress. More on that later.

Right-brain danger: Your right brain's preference for the path of least resistance can cost you money by letting seemingly small, recurring amounts escape scrutiny, by letting rebates go unclaimed, and by generally being lazy about financial matters.

What to do about it: Use a monthly budget (more on this in part II). If you buy anything on a rebate basis, do not allow yourself to use the product until you've done everything required to claim the rebate.

5. WHO ARE "YOU"?

I've been referring to "you" and "your" financial life. Who is this "you" that I am talking about, anyway? Every time I say "you," I am really referring to your household. If you are a household of one, then the distinction isn't too relevant. But there are many different kinds of households. An adult couple with no dependents might not seem much more complicated than a household of one, but if the two adults have differing philosophies about financial matters, watch out. Add dependents, or new household members moving in or out, or changes in employment status—you get the idea. Agreeing on the decision-making *process*, and deciding who will make which kinds of financial decisions, can become every bit as challenging as the financial decisions themselves.

Here is the danger: you might fail to develop a good financial plan—or you might fail to carry a good plan out effectively—if you don't have an agreed-upon and consistent way to make financial decisions in your household. I'll start with what *not* to do: don't avoid the topic. Even if you anticipate that the discussions might be awkward, start talking about it anyway. A strategy of "we'll just figure it out as we go along" is virtually guaranteed to cause problems, and disagreements about financial matters can be painfully divisive. The best approach is to start the discussion early, find common ground, and work from there.

Of course, my preference would be for everyone in the household to read this book from beginning to end, heartily agree on everything in it, and then all that is left to do is to divide up who does what. If it isn't quite that easy, though, you'll have more work to do. Ideally, you want an agreement that is as clear and explicit as possible about what the long-term goals are, how decisions will be made, who will make them, and with what limitations. Putting everything into writing is a good means of avoiding future misunderstandings. Patience and discipline are still important, but so are compromise, understanding, and goodwill. If you work together in that spirit, I have no doubt that you can come to an effective way of approaching financial matters together. Countless households have successfully done so, and so can you.

Right-brain danger: Your right brain may want to avoid the potentially awkward topic of how financial decisions are going to be made in your household. Operating without such an agreement can cause all kinds of serious problems in the household, including financial ones.

What to do about it: Address the subject, early and often. Make it a priority to have a well-understood and consistent approach to financial decision making in your household.

6. DECISIONS INVOLVING FINANCIAL AND NONFINANCIAL ASPECTS

If I have $1,000 to invest and I am trying to decide between two very different low-cost equity index funds (there's that phrase again), then I have a purely financial decision to make. My left brain can have a field day comparing statistics, looking at graphs, and eventually arriving at a decision. This is a purely left-brain decision process, and my right brain will be happy to sit this one out.

But what if I am considering a very different kind of choice? For $1,000, I can take a professional course that will give me some new skills and possibly qualify me for a higher-paying job. The additional income will benefit the entire household by brightening our long-term financial picture. Or I can send my daughter to a wonderful and highly praised summer camp that she has had her heart set on for months. I can afford one or the other, but not both.

Uh-oh . . . left brain–right brain gridlock!

In your financial life, you'll have some decisions like the index funds, but it is important to realize that you will also have plenty of "course vs. camp" decisions that involve a combination of financial and nonfinancial factors. When that happens, your right brain is likely to start agitating loudly for a fast, emotion-driven decision. It might play on your guilt by whispering in your ear, "You can't put a price on a child's happiness. Don't even dream of disappointing that innocent child because of your greed." Or it might try a fear-based approach like "The camp won't do the kid much good if we end up broke." Whatever tactic your right brain uses, if that's how you base your decision, you're likely to end up feeling uneasy about it later.

My advice is to stop your right brain in its tracks. Just because there are nonfinancial, or even heavily emotional, factors involved doesn't mean that you can't make a solid, thoroughly considered decision. You might end up needing both your left and right brains, but not at the same time. They ought to take turns, and when they do, the left brain goes first.

A good approach is the tried-and-true pros-and-cons list. Consider the pros, and then the cons, of the professional course, and then repeat the process for the camp. Write them down. That's four lists; that alone will quiet down the right brain. If an item on the list is quantifiable, quantify it. If it isn't, indicate its relative importance on a 1 to 10 scale or even just an indication of major, minor, or medium. Try to put everything on one page, so that you can more easily compare the lists. Going through this process (or anything similar to it) ensures that you give *all* relevant aspects careful consideration, not just the ones that trigger an immediate right-brain outburst. And in doing so, you might be led to start considering other lines of thought, which can prove useful. Will the camp, or the course, be offered next year also? Are there ways of getting benefits similar to the course, or the camp, in other, less expensive ways? Will the course *really* lead to higher income? How certain is that? How much more income? Does the child *really* have his or her heart set on the camp, or is your belief about that based on a one-time, now-forgotten comment?

See what I mean? Putting some left-brain structure into a decision like this can lead to a much-higher-quality decision, whatever it turns out to be. Your right brain will get its turn to provide input on the more emotional factors, but only once you've completed the overall structure first. The more important the decision in question is, the more time and structure you should put into it. A big advantage of this approach is peace of mind: you will be much less likely to regret or second-guess your decision afterward because you know that you've already considered each and every aspect carefully. Afterward you can instead turn your attention to implementing your decision in the most effective way.

Right-brain danger: Decisions that involve both financial and nonfinancial aspects are a fact of life. Often the nonfinancial aspects are emotional in nature and can trigger the right brain to try to take over the whole decision in impulsive and unpredictable ways.

What to do about it: Use a methodical, structured approach to such decisions. Make sure that all the aspects, whether emotional or not, are thoroughly and appropriately considered before reaching a decision.

SUMMARY

1. *Dead right* means being technically or procedurally correct, but in a way that isn't likely to do you much good. Personal finance is filled with potential dead-right hazards.
2. In the left brain–right brain model, the left brain is rational, quantitative, and linear, while the right brain is more creative, intuitive, and spontaneous. Most newcomers to personal financial management tend to see it as strictly a left-brain endeavor. But that is a mistake, because the right brain is fully capable of derailing any financial plan. The key is to understand ahead of time what some of the right brain's most common tactics are and to guard against them.
3. Personal financial management is a very, very long-term endeavor, probably at least 50 to 60 years in length. Operating in this kind of time frame is probably very new to you but is an essential habit to get into. Patience and discipline are at an absolute premium. Be aware that your right brain will object to your steady, methodical approach—but begin anyway.
4. *You* are in charge of your financial destiny—and nobody else. Although others may be involved in various ways, *you* are the one who will ultimately feel the effects of your decisions. Understand, accept, and fully embrace this essential fact of financial life.
5. Your right brain can come up with various sneaky ways of making unjustified spending decisions seem logical, but you can overcome these by remembering that all dollars are green, and they all count the same, no matter where they came from or what you compare them to. Adopt a windfall strategy of "100% of any windfall money will go straight into my savings account for a 6-month cooling-off period before I make any decisions about what to do with it."

6. It is human nature (maybe more like "right-brain nature") to seek the path of least resistance. This tendency can work against you financially by causing you to treat ongoing, automatic expenses like small expenses instead of realizing that they add up to big ones, by inducing you to avoid the resistance required to follow through on rebate requirements, or by generally being lax about financial matters. Counter this by using a monthly budget (more on this in part II) and by resolving to complete all rebate requirements before using the purchased item.

7. When I say "you" or "your financial life" in this book, what I really mean is your household. A common challenge that households face is how to go about making, and carrying out, financial decisions; and specifically, who has responsibility for what, and with what limitations. There is no one right way to establish this, but the most common wrong way is to avoid the discussion altogether. Discuss the topic directly, early, and often. Find common ground and build from there.

8. Many decisions have both financial and nonfinancial factors that are important to consider. The left and right brains may both need to be involved, but my recommendation is for them to take turns, and the left brain gets to go first. Do this by following a methodical, structured decision process. This allows a decision to be reached based on a thorough consideration of *all* important factors. You'll make better decisions this way and have more peace of mind afterward.

• 5 •

The Ultimate Acceleration Strategy

$\mathcal{A}$s the big-picture graphs made clear, income isn't everything when it comes to increasing net worth. At the risk of belaboring the point, what really matters is the *relationship* between income and spending. A high income is no guarantee of a strong net worth, and considerable wealth can be accumulated from virtually any level of income *if* spending is carefully managed. It bears repetition because a very different, and inaccurate, message is so often repeated in our popular culture and media—that income is everything and that a high income equals wealth.

But if income isn't everything, it isn't exactly inconsequential, either. If you save the bare minimum of 10% of everything that you earn, as recommended by the First Rule, then your financial river will begin flowing in the right direction. However, if two people are each saving 10%, the one with the higher income will accumulate net worth faster. The absolute level of income plays a role in building wealth, and a higher income *can* lead to more and/or faster financial success, depending on how much you spend.

What if you are already following the First Rule and saving the bare minimum of 10%, but you want to *accelerate* your progress in building net worth? How can you get the river flowing in the right direction even faster? There are two ways to do it. First, you can start saving *more than* 10%. Saving more means spending less, and that means taking a backward step in your lifestyle. That may not be a popular strategy in your household, and it certainly won't win the support of your right brain. But still, it certainly is possible, and it *will* accelerate the river. Another strategy would be to start earning more, while maintaining your 10% savings rate. Now you're saving 10% of a bigger income. Again, progress is accelerated, but this time, your household members and your right brain are delighted. Sure, you are now saving faster, but you're spending faster, too. Your lifestyle actually takes an upward step, because you're still spending 90%, but of a bigger income. If you have a choice between these two ways of accelerating your financial river, it certainly seems as if income growth is the way to go.

But how easy—or even possible—is it to increase your income? Most of the income lines in chapter 3 went continually up and never down. Is that realistic? Hold that thought: we'll address it directly a little later in this chapter.

THE ULTIMATE ACCELERATION STRATEGY

Assume for the moment that income growth *is* possible. What if you wanted to accelerate your net-worth accumulation by even more than either of the two methods we just described? What if you wanted to get your financial river flowing really, *really* fast? There is a very simple way to do it: increase your income but keep your spending and lifestyle exactly the same. Even though this strategy has been successfully used for centuries, it doesn't have a catchy, well-known name. We'll call it the Ultimate Acceleration Strategy. Just be advised that anyone who hasn't read this book won't know what you're talking about if you use this name. To see why we have given it such a powerful-sounding name, keep reading.

This strategy is one of those seemingly magic instances where the math works very powerfully in your favor, *and* it is very right brain friendly. How does it work? Let's say that Alex is following the First Rule, but just barely, by saving exactly 10%. Now let's say that Alex's monthly income increases by 10%, but that Alex keeps spending at exactly the same level as before (in dollars per month, not as a percentage). Alex's lifestyle doesn't change one bit, but Alex is now saving twice as much as before, and it didn't hurt a bit because no lifestyle change at all was necessary. Think of it like this: 100% of the income increase went directly into savings, while zero went into new spending. Alex's lifestyle is completely unchanged. A relatively small percentage increase in income resulted in a huge percentage increase in savings.

Alex could have said, "Wait a minute. My income went up, so I am entitled to spend more. I can keep my savings at 10% and my spending at 90%, but my income is bigger, so savings and spending can now *both* go up, and I'm still following the First Rule. What's wrong with that?"

Nothing is *wrong* with that. Alex will still be doing much, much better than the average household by continuing to follow the First Rule. Alex would get a better-than-average grade of "B" by doing this, just like household #1 in chapter 3. But to get an "A," Alex would need to follow the ultimate strategy and put *all* of the increased income into savings.

Now let's take it one step further: another year goes by, and Alex is accumulating net worth quite rapidly. But then Alex's income increases again by another 10%. What does Alex do now? Exactly the same thing: zero change in spending levels, and all of the income increase goes into savings. Alex's monthly savings are now more than *triple* compared with the starting point. Alex's financial river now features whitewater rapids; nature photographers show up regularly to capture its mighty force on film. But to anyone else, on the outside looking in, nothing is happening. Alex's lifestyle and spending habits remain unchanged; it is Alex's *net worth* that is experiencing explosive growth.

Okay, the nature photographer part of it was an exaggeration, but you get the idea: keeping spending flat while increasing income is an extraordinarily powerful way to grow your net worth. If you do it early in your financial life, you can apply the astonishing power of compounding to this now-considerable net worth, and the effect will eventually be nothing short of immense!

Now you know why the First Rule stipulates saving at least 10%. The 10% is a starting point. And now you know one of the most common strategies that the millionaire next door used to become wealthy. I'm not suggesting that you *never* increase your spending over the entire course of your financial life; inflation alone is likely to force at least some increased spending, and a growing household may force some more. (Go back and look at household #5's "A+" graph. It shows just such a picture.) But I *am* suggesting that you're missing a huge opportunity if you automatically increase your spending every time you increase your income—especially early in your financial life.

But the Ultimate Acceleration Strategy *does* require income growth, so we're back to the same question I asked you to hold earlier. How do you grow your income? Well, I am going to ask you to hold the question yet again, because answering it requires us to first understand some things about the different categories of income.

CATEGORIES OF INCOME

If you are like most people, you've got a single way of thinking about income: "I have a job, and my income is what I am paid for doing it, period." I'd like to encourage you to think much more broadly about this, though. Income can come from a variety of sources. One way of categorizing sources of income comes from (don't panic!) the U.S. Internal Revenue Service. The three broad categories of income used by the IRS are active (or earned) income, portfolio income, and passive income. It is possible to get into a very long discussion about the specific accounting definitions and tax implications of these three categories, but that's not our point here. Instead, I only want to get you to think of these from a purely conceptual basis. Let's look at them one by one.

1. **Active income.** This is income that is earned by, well, working for it. This includes all the usual ways that most people think about income, like wages and salaries, tips, commissions, and bonuses. If you own a business and you participate in either running or working for that business, then anything that you get in return for that is also active income. The main characteristic of active income is that whenever you stop doing whatever it is that you're getting paid for, the income stops, too.

   We can further divide active income into two categories (even though the IRS doesn't): *primary* and *supplemental*. Primary income is pretty simple; this is the active income that you get from your full-time job, including any bonuses. Supplemental income is separate from that. It is active income that you earn outside your primary job and is on top of your primary income. It includes part-time work, miscellaneous services that you provide for pay, or anything else for which you are paid on the basis of the amount of work that you do outside of your primary job.

2. **Portfolio income.** This is income that comes from your investments, including interest on savings, dividends, and any gains that come from buying and selling securities like stocks, bonds, or mutual funds, or gains from buying and selling other assets, like real estate, cars, or a stamp collection. We're not going to talk about portfolio income any more in this chapter because you've not yet arrived at the point in your financial life where it comes into play. It is important, though, and we'll give it full coverage in parts III and IV.

3. **Passive income.** Here is where it gets really interesting. Income is considered passive if it is earned *without* working directly for it (and if it isn't portfolio income). Some examples will help, and the most common example is income from a rental property. If you own a house and rent it out, then you'll get a rent check each month without doing any specific work for it; that's passive income. And as long as you own that house and keep it rented, that passive income stream will continue. Sure, there is *some* work involved; you probably have to advertise to find a renter, you have to evaluate each candidate's suitability as a renter, you have to make arrangements to collect and deposit the rent, and you have to either be available for repairs and regular maintenance or arrange for someone else to be. But the kind

of work involved is more about getting things set up and keeping everything running smoothly, as opposed to being paid specifically for the amount of work that you do. Do you see the difference?

Here's another example: when an author publishes a book, he or she is usually paid a royalty based on how many copies or downloads of the book are sold. The work involved, of course, is writing the book in the first place, although there is probably some additional work involved in promoting it, too. That work might take one author 30 years and another author a few hours, but in the end, the amount of work that the author put into the book has nothing to do with how much he or she will earn for it. And like the rental property, the income stream continues for as long as the book continues to sell. The Charles Dickens novel *A Tale of Two Cities* was first published in 1859, has sold over 200 million copies, and is *still* selling. Depending on the kind of contract that Dickens had with his publisher, there may be some great-great-great grandchildren around today who would be delighted to tell you all about passive income.

There is a very key distinction between active and passive income. Active income has a natural limit: the amount of time that you have available to earn it. If you have a full-time job and you have a great deal of energy and discipline, you might be able to manage another source or two of active income by doing other work on a part-time basis. But at some point, you'll hit the limit of what is humanly possible to do in a fixed amount of time. The only way you can increase your active income at that point is to substitute higher-paying active-income jobs—but then you'll just be at a new, higher limit.

Passive income is different. While it typically takes some time to get a passive income stream set up, it may or may not take much money. And once you've gotten the passive stream set up, it requires little if any time to keep it running. So the idea of a passive income stream limit is very different; because there is usually some time required to set one up, there is a limit to how quickly you can add new ones. But there is really no practical limit to how many you can simultaneously keep running. That is the beauty of passive income; once you've set it up, it keeps on coming your way, in addition to any passive income streams that you've previously set up, and in addition to any active income that continues to require the majority of your ongoing time.

There is still more to the story: passive income is a *perfect* Ultimate Acceleration Strategy opportunity. Your monthly spending, as limited by the First Rule, has probably been based on your primary income. But after you have gone through the effort to set up a passive income stream, as it arrives, it "feels" like a bonus or a windfall. You have the opportunity to put this passive income straight into savings, without alerting your right brain by spending any of it. If that's what you do right from the start, then this passive income will continue to follow a path of least resistance straight into your savings account, thereby directly increasing your net worth. Are you starting to see why passive income is a very powerful wealth-building idea? Are you starting to understand why the attitude of "I have a full-time job, and that's all the income that I am going to earn" is a very, very limiting position to take? Good!

While you may be convinced that passive income is a nice concept, you might still be skeptical that there is any realistic way that you could ever generate any. What I expect many of you are saying is, "Isn't rental property the most common example of passive income? How can I even consider rental property if I am just starting out? How can I write a book that anyone would want to buy if I don't even like to write e-mails? Couldn't you suggest some kind of passive income that doesn't require a lot of money or special talents?" The short answer is: research. Do a search on "passive income" and see where it leads you. A word of caution first, though: you'll have to weed out the many, many sales pitches for dubious "get-rich" schemes that such a search will inevitably generate. But what remains will be a very rich source of ideas. If you're like me, though, sometimes it helps to have an example, or story, that illustrates how a concept like this works.

MINI CASE STUDY: HOLLY AND MOLLY

Allow me to introduce you to two lifelong friends, Holly and Molly. The two friends shared a love of balloons, so it was no surprise when they each chose to major in Balloon Studies at the local university. And even though there wasn't much money in balloon-related careers, they were each thrilled to accept jobs at the Brilliant Balloon Boutique upon graduation. Their boss was delighted with their work and assured them both that they had potential for a long and fulfilling, if not particularly high-paying, careers in the balloon field. Molly's attitude was that she was happy to have a steady income and proud that she had worked so hard to qualify for it. She more or less accepted that she would never have a high income and would therefore never be able to establish much of a net worth; but still, she intended to work hard at BBB, with the hopes of earning raises each year.

Holly was grateful for the steady income, too, but her attitude was a little different. She focused on learning the ropes at BBB for the first several months but then began to explore ways that she could supplement her income in her spare time. The balloon field was demanding, so she didn't want anything that would interfere or be too time consuming. She considered several options for some modest part-time work and finally settled on tutoring. After all, she had done well in her Balloon Studies course work and she knew that there were always some students at the university (or their parents) who would be willing to pay for some extra help. After a year or two, she was tutoring as many students as she felt she could handle without interfering with her primary job. The money for doing so wasn't great; it totaled only about 5% of her BBB salary. Still, this was 5% that she looked at as extra, so she put this money all into savings, on top of the 10% of her BBB salary that she was already saving. There were many more students that wanted tutoring, and even though she would have welcomed even more extra income, she didn't feel that she could afford the time.

That's when another idea occurred to her; she knew lots of students that needed tutoring, and she also knew that with a little on-campus advertising, she could find even more. In addition, she knew lots of graduates from her own class who would be happy to earn a little extra income by tutoring. (She asked Molly if she'd like to tutor, but Molly said, "I already have a job.") Eventually Holly began to think that maybe there was some money to be made by matching students with tutors. So she set up a student–tutor matching service, earning a small commission for each successful match. This didn't take much time; but she thought she could do it in a way that would take virtu-ally *no* time if she could somehow automate the matching process. Holly was no computer whiz, but she believed that if she could set up a website where prospective students and tutors could register (for a small fee), then they could find each other without Holly needing to be involved at all. She took some of the savings from her own tutoring income and hired a professional to set up the website under her direction. It worked like a charm, and soon she was receiving regular income from the registrations without doing any work at all except some occasional monitoring; all the work had been done up front. So now she was earning 5% of her BBB salary actively by tutoring students her-self and another 5% passively by collecting registration fees—and saving it *all*.

That's when she got her next big idea; she already had a mechanism for matching Balloon Studies students and tutors from the local university. So how much different would it have to be to match up such people from *any* university? Well, it took her a few months to figure out how to publicize a nationwide Balloon Studies student–tutor matching service website to attract sufficient interest, but eventually she was earning registration fees from uni-versities all over the country. Since this required very little ongoing effort, she was able to still keep her full-time BBB income, her active tutoring income, *and* collect all of the passive income. After a year or two of this, Holly real-ized that without knowing it, she had built a very valuable asset: she now had, as a by-product of her nationwide matching service, the names and e-mail addresses of hundreds of balloon enthusiasts all over the country. You guessed it—she decided to start up a blog with an initial membership list already built and ready to go. Writing and administering the blog did take a little time, so she decided to stop actively tutoring herself. But the lost income was much more than made up by the advertising revenue that balloon manufacturers, balloon design services, and balloon educational institutions were willing to pay to place ads on Holly's blog site. Eventually, Holly's income consisted of her full-time BBB salary, *plus* another 50% from passive, or near-passive, ways like the matching service and the blog.

Even though an enterprising person like Holly is likely to keep discovering more new ways of generating passive income, I'll stop the story here because the point has become obvious: Holly's financial position is now vastly superior to Molly's in several ways, even though their primary job incomes are identical. First of all, Holly is saving at a much faster rate, and therefore she has much more to compound; even if she were to completely stop saving now, the amount she's already saved will continue to widen the gap between her net worth and Molly's. Second, she has far greater freedom from financial emergency than Molly. If the economy hits a downward cycle and layoffs come to the Brilliant Balloon Boutique, Molly's income will stop cold, while Holly will still have her 50% passive income regardless.

But the most fundamental and defining difference between Holly and Molly is what Holly has learned. Holly now has the skill to spot and capitalize on opportunities that will generate passive income, and that skill gives her the ability to thrive financially in almost any circumstance that will come her way. It is important to notice that she didn't build this skill all at once. The difference between her approach and Molly's wasn't that great to begin with. Instead, it was more of a small-step-by-small-step process, with each success built on the previous one. Just because you can't immediately see how you can generate passive income this minute doesn't mean that you never can; just keep your eyes open and look for small opportunities to learn from.

Be a Holly, not a Molly!

HOW TO GROW YOUR INCOME

It's taken a few pages, but now we are finally ready to address the question that we put on hold at the beginning of the chapter: How do you increase your income?

1. **Through your primary job**. Depending on the type of primary job that you have, you may be able to increase your income through

raises, bonuses, promotions, increased commissions, and/or by shifting to higher-paying employers or regions or specialties.

2. **Supplemental income.** You can add to the income that you get
   from your primary job by doing supplemental part-time work.
3. **Passive income.** The main effort involved is in establishing a stream
   of passive income in the first place. Because of that, there is a limit to
   how quickly you can add new streams of passive income, but no limit
   to how many you can add.
4. **Any combination of the above, simultaneously.** Of course,
   this is easier said than done. A lot depends on how much time and
   energy your primary job demands. If it is very demanding, supplemental income may be out of the question. But if that is the case for
   you, don't give up on the idea of establishing one or more passive
   income streams. Remember, the beauty of passive income is that it
   only requires a one-time effort to establish and is not time-intensive
   after that. It may take you quite a while to find the time to get one
   set up, but don't give up on the idea. I know the expression is a little
   overused, but where there's a will, there's a way.

INCOME MILESTONES

Let's close this chapter by looking at a series of milestones:

Milestone 1: first full-time, or primary, income
Milestone 2: first supplemental active income, in addition to your full-
time income
Milestone 3: first passive income
Milestone 4: supplemental and passive income exceeds your annual
income tax bill (now you get to keep *all* of your milestone 1 income).
Milestone 5: passive income exceeds your annual expenses (hm-m-m
. . . !)
Milestone 6: passive income exceeds your active (primary plus supple-
mental) income
Milestone 7: passive + portfolio income high enough to make milestone
1 income truly optional

The purpose of showing a list of milestones like this is not to suggest that
you'll have to progress all the way to milestone #7 in order to achieve financial success. Instead, it is to get you thinking in new and different ways about
income growth. Earlier, we noted that most Americans' notion of income is

"I have a job, and my income is what I am paid for doing it, period." The milestones above are intended to allow you to see how extremely limiting this typical attitude about income is.

Still, I know some of you are probably thinking that you don't have the time, ambition, opportunity, or luck to pursue any of these income growth ideas. Well, that's okay—you can still do just fine by following the First Rule. You won't get spectacularly fast results, but you will do much better than average if you consistently watch your spending. A solid "B" is well within your grasp. And if you're pessimistic about income growth now, keep an open mind—maybe your circumstances or opportunities will open up in the future.

But if the milestones have gotten you thinking that income growth is more possible for you than you had previously been imagining—good! To the extent that you can grow your income—and keep it growing—you have the opportunity to use the Ultimate Acceleration Strategy. This is how you can generate truly "A+" results.

When you first picked up this book, you probably didn't fully appreciate the truly amazing power of compounding, and you'd probably never even heard of the Ultimate Acceleration Strategy. But now you understand both of these concepts, and better still, you see how they can be used in combination with each other. This combination is nothing more than commonsense principles that have been around for centuries but can get your net worth on a path to tremendous growth. That's a pretty good beginning, wouldn't you say?

SUMMARY

1. Following the First Rule (saving at least 10% of everything that you earn) will result in an increasing net worth. To increase it at a faster rate, you can either increase your savings percentage or increase your income while maintaining the same savings percentage.

2. To increase net worth even faster, increase your income but keep your spending and lifestyle exactly the same. Then continue doing this each time your income increases. This is known as the Ultimate Acceleration Strategy and will get your financial river flowing in the right direction at tremendous speed.

3. The categories of income are active income from your primary job, supplemental active income from one or more part-time jobs, portfolio income (covered later in the book), and passive income. Most Americans, especially early in their financial lives, tend to think of income as only the first of these categories.

4. Active income is limited by available time. But passive income is limited only by how quickly you can establish it.

5. Relying on only one primary source of income leaves you completely vulnerable to the potential loss of that income; if you lose your job, are laid off, or your employer goes out of business, you lose 100% of your income. If you diversify your income sources by establishing supplemental and passive income, you are more protected from the possibility of interruption of any one of these sources.

6. The Ultimate Acceleration Strategy requires increasing your income; income can be increased through your primary job, through supplemental or passive income, or both.

7. The Ultimate Acceleration Strategy will result in very fast-growing savings (and therefore net worth). These savings can be grown further, via compounding. This combination of the Ultimate Acceleration Strategy plus compounding represents an extremely powerful means of building wealth. It is conceptually simple and requires no great sacrifice beyond simply maintaining a constant spending rate and lifestyle while increasing income.

Part II

BUILDING YOUR FOUNDATION

· 6 ·

Budgeting

$\mathcal{I}$n part I, you learned about the critical importance of carefully controlling your spending. If water is flowing out of the drain faster than it is coming in through the faucet—if the expense line is above the income line in your own big-picture graph—then your net worth is going *down*, the opposite of what you want. You also learned about the First Rule—save at least 10% of everything that you ever earn. These fundamental principles are vital for you to remember throughout your financial life.

Now that you've reached part II, though, the focus shifts to the practical aspects of applying these principles. The first subject that we're going to tackle is controlling your spending. This doesn't seem too complicated, and it isn't—in theory. All you have to do is decide how much you're going to spend in a given period of time, and then—well, you just don't spend any more than that. What could be simpler?

If that were all there is to it, everyone's bathtub would be full and we wouldn't need a chapter on it. But as you've guessed by now, there *is* more to it. From a practical point of view, there are definitely right ways and wrong ways to approach the job of controlling your spending. We'll spend some time in this chapter outlining how to go about it.

Before we get started, though, here is another practical consideration. From this point onward, I am going to assume that you have both a checking account and a savings account; both of them will be referred to later in this chapter. It is helpful if they are linked to one another (at the same bank or other financial institution), but it isn't absolutely necessary as long as it is relatively easy for you to move money back and forth between the two.

There are three other considerations to keep in mind when deciding where to place your checking and savings accounts. First, you want your deposits to be insured (more on this in chapter 8). Second, you want an institution that keeps fees low. Finally, now that you fully appreciate the power of compounding, you want to ensure that your savings account earns a competitive rate. Do some research to find out if your current checking and savings accounts meet all of these criteria; if they don't, now is the time to move them.

THE MONTHLY BUDGETING PROCESS

The right way to go about controlling your spending is through a monthly process called budgeting. The reason that we choose months as the time frame for the process is simple: a lot of your regularly occurring bills will come to you on a monthly basis. By process, I mean that each month, you go through the same consistent, predictable set of steps. This won't happen right away; at first you will need to invest some time getting the process set up and working the way you want it. Eventually you want to get to the point where the process itself is a smooth and simple habit. Once you've accomplished this, each month you will evaluate and make a few key spending decisions, do a little fine-tuning, and that's it.

The budgeting process has four cyclical steps (see figure 6.1).

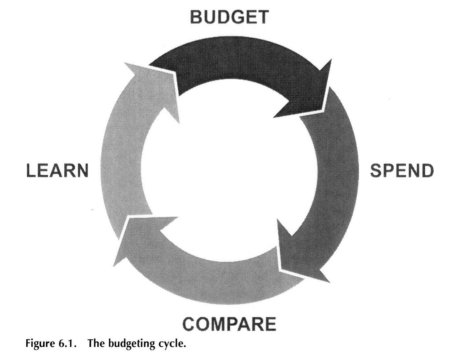

Figure 6.1. The budgeting cycle.

In the *budget* step (at the beginning of the month), you decide how much you are going to save and spend in the coming month and you break down the spending into logical categories like rent, groceries, utilities, and automotive expenses. Then comes the *spend* step (throughout the month), where you use the budget as your guide for how much to spend in the various categories during the month. In the *compare* step (at the end of the month), you compare how much you spent—within each category and in total—to your original budget.

The *learn* step is where you bring all of this together; this is where you have the opportunity to improve your skill in the all-important area of controlling your spending. Exactly what do you learn in this step? All kinds of things! Sometimes you learn that you need to improve your budgeting; you may have underestimated how much certain things actually cost, or you may have forgotten altogether about whole categories of low-visibility spending. That's okay; you can correct these in next month's budget. Other times, you learn that the budget was fine; it was your spending behavior that needs some improvement. The compare step highlights your problem spending areas for you; armed with that knowledge, you'll be better prepared for those areas *next* month.

Your goal is to apply what you learn to the *other* three steps in order for you to improve the next time through the cycle. Each time you go through the learning step, you get smarter about how to control your spending. Since everything you learn will build on what you already know, the process is like compounding—but now it isn't money that is compounding, it is your own knowledge and skill. In just one year of budgeting, you will have gone through twelve separate learning cycles, all focused completely on *your own* individual planning and spending habits. During that year, you will learn far more about how to control your spending than anything you could ever learn in this, or any other, book. In 5 years, you'll have 60 of these individually customized improvement experiences under your belt; you will be an absolute spending-control master!

The hardest parts about the monthly budgeting process are resolving to start it and then following through. Failing to control spending is a very common cause for people to fail to build wealth. If you don't budget, after 5 years you won't be any better at controlling your spending than you were at the beginning. Instead of 60 cycles' worth of continuous learning and improvement, you'll have 1 month of experience—repeated 60 times.

So why do people fail to utilize this simple process? After all, most people realize that budgeting is a very basic element of financial responsibility. Well, many of them have a very good reason, readily provided by their right brains: "it doesn't seem like it would be very much fun." But that won't be you!

I can't promise that budgeting is necessarily fun, but I can promise that once you get the basics down after a few months, it isn't nearly as much work as it seems like it is going to be. (Later we'll give some tips about how to automate the compare part of the process that really makes it simple.) And I can also promise that budgeting is much more fun than a low net worth. Budgeting is how you get the drain in your financial bathtub completely under control.

THE MOST IMPORTANT PART OF THE BUDGETING PROCESS

Get ready: here comes one of the most important recommendations in the *whole book*. It is a trick that makes your left brain happy by getting the power of compounding working in your favor but slips right by your right brain's bag of tricks. This recommendation *guarantees* that you will follow the First Rule, month after month and year after year.

It is called Pay Yourself First.

Here's how it works: the First Rule requires that you save 10%—minimum—of everything that you ever earn. So first you decide what percentage you are going to save and then convert that into a dollar amount. Next, make that amount the *very first* line item in your monthly budget. Think of this savings as a bill that comes to you every month—a completely nonoptional bill that you can't ignore or delay. Then as soon as the month begins, pay that "bill" first, before you spend any other money whatsoever. The way that you pay the bill is by transferring that amount from your checking account into your savings account. It's like saying "I know I have to pay my landlord, the electric bill, my phone bill, etc., every month, and of course I will. But I am going to pay *myself* first."

This changes your mentality about spending and saving in a subtle but extremely powerful way: you no longer save what is left after spending. Instead *you spend what is left after saving*. The difference may sound subtle, but its power is profound.

It works even better if you can make it automatic, which I highly recommend. Do this by preauthorizing an automatic monthly transfer, from checking to savings, in the amount that satisfies the First Rule (at least), on the same day that your paycheck is deposited. Your right brain's preference for the path of least resistance usually *hurts* you financially, but paying yourself first turns the tables and allows you to use this tendency to powerfully *help* you instead. The money is out of your account (and your mind!) before you even realize that it was ever there. You'll never miss it, so it won't feel like a sacrifice. You'll be consistently doing the right thing financially, in such a way that it doesn't hurt a bit. In fact, after you set it up, you won't even notice that it's happening. The only time that you'll notice it at all is when you happen to notice your savings account balance and are surprised by how big it is getting.

By the way, paying yourself first isn't a secret, and it isn't new—it's been around for generations. It's so well known for its rock-solid effectiveness that it's the primary technique used by the U.S. government for its own revenue collection. When you get a paycheck from your employer, you'll notice that an estimated amount for U.S. income tax has already been taken out *before* you get your hands on your pay. If the IRS doesn't want to take the chance that it won't get paid, why should you? Paying yourself first takes the chance out of increasing your net worth and makes it a sure thing. It's like money in the bank. Wait . . . it *is* money in the bank!

GETTING THE MOST FOR YOUR MONEY

So far, all of our emphasis in this chapter has been on keeping your *total* amount of monthly spending under control by using the budgeting process. As long as you do that, you'll be following the First Rule and your net worth will grow. In addition, the learn step in the budget process will increase your spending skills, and *this is important.* Two people can spend the same amount of money in a month, but the one with the superior spending skills will be able to afford more goods and services for the same amount spent. Alternatively, two people can buy an identical set of goods and services in a month, but the one with superior spending skills will buy them for less, and therefore will be able to save faster.

People who have mastered the art of spending waste less money and get more for the money that they do spend. You'll learn how to do this yourself as you continue to repeat the learn step in the budget process, but I'd like to give you a head start by outlining some of the key elements of spending skills. Here are seven of them.

1. **Don't make individual yes/no decisions—*prioritize.*** The most basic level of prioritization is separating needs from wants. There is no debate that you *need* a basic level of food, clothing, shelter, and health care. But everything beyond that is a want. What prioritization is all about is ensuring that your needs are paid for before any wants and deciding which of your wants you want the *most.* Because you are committed to staying within a fixed amount of spending each month, every time you say yes to a want, you're saying no to other ones. Your goal at the end of the month is to look back and be satisfied that you got the most for your money—that you spent it only on your needs and your very highest-priority wants.

The *worst* possible way to get that result is to make your spending decisions one at a time, as they come up or as they occur to you, as if every spending decision were completely independent of every other one. Decisions will come at you at disjointed, random times—so you'll get disjointed, random results. Without prioritization you just spend your way through the month, saying yes when it seems like a good idea, and you run the risk of spending your monthly total before the month is over. (The technical phrase for this is "running out of money before you run out of month.") The only possible way to end up close to a good prioritization is to look at all of your possible spending alternatives *together*, at the same time, so that you can compare them against one another. The wrong question to ask is "Should I buy X, yes or no?" The right question to ask is "I can afford to buy X, Y, or Z, but only one of the three. Which *one* of them makes the most sense for me right now?"

The budget process forces you to prioritize your spending in just this way, *in advance*. This kind of "advance comparative thinking" will become a habit and will give you a much higher level of satisfaction with your spending decisions than the "serial yes/no" approach. You'll become much less tempted to make spontaneous exceptions to your budget, because you'll know from your own experience that you'll have to pay for them by doing without something else that you wanted even more.

2. **Be a smart, well-informed consumer.** We're all bombarded by advertising around the clock. This virtually guarantees that we get a constant, unrelenting view of exactly one side of the story. Everybody knows what this side of the story looks like: the benefits of buying are mind-bogglingly wonderful, the price is unbelievably low, you'll be admired by everyone you know, and unless you act now, you'll really be missing out. Is that all you need to know, or is there *another* side to the story?

Of course there is—but you'll have to do some of your own homework in order to get it. If you put some effort into this kind of homework, I'll promise this: you'll be amazed by how much you can save, easily. Become familiar with consumer-oriented publications and forums. Check out user reviews on the Internet. Get educated about the real trade-offs between new vs. used, and about branded vs. not. Ask friends or colleagues who have made similar purchases what they learned in the process. Spend a few minutes looking at coupons in the mail before throwing them out as junk. Learn which things you should *never* pay the full asking price for. Understand why Homer

Simpson says, "Extended warranty? How can I lose?" If you've never done this kind of research before, it might sound like a lot of work. But like many other areas that we've been talking about, the key is to establish a habit. There is no real shortcut to becoming a smart, well-informed consumer. It takes a commitment to doing the homework, but the payoff for doing so begins early and is well worth it.

3. **Smooth out nonrecurring expenses.** Most of the expenses in your budget come to you in relatively predictable monthly amounts. But some of your expenses won't follow this kind of monthly pattern. You might have some that are once a year, like membership fees, holiday gifts, or annual vacations. Others might be one-time expenses, like purchasing a major appliance, a new computer, or a training course.

   This is where your emerging habit of long-term thinking can come into play to improve your financial life. The idea is to begin planning for these expenses early, well before you need the money to pay for them. How do you do that? By including them in your budget, in small, regular monthly amounts. Similar to paying yourself first, you simply transfer these amounts to savings each month, where they'll earn interest in the meantime.

   Financially speaking, not every month is the same. But the trick is to use your budget to make every month *seem* roughly the same. When it's time to pay the nonrecurring expense, since you've saved for it in advance, your monthly process won't skip a beat. For those without budgets—or who don't use their budgets to anticipate these kinds of expenses—financial life can be a chaotic series of up-and-down months. Smoothing out your nonrecurring but perfectly predictable expenses frees you up from all of this unnecessary stress. This feeling of being in control of your monthly expenses is one of the more immediate benefits of budgeting; you'll be surprised by how easy it is once you've gotten the hang of it.

4. **Plan for unplanned expenses.** Your car needs new brakes much sooner than expected, your doctor prescribes some new and expensive medication, or your microwave blows up and needs to be replaced. All kinds of things like this invariably pop up, and the one thing that they have in common is that they *weren't in the budget.* We're not talking about huge financial emergencies here—we'll cover those in a later chapter. Instead we're talking about those bothersome, unplanned expenses just big enough to put a painful dent in this month's budget. That means that you'll have to scramble to find the money by doing without some other things that you'd been planning on. Unless, that is, you've taken some precautions.

Look at it this way. Even though events like these are rarely planned, what is the probability that your car will *never* need an unexpected repair, that you'll *never* get sick, or that a household appliance will *never* need replacing? What to do? Build a contingency fund into your budget, that's what.

Let's say that your goal is to do a little better than the First Rule minimum, and you intend to save 15% of everything you ever earn. The way that you plan for unplanned expenses is to put a line item in your budget called "contingency fund." If you budget for 3% of your earnings on that line, all of your other—planned—spending will be set as if you were planning on saving 18%. The difference between the 15% and the 18% is a pool of excess savings that you can draw on when these unplanned expenses occur. At the end of the year, if it turned out that you needed the 3%, you've got it—and you still achieved your goal of saving 15%. If it turned out that you didn't need the 3%, then you've saved more than you planned and your net worth is increasing faster than you'd planned—oh, darn!

5. **Avoid using currency.** There are many forms of what economists call *cash* and *cash equivalents*—we'll learn more about them in upcoming chapters. But probably the most familiar of all the forms of cash is currency—coins and bills—whether in your pocket, purse, wallet, piggy bank, or between the cushions on your couch. Do you understand now what I mean by *currency*? Good. Now, stop using it.

When you spend coins and bills, they leave no trail. Unless you want to collect paper receipts all month, or keep some kind of transaction-by-transaction record, using currency short-circuits the compare and learn steps in the budget process. It's like mystery spending—who knows where, when, or how it was used? All you know is that it's gone.

When you spend with a debit card, a credit card, or by check, you leave a specific record of what the purchase was for, which greatly facilitates the budgeting process. The best approach of all is to select just *one* of those three (debit card, credit card, or check), and use that for every transaction. (We'll cover which one of the three is best a few chapters from now.) That way, the results for the entire month are available online, all in one convenient place, in downloadable form. This makes the compare step a snap, and you can spend more time in the learn step.

Yes, there are exceptions. It may not work particularly well to pass your debit card down the aisle at a baseball game to a hot dog vendor or to write a check at an automated turnpike toll booth. But the more you can avoid using currency, the smoother your budget cycle will be.

6. **Small transactions repeated a large number of times add up.** Sounds obvious, doesn't it? But this is one of the most common spending traps that those who don't budget fall into. Why go to the trouble of bringing your lunch to work? It's always easier to go out; bringing your lunch might only save $5 or $10. The key is to understand that it is not a $5 or $10 decision—multiplied by 200 lunches a year, it is a $1,000 or $2,000 annual habit. Maybe those lunches are worth that much to you, or maybe they're not, but the point is to make the decision *consciously,* prioritizing the lunches against other things that you could spend that same amount of money on.

   Budgeting *forces* you to look at the small-dollar, high-volume transactions and see them realistically. Operating without a budget, or letting these kinds of expenses escape scrutiny by using currency to pay for them, will allow you to be lulled into thinking they're much smaller than they really are.

7. **Beware of the subscription effect.** Many service providers charge for their services on a regular monthly basis. Often it is convenient for both you and the service provider to set up an automated payment scheme, which calls for you to preauthorize payment from either your bank account or a credit card. Examples include services like cell phones, cable or satellite television, club memberships, and insurance coverage. If you are completely certain that the monthly amounts will never change and that the duration of the agreement cannot be extended without your explicit permission, then you are on safe ground. But if the monthly charges are subject to variation, or if the agreement can be automatically extended or renewed automatically, then watch out! This situation leaves you vulnerable to what is sometimes called the *subscription effect,* and it is financially dangerous; you might end up paying much more, and/or for a longer period of time, than what you had originally preauthorized. Here's how it works.

   It starts with highly visible advertising for a very low monthly rate for a certain set of services. (The rates are often especially low if you are switching over from a competitor.) These low rates are only temporary, but you will only find that out in the fine print. These temporary low rates are called *teaser rates.* Before long, the teaser rates go up—sometimes very substantially. The seller heavily encourages you to preauthorize an automatic monthly payment, allegedly for your convenience. But the seller's real motivation is to encourage an "out of sight, out of mind" situation so that you (hopefully) won't notice when the teaser rates expire and the higher rate takes effect. After several more months, the seller may implement yet another price increase. If you're notified at all, the communication is usually in the tiniest print available and specifically designed to encourage you to ignore it. A similar tactic may be used when it's time to renew your agreement; it isn't uncommon for service providers to automatically assume that you want to renew unless you specifically notify them to the contrary.

Here's another twist. Let's say that the seller has three levels of service: red, white, or blue. You sign up for blue. A year or so later, the seller redesigns all their service packages and now has *four* levels: bronze, silver, gold, and platinum. The seller notifies you of this exciting new development and advises you that "gold" is the closest to what your current "blue" service level is. So, supposedly for your convenience, they offer to make the assumption that your choice is to switch to gold, and if you agree, you don't have to do anything—they'll take care of everything automatically! Well, gold may be the closest to blue, but it is a safe bet that gold has a *higher* price than blue. Unless you are the type to read every line of fine print in what looks like a routine piece of mail, you've just "agreed" to pay a higher price—by doing nothing. Suffice it to say that these sellers know all about the paths of least resistance. The idea is that they've got a little hidden drain in your financial bathtub, and they want to steadily open that drain up as wide as possible without your noticing a thing.

Your budget process *stops* this tactic cold. They're hoping you won't notice the steady increases, but your budget *forces* you to notice every increase. Each increase is a trigger for you to reprioritize the spending against all of your other spending and make conscious decisions about whether to accept the increase, downgrade your service level, or cancel it altogether. If it sounds like I'm making a big deal out of one small part of your spending, wait until you set up your first budget. If you're like most people, you will be surprised by the large percentage of your total spending in the automatic monthly billing category. It *is* a big deal!

DECISION TIME

Earlier in this chapter, I noted that many people choose not to adopt a budget process at all because it doesn't seem like much fun. And even though I've done my best to convince you, point by point, of the many advantages of a basic budget process, I'm sure that some of you still aren't ready to commit to it. I won't sugarcoat it; even though the budget process eventually becomes a breeze, the first few cycles are likely to be time consuming and maybe a little bit frustrating. That's because you're learning lots of very valuable lessons in a concentrated period of time, and I highly recommend that you begin right away.

But for those of you who just can't stand the idea, let me offer this alternative. Strictly speaking, you don't have to use a monthly budget process, but if—and *only* if—you faithfully follow the First Rule (which, as you'll remember, precludes any form of borrowing whatsoever) and pay yourself first every month without exception. If you follow these two rules, you can just spend each month until you run out of money—and then stop.

If you choose this alternative, there is good news and bad news. The good news is that your net worth will continuously grow—maybe even as fast as it would if you were doing monthly budgeting. You'll also be able to use every other tool and recommendation in the book; none of them are dependent on your doing a monthly budget. Now here is the bad news: your financial life will be quite chaotic. Especially when you are in any kind of transition (a move, adding a spouse or partner, new dependents, new job, etc.), you'll find yourself running out of money before you run out of month and having to scramble. And you definitely won't get as much for your money as if you'd budgeted. Once you've had enough of this bad news, you can always change your mind—when it comes to budgeting, better late than never!

The choice is yours: implement the monthly budget process as was just described, or skip it and instead rely only on the First Rule (which precludes any form of borrowing) and Pay Yourself First shortcut.

Before you decide, consider this: would you invest in a company that doesn't budget, when there is overwhelming evidence that most successful companies do? Isn't investing in your own financial future *at least* as important?

SUMMARY

1. The best way to control spending is through a monthly budgeting process. This process has four cyclical steps: *budget, spend, compare,* and *learn.* Consistently following this process allows you to continuously improve your skills in managing your spending.
2. One of the most powerful and effective tools in all of personal finance is called *Pay Yourself First.* To do this, you transfer your intended amount of monthly savings out of your checking account and into your savings account as soon as your paycheck is deposited, before you have a chance to do any other spending. This forces you to *spend what is left after saving,* instead of saving what is left after spending.

3. A key advantage of budgeting is that it enables you to compare various spending alternatives with one another on a side-by-side basis, in advance, rather than as a series of independent yes/no decisions. This ensures a result that is much closer to your intended priorities.

4. Becoming a smart, well-informed consumer involves a commitment to do the required research before making spending decisions, but pays off in the form of much less wasted money and more satisfaction with your purchases.

5. Most of your expenses occur monthly, but some of them are non-recurring. Plan for these expenses in advance, before you need the money to pay for them, by including them in your budget in small, regular amounts. Not every month is the same financially, but the idea is to smooth your nonrecurring expenses out in order to make each month *seem* the same.

6. Anticipate that you'll have some unplanned expenses; they are inevitable. Deal with them by including a contingency fund in each month's budget. If needed, the money will be there; if not, this defaults to increased savings and net worth.

7. Avoid using currency (coins and bills) whenever possible; it leaves no trail and thus short-circuits the *compare* and *learn* parts of the budget cycle.

8. It is very easy to underestimate the true annual impact of small-dollar decisions repeated a large number of times throughout the year, especially when paid for in currency. Budgeting is the best means of detecting and accurately assessing these kinds of expenses.

9. The *subscription effect* refers to the practice of service providers collecting payment via automated monthly payments. This usually involves low initial rates to attract you to the seller, but these rates are then increased over time, sometimes gradually and sometimes abruptly. Again, the budgeting process is the best defense, providing full visibility to every increase.

10. A complete budgeting cycle, as described in this chapter, is optional but highly recommended. A substitute way to bypass the budgeting process, but strictly commit to the First Rule, is to use the Pay Yourself First technique and the No Borrowing Ever rule.

Case Study: Billy Bigshot

In the last chapter, we covered the essential elements of budgeting. Like most of what I recommend in this book, budgeting is conceptually quite simple, but if there ever were an example of "the devil is in the details," it's budgeting. For most people, an example is very helpful in getting the hang of what successful budgeting is all about. That's why Billy was invented, and he's about to become your budget buddy. Billy makes just about all possible bathtub drain management mistakes, so that you don't have to. You can learn, along with him, what those mistakes are and how to fix them—or better still, how to avoid them in the first place.

$\mathcal{B}$illy Bigshot was on top of the world! Here he was, 21 years old, and he'd managed to land a really great job that promised financial independence and a bright future. This was no ordinary job—it paid $50,000 a year! A lot of Billy's friends weren't earning anything at all—in fact, they were *paying*. The way Billy saw it, his friends were living like prisoners in cramped college housing, paying exorbitant amounts for tuition, fees, and books, frantically studying around the clock for no pay, and too poor to afford anything fun or nice. And for what? The possibility—not the guarantee, only the *possibility*—of a good job afterward. And even if they got one, they'd be lucky to find one that paid as much as $50,000, and Billy had that now. Billy knew what college life was like because he had just left it. He had been getting pretty good grades at the local university for a couple of years and actually got to the point where he was enjoying the experience. But that's when opportunity knocked. When his uncle offered him the job of a lifetime, Billy jumped at the chance, even though he hadn't yet completed his degree.

You see, his uncle Barney Bigshot was president and CEO of Rotary Telephone Repair Corporation (RTRC), a company that had been founded in the 1950s by Billy's grandfather Benjamin Bigshot. Benjamin had built the company up from nothing, and as he neared retirement, he hired his son Barney and groomed him to eventually take over. And now that Uncle Barney was getting a little older, Billy felt that there was a pretty good chance that *he* might actually run the company someday. A few of Billy's friends had commented that there didn't seem to be much of a future in rotary dial phone repair, but Billy knew they were just jealous. So at 21, Billy was already making $50,000, had bypassed much of the drudgery and expense of college, and dreamed of becoming the leader of a company destined for greatness. How could he go wrong?

Billy knew that it was important to be responsible with his money, so he tried to make a point of showing some degree of restraint in his spending decisions. For now, he lived in an apartment in the "young professional" part of town. But he'd heard many times that paying rent was like throwing money away. With the kind of money he was making, he was thinking that he really ought to buy a house and start building up some equity. He didn't know exactly how that worked, but he knew that getting a mortgage was somehow involved, and that this in turn would mean that his credit was going to be evaluated. So when he happened to see an ad on TV about how to have his credit score sent to him, he thought "Bring it on!" Imagine his surprise when the credit score came back *below* the level needed to qualify for a mortgage. Way below! Gulp . . .

Billy knew that something had to be wrong about this. Even though he considered himself pretty smart about money ("Duh! I'm making $50,000 a year!"), he didn't know how to go about figuring out exactly what the problem was. That's when he remembered his old neighborhood friend Bobby Budget. Bobby was a few years older than Billy, and although he didn't drive a new car or live in a big house, most people considered Bobby a pretty solid guy when it came to personal financial management. He called Bobby and explained his situation. Bobby replied by saying, "Offhand, I'd say all you need to do is keep your spending to about $2,500 a month, and you should be fine. Or maybe $2,000 if you are trying to pay off some debt."

"How can you tell that without even looking at what I'm spending my money on?" Billy asked.

"Easy," replied Bobby. "There's an old rule of thumb for people just starting out that says if you keep your monthly spending to within 5% of your annual income, you'll be fine and be able to save. If you're in the hole, though, you probably need to keep it to 4% or less. It doesn't always work perfectly, because it depends on your withholding, but for most people it's pretty close. So . . . how much per month are you spending, Billy?"

"Um-m-m . . . I'm not really used to looking at it that way," replied Billy. "All I know is that I've got a good salary and all my bills are paid, so

I must be doing fine. But still, somehow I've got a low credit score. Maybe you'd better come over."

The next day, Bobby arrived, laptop in hand. The first thing he said was, "Okay, let's start with your faucet. Let me see your last several pay stubs." Billy had no idea what any of this had to do with faucets, but he did know what a pay stub was. He was paid monthly and was able to find the stubs for the past few months. He had to admit to Bobby, though, that he hadn't spent much time studying them. There were lots of lines and amounts that just looked to him like a lot of bureaucratic bean counting. He told Bobby that he figured as long as the pay stub verified that he was making $50,000 annually, that was all he needed to know to manage his expenses. Bobby listened to Billy's theory of expense management while he studied the pay stubs and then entered some numbers into his laptop.

What Bobby told him next came as a shock. "Billy, you keep saying that you make $50,000 a year. In fact, you keep saying it over and over. But that's just not a very helpful number to use in planning your monthly spending. I think you need to *stop* thinking in terms of the $50,000 a year coming in. After looking at your pay stubs, the rule of thumb was right. You need to stop thinking about your annual salary and start thinking about limiting your spending to no more than $2,000 a month."

Billy shot back, "$2,000 a month? That is *nothing*! My rent alone eats up over half of that. A decent car costs *ten* times that. Houses in this neighborhood cost one or two *hundred* times that. That *can't* be right! How on earth do you get that number?"

Bobby patiently replied, "Billy, number one, you are jumping back and forth comparing annual numbers (like your salary) with monthly numbers (like your rent) with one-time numbers (like the price of a car or a house). From now on, we're going to talk about all your spending on a *per month* basis. Number two, you don't know the difference between gross pay and take-home pay. All your bills and expenses have to be paid with your take-home pay, so let's start with that."

Bobby continued, pointing at lines on Billy's latest pay stub as he spoke. "Look at the top line, which is your monthly gross pay. It's $4,167, and sure enough, that is $50,000 divided by 12. But now, look at all the things that are *subtracted* from that before you get to start spending anything. See this number down at the bottom, called *Net Pay*? That's your take-home pay, and it's $2,833, which is about two-thirds of your gross pay."

"What? I'm only getting to keep *two-thirds* of what I earn? Where is the other third going?" asked Billy with alarm.

"Actually, that is a pretty typical ratio. Here is how yours breaks down: about 22% of your gross pay is getting withheld to pay for federal and state income tax. Your actual tax bills might be more or less than what's getting withheld, but based on what you put on your W-4, this is what's getting taken out now." Bobby could tell from the look on Billy's face that he had no idea what a W-4 was, but he continued anyway. "Another 7% or so is what you're contributing to Social Security and Medicare. You pay into this as you earn, and at least in theory, these programs will be available for you when you reach retirement age. And another three or so percentage points is to pay for your health insurance plan. The cost for this is split between you and RTRC; they pay quite a bit of it, but you pay the rest. Believe me, if they weren't subsidizing this, you'd be paying a lot more for your plan, so you're getting off pretty easy on that. Add all that up, and that comes to about a third of your gross pay."

Billy just shook his head, now realizing that there wasn't much he could do about the big difference between his gross pay and take-home pay. Suddenly his face brightened. "Hey! At least I did one smart thing, and now I'm even happier that I did it. See that line called '401(k)' with a big zero next to it? Human Resources came around asking how much I wanted to contribute. They told me it would be an automatic payroll *deduction*, so I told them to forget it. Pretty smart, huh? What is 401(k) anyway? Some kind of charity?"

Bobby replied, "Billy, that's the *best* deduction to have! RTRC has a fantastic 401(k) matching program, and you want to contribute the maximum allowed. It's a charity alright, but the recipient is the future *you*. And the giver is the present you, along with the IRS and RTRC. But it is too late to sign up for this year, so let's put that aside for now."

Just then Billy noticed something. "Hey, you said I need to keep my spending below $2,000 a month, but my net take-home pay is over $2,800 a month! Looks like you screwed up; I'm not as bad off as you thought, right?"

"Well, no," Bobby replied. "There is something that's not on your pay stub, that some of us refer to as the First Rule of personal finance. But we'll get into that later. Right now, let's take a look at your drain. Tell me about your monthly expenses."

Again, Billy didn't quite get what drains had to do with any of this. But for a change, he began to feel a little better about his financial understanding. You see, he had anticipated that Bobby was going to ask him about this, and he'd already made up some rather extensive notes about his spending. So referring to his notes, he took a deep breath, and told Bobby the following.

"Well, I pay $1,200 a month in rent. I felt like this was quite a responsible choice. It's a pretty nice apartment, but definitely on the modest side for a guy making $50,000 a year. It's a smart deal, too, when you consider that the $1,200 includes all utilities. Besides, the apartments downtown with a view of the water can run double or triple this. I saved even more money by buying the Triple Whammy package from Cable Giant. This gives me a land line, long distance, cable TV with all the premium channels, and wireless for one low 'bundled' price. Not sure what it is now, but it started at only $59 per month, and it would be way more if I didn't bundle. Let's see, I have a cell phone—can't remember the monthly rate, but it's really low, too. My car? Well, you have to understand—I am passionate about cars, and since I can afford it, I got a pretty sweet one. I bought it brand new, and I've customized it quite a bit. But I didn't want to go completely overboard with spending, so I actually bought a less expensive one than the car that I *really* wanted. That's what I'll get next year if I get a raise. On top of that, the financing package was really good, so I pay only $220 a month. Mileage isn't too great, though, only 15 mpg, but the tank is really big, so I don't have to fill up too often."

"I'm with you so far, keep going," said Bobby, busily typing as Billy continued.

"When it comes to food, I don't really spend much. I'm always in a rush to get to work in the morning, so it's perfect to just go to the drive-through coffee bar for a Double Reverse Mocha Blaster and a cinnamon roll, 10 bucks max. I usually go out for lunch with my friends at RTRC, but that doesn't really count because the only other choice is the ultra-boring corporate cafeteria. For dinner, I usually eat at home. Upscale Market is right on my way home, and the premade Gourmet Yuppiepalooza dinner specials they have are great. Since I'm there, I pick up any other household stuff that I need, too, although I have to admit that the lavender-scented organic toilet paper isn't much of a bargain. Now, I do treat myself once in a while and go to a nice restaurant, if I have a date. No more than once a week, though—I don't want to spend *too* much. And speaking of dates, how is an up-and-coming guy like me going to meet the woman of my dreams by staying home all the time? Besides, you know what they say about all work and no play. If you want to hang out with nice people, you have to go to nice clubs, and those aren't exactly cheap. But like I say, I don't want to be irresponsible, so no more than once a week. Some of my friends go almost every night! Clothes aren't a big expense for me either, since we dress informally at RTRC. So one or two trips to the mall a month, at the most. The only other monthly expense I have is my credit card, but I got one on a special promotion with great interest rates and really low minimum payments. So that only runs me $25 a month. I have some other expenses, but they aren't monthly. Most of the time, they aren't really optional—like getting my car repaired when it needs it, buying furniture for the apartment, presents at birthday and holiday times, those kinds of things. Of course, as hard as I work, I need a vacation a couple of times a year. I figure that because I am so responsible with my money for 50 weeks a year, I can afford to splurge a little bit for the other two. What the heck, I'm making 50 grand a year—I can afford to go some pretty cool places."

Well, Billy was quite happy with his speech. Not only did its length show just how on top of his spending he really was, but it was filled with examples of how responsible he was by making less-expensive choices than he could have made. Meanwhile Bobby continued typing into his laptop; then he asked to see all kinds of receipts, credit card statements, bills, and invoices. Fortunately, Billy had most of them. He'd made a habit of throwing all of his receipts into an unoccupied corner of his living room. Bobby went through every one of them, but his calm expression gave Billy no clue about any conclusions he was forming. Finally, after a few final keystrokes, he looked over at Billy.

"Billy, before I say anything else, I just have to set you straight on a very key word you keep misusing. The word is *savings*. When you buy something, but you say that you could have spent more, the difference is *not* savings! Same thing with spending less than your friends are spending—that doesn't save you anything! Think about it. Absolutely every single thing you or anyone else buys, you could have spent even more by buying a bigger, better version, or by buying the same thing somewhere else for a higher price, or by buying two instead of one. If that is savings, then we're all "saving" millions of dollars a month! It's a comparison that isn't much use; it's like the captain of the Titanic pointing out that he missed a couple of even bigger icebergs before he hit the one that sank him. You need to think about the *actual* dollars and cents that you're spending, not the artificial, hypothetical savings compared to what you could have spent. That's how advertisers want you to think, and the advertiser's job is to get you to spend."

"Okay, then," Billy asked, "what's your definition of savings?"

"Depositing money that you *don't spend* in a savings account."

Billy replied, "Okay, I get it. But really, Bobby, enough with the lectures; I can't stand the suspense. You've just spent 10 minutes pounding numbers into that laptop, and now I gotta know—how am I doing? Do you think I'll be able to buy a house after all?"

"Not anytime soon," Bobby said seriously. "Listen, Billy, I'm going to give it to you straight. Right now, your financial condition is a mess. Your net worth is already negative to the tune of several thousand dollars, and it's getting more and more negative every month that goes by. If you keep on going the way you have been, you'll end up owing over *a million dollars* 10 years from now. Of course, you won't ever get to the point of owing that much, because your creditors will never let the debt get that high. Instead you'll be forced into bankruptcy, meaning that you won't be able to borrow any money at all, get any kind of credit, or buy any kind of house, for a very, very long time. So . . . *that's* how you're doing."

"But, but . . . " Billy blustered belligerently. "How can that possibly be true? There's no way! I make . . . I make . . . fifty . . . thou . . . " His voice trailed off, as he realized that he was about to tell Bobby his annual salary for the sixteenth time that hour. Finally, his tone now somber, he managed to ask, "How could this have happened? I thought that things were going so . . . well."

"It's your spending, Billy. You *do* make a good salary. Lots of people would love to have your salary. But your spending would be pushing the limits for somebody making twice what you make, and that's what's killing you. You are spending way, way too much—month after month."

By this time, Billy was stunned enough to believe that he was actually going broke on $50,000 a year, but he still couldn't fathom how. He asked Bobby to show him. Bobby turned the laptop to Billy and showed him a spreadsheet (see figure 7.1).

MONTHLY SPENDING FOR BILLY BIGSHOT	
Take Home Pay	2833
Expenses:	
Rent	1200
Triple Whammy	125
Cell phone	80
Car payment	220
Gas	300
Car insurance	90
Car maintenance and customization	150
Morning coffee and cinnamon roll	200
Workday lunches	150
Restaurant dates	260
Groceries	320
Clubs and other entertainment	200
Clothing	150
"One-Time" expenses: vacations, gifts, etc.	400
Total Expenses	**3845**
Income Minus Expenses	**-1012**

Figure 7.1.   Monthly spending for Billy Bigshot.

"Look, Billy, you're spending $3,845 a month, on the average. But your take-home pay is only $2,833. So you're not just failing to save, you're getting deeper in the hole by more than $1,000 a month. But it gets worse. Where do you get that extra $1,000 from? Your credit card, that's where! You think you're paying off your car, but you're fooling yourself. You're just transferring your debt from the car dealer to the credit card company. Another way to put it is that you're converting secured, medium-cost debt into unsecured, extremely high-cost debt. Your unpaid credit card balance just keeps growing and growing. If it grows at $1,000 a month, that's over $12,000 a year. *This* is what's killing your credit score.

"But it gets even worse. You said that your credit card had a very low interest rate. But that was just a temporarily low rate to get you to switch. Since then, they've moved you to a much higher rate. If you miss a payment or two, then your rate will go even higher. These rates can get unbelievably high. I know it seems hard to believe, but trust me—it would total over a million dollars in 10 years. That's the power of compounding for you . . . or, I should say, *against* you.

"Now, you asked how it happened. To put it plainly, you failed to do two very important things. Don't feel too bad, because many other people fail to do these things, too. First, you don't have a budget. A budget is a plan for how you're going to spend your money each month. Your budget needs to be a strict, absolute limit, which you determine *ahead of time*. The limit has to be low enough to allow you to save a good part of your monthly income. But since you don't have a budget, you have no basis on which to decide whether you can afford something or not, other than a vague comparison to your annual salary. You aren't able to see how seemingly small decisions can add up to a big problem.

"Let me put it another way. There is no one, single spending decision or habit that has put you into trouble all by itself. What has you in trouble is the combined effect of *all of them together*. You've been looking at each decision one at a time, as if each one were completely independent of the other, and then justifying each one. I can't stress strongly enough that that approach will *never* work—it will always result in too much spending. The only way to make effective spending decisions is to determine, ahead of time, how much *total* spending you can afford each month. At the end of the month, *total* spending is all that matters. Then you prioritize what you are going to spend it on and you stick to your decisions. That's what making a budget, and living within it, is all about. This is one of the most basic cornerstones of being financially responsible.

"The second reason for your problems is that you don't do your homework. Since you're not a well-informed consumer, you end up wasting a lot of money without realizing it. You're falling for all the advertisers' tricks, instead of doing research to find the best deals. It might not seem like research makes that big of a difference—but it does!"

Picking himself off the floor, Billy dejectedly stared at the laptop and then asked, "Bobby, I can't believe how badly I've messed up my financial life. I had no idea. Not only are my dreams out of reach, but I am digging myself deeper and deeper into the hole each month. Tell me . . . is there any hope? Is there *anything* I can do?"

For the first time that day, Bobby smiled. "Billy, the first thing to do when you find yourself in a hole is to *stop digging*! Listen—even though I gave you a hard time about bringing up your salary over and over, it is still an important part of the picture. You have something that a lot of people don't, which is a good, steady income at a pretty high level. That's a great starting point. Your salary isn't the problem; your *spending level is*. So what you need to do is to establish a new, lower spending level that makes sense with the level of income that you have.

"Here is some more good news. Even though you've been digging yourself a hole at a pretty alarming rate, you've only been digging for about 6 months. If you'd called me 2 years from now, this conversation would be very different. You know, in a way, the fact that you're young is an advantage. It's never much fun to scale back from a high-spending lifestyle, but it's definitely easier when you haven't had much time to get completely used to it.

"I won't sugarcoat it—you are going to have to make some very major changes. But if you can do that, you can get yourself turned around. It won't happen overnight, but the sooner you reverse course, the sooner you can get yourself out of debt and start building some net worth with that nice salary of yours. So tell me: are you willing to give it a try?"

Billy listened to every word and started to feel like there might be a way out. "Bobby, let's do this right now. Let's you and me sit right down at this laptop and figure out how I can get out of this situation!"

But Bobby shook his head. "Billy, at this point, it's really important that *you* take over. I've told you that you need to establish a budget, and I've told you that you need to become a smart, well-informed consumer. You are going to need to keep both of those habits going for the rest of your life. I am not going to be here to help all the time, and besides, *you* are the one who's going to live with all of the decisions that you make, so *you* have to be in charge.

"But I'll tell you what I'll do. I want you to spend the next week thinking about everything that we've talked about and then take a shot at putting together a budget for the next few months. The first few tries you take at it, you might get discouraged. But this is not wasted time; the things you learn from your first few failures will be *very* valuable lessons that you'll remember the rest of your life. I don't want to deprive you of those lessons by holding your hand the whole time. Just don't give up.

"Now here's what I want you to do: I want you to build a monthly budget for yourself. Remember when I told you about the First Rule? That rule is to save at least 10% of everything that you earn. In your case, since you're in debt, I think you should shoot for double that amount—20%. The only way to make that happen is to *pay yourself first*. So the very first part of your budget should be to subtract 20% of your gross pay from your take-home pay; you don't want to even dream of considering that as money available to spend. Your take-home pay is $2,833 a month, and 20% of your gross pay is $833; so that leaves you with an absolute maximum of $2,000 a month to spend. Hey, that's exactly what the rule of thumb predicted it would be! Anyway, will you give it a try?"

Billy, feeling a little bit less of a big shot now, was willing. "I already have some ideas," he told Bobby. "But they seem kind of small. I'm not sure I can get all the way down into the $2,000-a-month range, because I don't really think I've been all that extravagant. But yes, I'll give it my best shot—I have no choice. See you next week."

Before going on, go back and take a look at Billy's monthly expenses in figure 7.1. You are probably already convinced that he can get his spending down to $2,000 a month if he really tries; but where do you think the big opportunities are? Do you think that getting spending that low will be hard or easy?

A week later, Bobby knocked on Billy's door, and Bobby immediately saw that Billy was a changed man. His kitchen table was covered with bank statements, bills, and spreadsheets, all neatly arranged into organized stacks. Cardboard boxes filled the room, and it was clear that Billy was in the process of packing. But the most important thing that Bobby noticed was Billy's big smile.

"Bobby, I can't wait to show you! I can't believe how much I was able to figure out in just a week. After a while, I realized that there was just no way that I was going to make any headway living in this $1,200-a-month apartment. Well, it turns out that two of my college buddies are living in an old rental house, and their third roommate just transferred to another college. So I'm moving in with them. Their rent is $800 a month including utilities, and all I have to pay is one-third of that. No more triple whammy, either. All they have is basic cable TV, and I'll pay a third of that. Why even have a land line when we've all got cell phones? Speaking of cell phones, I canceled the contract on my fancy one and got a much cheaper pay-as-you-go phone. As far as wireless, there are free spots all over town, including the public library, which is just two blocks from their place. My 6-month lease here is just up, and my buddies are ready to take me right away, so I'm moving this weekend. Living over there is going to save me *lots*."

"Congratulations," Bobby said with a smile. "I see you have a new definition of savings—spending less money than you used to spend. Very good. Tell me more."

"Well . . . about the car. As much as I love it, when I saw just how much it was costing me, month after month, I knew I had to do something about it. I did a little research, and now I can see that I was a real sucker for buying a new car; I can't sell it now for anywhere near what I bought it for. And all that customizing I did only made it worth even *less*. But I got lucky! It turns out that Harry Hotshot, who is a guy I know a few years younger than me, has had his eye on my car ever since I bought it. And he actually *likes* the custom-painted flames! We were able to agree on a price that was exactly what my loan balance was. So I sold it and paid off the loan, with no profit, no loss. I can't believe I'm saying this, but I've decided to completely do without a car of any kind, at least for now. I realized that most of the miles I was driving were back and forth to work. At first I wasn't too crazy about the idea, but there is a bus stop right near my new place. And of course, there's another one just two blocks from RTRC. I'd never really checked this out before, but public transit in this town is really cheap, just a buck each way to and from work. But there's no way that I'm going to pick up a date on the bus, so I've worked out a deal with one of my new roomies. He's got a 'nice enough' car, and he's willing to loan it to me once in a while for 50 cents a mile. I figure that the most I'd ever drive the borrowed car in a month is 100 miles—50 bucks a month, max. The bus will run me another $40. So now my total cost for transportation in a month is under $100! No car payment, no insurance, no oil changes, all of that is gone. And now that I've ridden the bus a few times, I've found out that it's not so bad. In fact, now I'll have time to read *Rotary Phone Illustrated Weekly* on the way to work, which will definitely impress Uncle Barney.

"There's more: I couldn't believe how much I was paying on everyday expenses like food. Forget the drive-through coffee bar; now I'll have the same thing for a fraction of the cost at 'Billy's Place.' All I need is a pound of coffee and a couple of dozen cinnamon rolls from Cheap-O-Mart, and I'm good for a month. Speaking of which, that's where I'm getting *all* my groceries and household items from now on, no more Upscale Market. Cheap-O-Mart's freezer section is three times as big as their deli; it's the other way around at Upscale. And as much as I like hanging out with my work friends over lunch at the restaurants, there are just as many friends who stay in at the 'boring' company cafeteria, so that will be fine. Better still, I plan on bringing my own lunch most of the time. Between that and skipping the coffee bar, I'll save money *and* time every day. Clubs? Well, I'll still go, but once a month instead of once a week. And I still plan on dating just as often, but every single date doesn't need to be a dinner out. Again, maybe once a month instead of once a week, and there are plenty of less-expensive things I can do for the other dates. As for clothes, well, I figure that I've bought enough new clothes over the past 6 months to last for at least the next several. But I'll put in a small monthly amount in case I need something special.

"Now, what about this $400 a month for one-time expenses? When I really looked at it, the majority of it was for vacations. I ended up deciding that since I'm only 21, I have the rest of my life to explore exotic beaches. I'll just skip those kinds of destinations for a few years until I'm in much better financial shape. In fact, I talked to the landlord at my new place, and he said that he has some other properties that need painting this summer. So maybe I'll take those vacation weeks and *earn* some extra money instead of *spending* extra money. The last thing is that I know I'm new at this, and I might have forgotten something, or I might have overestimated how much I can save on certain things. So I put in a 3% contingency, just in case. If I don't need it, I'll save it.

"Anyway, I put it all into a spreadsheet, and here's what it looks like." See figure 7.2.

Before going on—how did Billy's result compare to how hard or easy you imagined that this would be? Now take a look at each line in Billy's old and new column. For each line, think about what changes Billy had to make in his life to get from the old amount to the new. This may seem a little tedious, but it really gets to the heart of what building a budget is all about. Once you get a feel for this kind of thinking, it becomes a lot more natural and goes more quickly.

Bobby took a look at Billy's numbers, shook his hand, and said, "Billy, I'm very impressed! You used to spend $3,845 per month, and I asked you to try to get it below $2,000. But you've gotten it down to $983. That's about *one-quarter* of what you used to spend. Fantastic! Now let me ask you, Billy: living on less than a quarter of your old spending level sounds like it ought to be really, really painful. It sounds like a plan that would have to involve some enormous sacrifices in your standard of living. Is that how it feels to you?"

"Well, I haven't done it, yet," replied Billy. "All I've done is plan it. But to answer your question—no, it doesn't seem like it's going to be as painful as I thought. Sacrifices, yes, but not big, scary ones. I'm moving back in with some roommates, but I've done that before, and it was a blast, so what's the big deal? Getting rid of my car seemed like it was going to be huge thing, but I've been carless before, and I always managed to get wherever I needed to go. In a way, it's nice—I actually feel kind of freed up from always having to take

EXTREME FINANCIAL MAKEOVER for BILLY BIGSHOT

	OLD	NEW	CHANGE
Take Home Pay	2833	2833	
Pay Myself First (20% savings)	0	833	
Available to Spend	**2833**	**2000**	
Expenses:			
Rent	1200	266	-934
Triple Whammy	125	17	-108
Cell phone	80	30	-50
Car payment	220	0	-220
Gas	300	50	-250
Car insurance	90	0	-90
Car maintenance and customization	150	0	-150
Morning coffee and cinnamon roll	200	20	-180
Workday lunches	150	80	-70
Restaurant dates	260	65	-195
Groceries	320	160	-160
Clubs and other entertainment	200	50	-150
Clothing	150	30	-120
"One-time" expenses: vacations, gifts, etc.	400	50	-350
Public transit	0	40	40
Contingency (3%)	0	125	125
Total expenses	**3845**	**983**	**-2862**
Difference (available vs. spent)	**-1012**	**1017**	

Figure 7.2.   Extreme financial makeover for Billy Bigshot.

care of it, always worrying about parking, that sort of thing. Besides, I'll get another one when I'm in better financial shape, so I look at it as a temporary situation. As far as all of the other changes, it just feels more like I'm cutting back a little. I guess it's because once I had all my spending down on paper, in front of me, I was able to take out the easiest things to live without first. And I'll still do a lot of the things I was doing before, just not as often. So what do you think, Bobby? Have I stopped digging that hole?"

"You bet—*if* you stick to this plan. Instead of digging, you're on the way *out* of the hole. First, you're saving $833 a month up in the pay-yourself-first line. Then you're saving another $1,017 on top of that. That totals up to about $1,850 a month savings. The usual First Rule guideline is 10% of your gross pay. I asked you to shoot for 20%, and you've come up with a whopping 44%. You might even end up saving more than that, if you don't need your entire contingency . . . wow!"

"Okay, that's exactly what I was going to ask you about," said Billy. "Now that I'm going to be taking in more money than I spend, what exactly do I do with the extra money each month? Save it? Pay off the credit card debt?"

"Believe it or not . . . both," replied Bobby. "You see, you've got what some people call a *financial red alert*—but you have two of them at once. That means that you have two urgent, major financial problems, and they both need immediate attention. The first one is your credit card debt, and the second one is that you don't have any savings at all. When you've got a double financial red alert, I recommend going with a 50–50 plan.

"First, let's talk about your savings. I know you're excited about your prospects at RTRC, but it's important to realize that *no* job is completely safe these days: not mine, not even your uncle's, and definitely not yours. If you were to lose your job anytime soon, you would have absolutely nothing left to fall back on to pay your bills. It's a vital part of managing your financial position to have some cash held in reserve in a nice, safe place, where you can get your hands on it right away in the case of an emergency. Some people call this their *cash bucket*, and you urgently need one.

"And by now, you know how I feel about credit card debt—it's financial poison," Bobby continued. "When we started, you had two kinds of debt: a car loan and credit card debt. Well, you sold your car—brilliant! Now what you've got left is your credit card debt, and that requires urgent attention. So start paying it off, and if you stick with it, eventually you'll have it down to zero.

"So here's the plan: you've got two financial emergencies, and you have to deal with them both. At the end of each month, I recommend that you take 50% of the money that you've saved and put it into your new savings account, and use the other 50% to pay down your credit card debt. Keep doing that, month after month, until your credit card debt is all the way down to zero. As soon as that happens, you might be tempted to increase your monthly spending a little bit: don't do it! Instead, now you can take *all* of your monthly savings and put it straight into the savings account. Got it?"

"Absolutely!" Billy said with determination. "I've learned my lesson. Now that I see what a mess I'd gotten into, I never want to be in a position like that again."

Bobby went on: "Now, my last bit of advice: you've made a really excellent start, but you can't stop here. First of all, it's one thing to make these kinds of changes on a spreadsheet, but it is another to turn them all into reality. In order for this to really work, you've got to *follow through*. You've already told your landlord you're moving out and you've started packing—good. You've already sold your car and developed a plan to do without—good. You know, it usually works like this right after somebody goes through a big budget exercise. The big, one-time decisions get made, and these get followed through on right away. Now comes the trickier part: the smaller, everyday expenses. You'll be tempted every day to go back to your old habits, especially at first. You'll tell yourself that you've done a good job with the big things, so what's the big deal if you overspend on the little things once in a while? But remember what you just learned about small habits repeated a large number of times: they add up. So stick with the budget, for large items *and* small. At the end of each month, total up all your spending, compare it to your budget, and see how you did. Don't be discouraged if you get some unpleasant surprises at first, because you're still pretty new at this. But every time you get a surprise, learn from it.

"And speaking of learning, you've done a lot of it over the past week. So tell me . . . what do you think the most valuable spending lessons you've just learned are?"

Billy replied, "Give me a minute . . . this is too important not to write down." So he sat down and started making some notes. When he was finished, he showed this list to Bobby and explained each item.

1. **The First Rule—save at least 10% of everything that I ever earn and pay myself first.** In my case, I'm in a hole, so my plan is to go way past 10%.
2. **A monthly budget is vital.** Before, I was making all my financial decisions one at a time, regardless of any other decisions that I'd made. I never added them all up. And I was comparing everything to my gross pay, not my take-home pay. Basically I had no idea what I was doing or where I was going until I worked out a monthly budget.

The rule of thumb about limiting monthly expenses to 5% of annual salary—and 4% if you have debt—was a good place to start, but I ended up doing even better.

3. **Research matters.** I definitely wouldn't have found out how much I could save on some of those automatic monthly payment items if I hadn't done some homework. And I wouldn't have been brave enough to ditch my car until I'd spent some time studying the bus routes. A little study time to become a smarter consumer goes a long way.

4. **I have to do this myself.** I was all ready to have you put together a budget for me; now I'm glad you wouldn't do it. I had to make tradeoffs about what was and wasn't important to me, and only I could have done that. More importantly, since I made all these decisions, I am more determined to stick to them and make it all work.

5. **It is all about attitude.** Before we did this, my attitude was "I make $50,000 a year, and therefore I am entitled to a certain lifestyle no matter what." Going through the budget made me change my thinking. Now my attitude is "I am responsible for my financial position, nobody else. So I am going to make a plan that will get me where I want to go, and stick to it!" Without changing that attitude, I never would have done a thing.

6. **Little things add up.** Sure, the biggies were where I live and what I drive. But what really surprised me was how much I can save by just changing my smaller, everyday spending habits. What I'm going to save in food, clothes, and entertainment has turned out to be a huge part of the picture, too.

7. **It's a lot easier to change spending levels than I thought.** I have to admit, when we first started talking about this, I thought I was going to make big, drastic sacrifices just to get a 10% savings. The key was going through everything, line by line by line, with my new attitude. When I added it all up, I was stunned at how much money I could save.

8. **Follow through.** I guess I can't buy a house by taking my spreadsheets to a mortgage broker. A good plan is the start, but it doesn't count for anything unless I follow it.

Bobby smiled and said, "Billy, first of all, I just want to congratulate you on how far you've come in such a short time. The list of what you've learned in the past week is pure gold and will serve you for the rest of your financial life. You get an 'A' in 'Extreme Budget Makeovers,' which I think is just as important as any of the other subjects you were graded on in school. As far as buying a house goes, if you really stick with this budget, it just might be possible—but not for a while. I'll tell you what. Follow your plan, month after month, and give me a call about a year from now. Then we can talk about how to tell when you're financially ready to consider a house, okay?"

"Okay, will do. Any last words of wisdom?" Billy asked.

Bobby hesitated. He was thinking about advising Billy to do an Internet search on rotary telephone repair and take a look at what the stock analysts had to say about future prospects in that industry, but he didn't have the heart. Right now, Billy was flying high with his new budget, and there would be plenty of time in the coming months to call Billy's attention to the somewhat shaky status of his $50,000-a-year faucet. In the meantime, he needed some practice managing his drain. So he smiled and waved as he headed for the door and said, "Not for now, maybe later. Good luck, Billy!"

SUMMARY

This chapter doesn't need a summary; your budget buddy Billy just did it for you.

· 8 ·

Your Cash Bucket

*W*hat if you lose your job?

It happens all the time; cutbacks, outsourcing, and economic slumps can result in layoffs in virtually any industry. Even in good times, your employer could decide to change business direction, relocate, or consolidate—any of which might mean the elimination of jobs like yours. If that happens where you work, you could suddenly find yourself, through no fault of your own, without your primary income. And I hate to say it, but it's at least possible that you could lose your job *through* your own fault.

As long as we're considering worst-case scenarios: what if you or a dependent develops a medical condition that isn't covered by your health insurance? What if you are involved in a car accident where you are liable for damages that exceed your insurance coverage? Just because the chances of these kinds of things happening are small, it doesn't mean that they can't happen to you—they can.

The point is, you need some emergency funds. Yes, many worst-case scenarios can and should be insured against, and we'll talk about how to do that in a few more chapters. But some things can't be insured against, or the cost of doing so is too high to make good financial sense. These kinds of risks have the potential to completely derail your financial future if you have no means of dealing with them.

Well, you *are* going to have a means of dealing with them, and that means is what we're going to call your cash bucket. Think of it as your margin of safety, your *self-insurance* against the unforeseen, your security blanket, your safety net, your financial crash helmet, or any other term that will help you remember what it is for, which is a healthy supply of quick-access emergency money to fall back on in the case of a *true* financial emergency.

Notice the emphasis on the word *true*. The instances that we've brought up already—losing your primary income, an uncovered medical condition, or an over-the-coverage-limit car accident—are good examples of true financial emergencies. Suddenly remembering that tomorrow is your boyfriend/girl-friend/spouse/partner's birthday and you haven't gotten a present yet might be a relationship emergency, but it isn't a financial one. A great price on the perfect car/boat/vacation/fill-in-the-blank that you've wanted all your life is something that you budget some extra savings for, delay until after your cash bucket is full, or forgo altogether—not a financial emergency.

Think of your cash bucket as your last line of defense against financial emergency—so *you don't touch it* unless there is no other option.

Why are we using the term *cash bucket* instead of one of the more tradi-tional terms, like *emergency funds* or *cash reserves*? Simple: a bucket is either full or it's not. It's all too easy to feel financially safe if you have some emergency funds—but "some" is too vague of a concept. Referring to it as a bucket forces you to consider whether you have *enough* or not. Each time you think of your cash bucket, you'll think in terms of "yes, I have a cash bucket, but is it full or isn't it?" And if it isn't, you know you have some work to do to fill it.

In the next section, you'll learn that filling your cash bucket is simple to understand but requires a significant commitment of time and sacrifice. But filling it is a *requirement* before you can proceed to buying a house or getting started in any long-term investing. Think of filling your cash bucket as the price of admission for all of the other, more fulfilling financial goals that you hope to achieve later.

THE BASIC CASH BUCKET FAQs

Q: Where does the money for my cash bucket come from?

A: From the money you save, month after month. This is the first place that your First Rule money goes; when you pay yourself first, those payments go to your cash bucket until it is filled up.

Q: Okay, then, how much do I have to put in the cash bucket before I can consider it full?

A: For most people it takes an amount equal to *6 months of your primary income*. In other words, if your primary income is $3,000 per month, you'll need $18,000 in your cash bucket in order to consider it full. If you're making $5,000 per month, you'll need $30,000, and so forth.

Q: Gulp . . . that's a lot.

A: Yep.

Q: What do you mean "for most people"?

A: How big your cash bucket needs to be depends on what your own risk level is. To keep things simple, let's arbitrarily say that everyone falls into one of just three risk categories: high, medium, and low. Those at medium risk should use 6 months of primary income as their cash bucket size, but if you're at high risk you should use 8 months, and if you're at low risk, you can use 4. Start by assuming that you're at medium risk and you'll need a 6-month cash bucket. However, if *any one* of the following applies to you, then you're at high risk and should use 8 months:

1. Your primary income is two-thirds or more of the total household income and you have one or more dependents.
2. The industry where you work, or the particular job that you have, is more susceptible than average to ups and downs in the economic cycle, to outsourcing, or to seasons of the year.
3. Your job involves very specialized skills, which are applicable to a relatively small number of employers. In other words, if you were to lose that job, it's likely to take quite a long time to find another job of that type with another employer.
4. Even if your job type is stable, your individual hold on it might be weak. If you are one of several people in your workplace doing a particular job but you have low seniority or have a relatively low performance ranking, then you would be among the first to go in the event of cutbacks; this puts you at relatively higher risk.

On the other hand, you may have lower than average risk. If *any one* of these applies, then you can use 4 months of primary income as your cash bucket size:

1. There are multiple incomes in the household, and no one of them is more than two-thirds of the total household income.
2. You have some regular supplemental or passive income, in addition to your primary income, that is one-third or more of your total household income.
3. Your job is relatively recession-proof—you have skills that are routinely in demand, by a large number of employers, in good and bad

economic times. If you lost your current job, you are reasonably sure that you could find another, similar one, fairly quickly.

4. The hold you have on your job is strong: within your work group, you have high seniority and/or a relatively strong performance ranking. In other words, you are fairly certain that if there were cutbacks, you would be among the last to go.

Stop now, before you go on reading, and put yourself into one of the three categories: Is your cash bucket size 6 months of primary income, like it is for most people? Or should you use 8 or 4 months?

Q: Let's say I have average risk and I need a 6-months-size cash bucket. If I save 10% of my income, won't that take me 60 months to fill up my cash bucket—*5 full years?* Isn't that a really long time to be on financial red alert?

A: Yes, you've done the math right, and yes, that's a sobering length of time.

This is the part that comes as a surprise to most people, and not a particularly pleasant one. You have probably been thinking that when you start out in your financial life, this is when you begin making some money of your own and things ought to start looking up, right? If you've been a student, you're going from a life of writing checks to one of *collecting* them. If you've been dependent on someone else financially, now is the time for financial freedom. So what's with this "5 years of financial red alert" stuff? Believe me, if that's your reaction, I can understand—that was mine, too. There's just no getting around it, though; if you don't have a full cash bucket, then you're financially exposed in ways that can take far longer to recover from than the time it takes to fill that bucket.

But even though the math used above says that it will take 5 years, there are ways to shorten this. How about this: if, at least during the cash bucket–filling period, you can manage to save 20% instead of 10%, you can cut the required time in half. If you can store this money in such a way that you earn some interest on it (more on this shortly), then you can cut it a little bit more. If you can get some supplemental income, you can put virtually *all* of that into your cash bucket and really cut down on the time. The same goes for any windfalls that might come your way—straight into the cash bucket. Finally, there may be some things that you can do to lower your risk category and cash bucket requirement, such as changing to a more secure type of job or improving the hold that you have on your current one. Adding all of these together, you could be looking at a much shorter period of time than 5 years.

When you consider that your financial life might last roughly 60 years, a financial red alert filling period of a few years isn't all that long, especially when the benefits of doing so are so great. My advice is to just bite the bullet and be done with it.

Q: So what does *financial red alert* mean?

A: It means that you and your dependents are at high financial risk, so your top financial priority is to get out of danger as soon as you can. It means that you must approach each and every spending decision with a red alert mindset. Before you spend or budget a dime on *anything*, ask yourself "Is this more important than getting out of serious financial danger?" Unless you can answer yes, then don't do it!

Our First Rule is to save a minimum of 10% of all income. When you're in financial red alert, your focus changes in a very fundamental way. Your goal is no longer to save a predetermined amount; it is to spend the *minimum* amount. Minimum means minimum; it's as simple as that.

The only way that your cash bucket will get filled is through your own efforts—nobody is going to fill it for you. The more disciplined and committed you are, the faster it will be filled, and the faster you can get out of financial red alert status.

Q: But once I get it filled, I can just leave it filled and forget about it—right?

A: Well, not really, because the required size is likely to grow. As you continue through your financial life, your primary income is likely to increase. So that means that the amount you need to keep set aside for an emergency, such as the loss of that income, will need to grow, too. But it's also true that once you've gotten your cash bucket filled the first time, it's a much smaller matter to top it off occasionally as your income grows. If you forget to do this regularly and dependably, though, you can find yourself behind. A good practice is to review your cash bucket strategy once a year. Is your risk level still the same or do you need to adjust it? Is your average primary income still the same or has it increased? Once you've determined the answers, take the appropriate steps with regard to your cash bucket before continuing with any other investing.

Q: Now that I understand what you're recommending with this whole cash bucket idea, I'm not so sure that I'm ready to sign up for it. Do I really need to do this?

A: I thought you might have some second thoughts, especially if this is the first time anything like this has been explained to you. So the next section of this chapter is designed to help you think it over.

YOUR CASH BUCKET DECISION

Now that you know what's involved in filling your cash bucket, it's up to you to make a decision about it. It's not possible to be neutral on the subject of emergency funds; you either have a full cash bucket or you don't. Here are your choices:

1. Do completely without a cash bucket and hope that no financial emergencies ever arise.
2. Deal with financial emergencies some other way than having a cash bucket.
3. "I'll fill it, but slowly" or "I'll fill it, but I won't start right away."
4. Resolve to fill up your cash bucket as quickly as possible, beginning now.

Let's go through them one at a time.

1. **Doing without a cash bucket.** If this is your choice, then you will certainly have a lot of company. After all, most people don't have a cash bucket, generally because they've never learned about how important it is to have one. But you no longer have that excuse. Now that you've read this far, for you to decide against a cash bucket involves a conscious choice. You will have to make a deliberate decision either to hope for no financial emergencies or to prepare for the possibility.

    If you're considering this kind of choice, it is probably because the prospect of going through the sacrifice and discipline of filling your cash bucket isn't too appealing. That's fair enough—it really does require sacrifice and discipline. But ask yourself: which is really the more unpleasant prospect? A temporary period of sacrifice and discipline that lasts for a few years or the stress and uncertainty of worrying about a potential financial emergency for the rest of your financial life? A cash bucket–filling period that begins at a time of your choosing or a financial emergency that could happen virtually any time? Delaying buying some things that you'd really like until after your cash bucket is full or taking a big step backward, without warning, in the lifestyle to which you (and your dependents) have already gotten accustomed?

    Maybe you're thinking that the whole prospect of a financial emergency is so remote it really isn't necessary to take the extreme step of taking a few years to fill your cash bucket. Okay, then: let's look at it quantitatively. What do you think the chances of a financial emergency—like losing your job, developing an uncovered medical condition, or being involved in a car accident beyond your insurance coverage—are for you, in the next year? Really small, right? Probably less than 5%, maybe even as low as 1%. But remember—your financial life is likely to be something like 60 years long. I'll do the math for you: the probability that a 1%-per-year chance will occur at least once in a 60-year period is just about 50–50. The probability that a 5%-per-year chance will occur sometime in a 60-year period is overwhelming! Even if the prospect of a financial emergency in any one year seems remote, the prospect that one will *never* happen throughout your financial life is also very improbable. If you choose to take your chances, then you should know what your odds are—not good!

2. **Alternatives to a cash bucket.** If you're serious about wanting to manage your personal finances successfully, then ignoring the possibility of a financial emergency simply isn't a defensible choice. But aren't there some other ways of guarding against them? Ways that *don't* require a financial red alert, and all that sacrifice and discipline? Well, there are two different approaches like this that some people take; let's take a look at them.

The first one involves credit cards (uh-oh!). The strategy is simple: after a few years of successfully managing a credit card or two and increasing your credit limits, you can use these credit limits as your cash bucket. If a financial emergency occurs, you've got credit already in place, which can tide you over until you've recovered. What's wrong with that? First of all, achieving a combined credit limit equal to 6 months' pay is very difficult, especially early in your financial life. The second problem with this strategy is one that you already know about: extremely high interest rates. And of course, these very high rates compound, and you know what this means, too. Relying on credit cards to see you through a financial emergency carries the risk of turning one financial crisis into *two*.

The second alternative strategy? Well, since you are early in your financial life, that means that until recently, you were dependent on somebody else financially. For most of you, that somebody else was one or both of your parents. And since they took care of you for so many years, it seems only natural that they might be the first place you'd look for a rescue in the event of a financial emergency. You probably don't need me to tell you that this isn't the world's best strategy to put in place for the rest of your financial life. Especially if your parents did a good job of financially providing for you while you were dependent on them, the last thing you want is to be an ongoing burden. Wouldn't it be far better to show your gratitude by becoming completely financially self-sufficient as soon as you can?

Before you completely dismiss these ideas, bear in mind what you've just learned about how long it is likely to take you to fill your cash bucket. During the time you're filling it, you'll need some kind of backup plan in case of emergency. These two strategies might be useful as temporary, stopgap alternatives but definitely not as substitutes for a full bucket. If anything, the unsuitability of these temporary strategies should serve as motivation to get your cash bucket filled as soon as you can.

3. **The gradual- or deferred-start strategies.** These are sort of uneasy compromises. On one hand, they acknowledge the importance of emergency funds, and on the other, they seek to minimize the commitment. If you're drifting toward this line of thinking, you're on the right track—the *dead-right* track. You're creating an ideal opportunity for your right brain to come in and sabotage the entire effort. How do I know? You guessed it—in my early financial life, this was my approach. And no, I never got anywhere until I finally switched to . . .

4. **Resolve to fill your cash bucket as quickly as possible, beginning right now.** Now you're talking! Remember in the introduction when I described how common it is for older people to realize what they should have done early in their financial lives, but they came to the realization too late for it to do them any good? Let me share with you a few comments I've *never* heard from people in the 2nd or 3rd third of their financial lives.

> "I took a really long time to begin saving any money because I thought it was more important to buy some really cool stuff and to party. Well, I still have all that stuff, and now it's cooler than ever. And the memories that I have of all that partying are absolutely priceless. Now I'm completely exposed every time the economy turns bad, and I barely have any long-term investments at all, but I would never trade my cool old stuff or my priceless partying memories for financial security—no way!"

> "Yes, I sacrificed early in my financial life in order to build up some cash reserves. But I never faced any financial emergencies at all, big or small, so all of that effort was completely unnecessary. By filling my cash bucket, I developed my discipline skills and self-confidence—but as it happened, discipline and

self-confidence turned out to be completely unnecessary for me in any of the other areas of my life. So I look back on my cash bucket–filling period as one big waste of time."

Get the idea? Now that you've had a chance to really think through all of the alternatives, I hope you'll take my advice and simply resolve to do it, as fast as you can, beginning right now.

WHAT TO FILL YOUR CASH BUCKET WITH

You already know that your cash bucket needs to be filled up with money, but in what form? Remembering that this is your emergency fund, you'll want to keep this money in a form that guarantees you'll be able to access it at a moment's notice, without penalty and without delay. Of course, you would prefer to earn at least some interest on it, but definitely not at the expense of putting the amount saved at any kind of risk whatsoever. Think of your cash bucket as sacred: you don't spend it and you don't risk it. It is there for emergencies only.

Keeping all that in mind, my recommendation is that you divide your cash bucket into pieces, and keep it as follows.

1. **Household cash (actual currency).** This is actually the least safe way to store money, and it earns zero interest. Therefore, I recommend that you keep this part of your cash bucket very small—no more than a few hundred dollars. The reason you have any cash lying around at all is for the rare occasion, probably after business hours, when you need to pay for something where your debit or credit card won't work. Keep it secure and hidden; money in this form is not insured and nearly impossible to recover if stolen.

2. **FDIC-insured checking account.** In the United States, the Federal Deposit Insurance Corporation (FDIC) insures individual accounts at commercial banks and savings and loans located within the country. So if your bank is robbed, engulfed in flames, or goes out of business, you are automatically insured (up to $250,000 at the time of this writing). That covers the "safe" part of our requirements. Still, money in a checking account doesn't earn interest, so you should limit the amount here to no more than 1 month's average primary income.

3. **FDIC-insured savings account.** This money is just as safe as the money in your checking account, but here you begin to earn some

interest. The amount of interest you earn isn't high and rarely even keeps up with inflation, but it's better than nothing. A typical pattern would be to spend from your checking account and then replenish each month's spending with money from your savings account.

Note: Credit unions are not covered by the FDIC, but most are covered by similar insurance. All federal credit unions are insured by the National Credit Union Share Insurance Fund (NCUSIF). State-chartered credit unions may be insured by the NCUSIF or might have their own state or private insurance. If you've chosen to bank at a credit union, make sure that your checking and savings deposits are covered.

In the early part of your cash bucket–filling period, these three elements are all that you'll need. But once you've gotten up to about 3 months of primary income in the total of these three forms, you can begin seeking a higher interest rate than what you'll be able to earn from your savings account. There are some ways to earn *a little* more interest without putting any of your money at risk. One of the most common ways to do this is through buying:

4. **Certificates of deposit (CDs).** CDs are a common offering of most banks, savings and loans, and credit unions. Here's how they work: CDs come in various *maturities*, or lengths of time, ranging from as short as 30 days, up to 5 years or longer. CDs require a minimum investment, sometimes as little as $500. Usually longer maturities mean higher rates, and larger investments can mean higher rates, too. Why do CDs generally pay higher than savings accounts? Because you're agreeing to leave your money in the CD for the entire time until maturity, whereas you can withdraw from your savings account without penalty anytime you want. If you withdraw some or all of your investment from a CD before maturity, you'll pay a penalty. The extra interest that you get from a CD is only worth it if you're quite sure that you'll be able to leave the money in your CD alone until maturity. Finally, the interest earned and the minimum required deposit both vary quite a bit from one financial institution to another; research is essential.

So your cash bucket isn't in one single place, nor is it in one single form. A typical breakdown might be a small amount in household cash, 1 month of average primary income in checking, another month or two of average primary income in savings, and the balance in one or more CDs of various maturities. (You'll spend from checking and savings first; that's why you're safe with CDs that will mature before those sources are exhausted.)

SUMMARY

1. Insurance can't cover every possible financial emergency; that's why you need emergency money, funded by your own savings, which we call your cash bucket.
2. Until your cash bucket is full, you should consider yourself on financial red alert, because you are exposed to financial emergencies. Financial red alert means that your highest financial priority is to fill your bucket, and you should say "no!" to any financial decision that is contrary to that priority.
3. The size of your cash bucket depends on the degree of risk you're facing. The default-size cash bucket is *6 months' average primary income.* Those at higher-than-average risk should use 8 months; those with lower-than-average risk can use 4 months. Your risk level is determined by the likelihood of job loss, the difficulty that you would have finding another job, whether yours is the only (or predominant) income in the household, and the presence or absence of supplemental or passive income.
4. It may take you 5 or more years to fill up your cash bucket, but you can accelerate this by saving more than the 10% minimum, earning supplemental or passive income, putting any windfall or unscheduled gains directly into your cash bucket, and/or by taking steps to earn interest on the money in your cash bucket.
5. The required size of your cash bucket is likely to grow as your average primary income grows. A good practice is to review your cash-bucket requirements and status once a year; you're likely to need to top off your cash bucket from time to time.
6. The length of time required to fill your cash bucket, as well as the discipline and sacrifice involved, makes some people hesitate to commit to fill it as soon as possible, starting now. But the high risk or ineffectiveness of any of the alternatives makes filling it ASAP your best choice.
7. Your cash bucket should be filled up with money that you can access without delay and without penalty. You would like to earn some interest on at least part of your cash bucket, but because this money is for emergencies, you won't risk any loss of principal. A typical breakdown would look like this: a small amount of currency to serve as household cash (less than a few hundred dollars), an FDIC-insured checking account (no more than 1 month of average primary income), an FDIC-insured savings account (about 1 to 2 months' average primary income), and the balance in one or more certificates of deposit (CDs).

· 9 ·

Borrowing, Lending, and Credit

It's time to pick up the pace. So far in part II, we've covered budgeting and your cash bucket in quite a bit of depth. This is because these two essential topics require a solid understanding of the details, and these details were probably new to you. Now we'll move into some areas of personal financial management that are equally important but probably more familiar. In this chapter you'll learn about borrowing and lending, the best way to pay for what you buy, as well as your all-important credit score and how to maximize it. Where details are important, they'll be included; but in general, you'll notice a brisker pace.

BORROWING

Here is the rule when it comes to borrowing money:

Don't borrow any money.

Yes, there is one—and only one—possible exception, and that is a mortgage on a house. We'll talk about all that in part III, including the very specific conditions that you'll need to meet before it makes sense to even start thinking about buying a house. Until then don't borrow any money, period. Borrowing money isn't always called that—sometimes it goes by other names like "installment payments," "buy now pay later," "financing," or "lease with option to buy." Whatever it is called, though, it involves paying interest, and you don't do it. For anything that you want or need to buy, your approach is to pay in full at the time of purchase, saving up if necessary.

115

Most people intuitively understand that borrowing money isn't a good way to improve their long-term financial position. So why do so many people get into trouble with debt? Mostly because they start small, fully intending to repay quickly, and promise themselves that it is an exception "just this once." As soon as they do, though, that's just the opening the right brain needs. Before long, the right brain is teaming up with the amazing power of compounding, and that sound you hear is water draining out of their financial bathtubs.

What if you really, truly have no choice? Be careful when you think about this possibility, because there simply aren't many examples where this is really true; it's usually just a right brain–generated excuse. It could be true, though, in the case of a genuine financial emergency that occurs before your cash bucket is full enough to deal with it. If you are truly forced into borrowing, you'll want to proceed with extreme caution. Here is how to do it: borrow the smallest amount necessary to see you through the emergency, but first use any other funding that's available to you, including your cash bucket, and borrow only what can't be covered some other way. Borrow at the lowest interest rate possible and pay it back as soon as you possibly can. Deal only with a reputable professional lending institution such as a commercial bank where you already have an account (not with a pawnbroker or a well-meaning friend or relative). Then once the loan is secured and the emergency dealt with, tighten your budget to the red-alert levels in order to get the loan repaid and your financial condition back to normal as soon as possible. As long as you've been forced into borrowing, you may as well take advantage of the opportunity to have it favorably reflected in your credit score after you've repaid (more on this later).

Here is one last bit of advice about borrowing. Let's say you have a friend who is borrowing money from a bank, but the bank is requiring that someone else cosign for the loan. Your friend asks you to be the cosigner. Should you do it? After all, the friend is borrowing, not you. And the word *cosign* sounds innocent enough, like you're vouching for your friend's character. What's the harm? Here's the harm—if your friend can't make the payments, the bank will come after *you* to make them. Cosigning is even worse than borrowing; your friend gets to enjoy the money the bank loaned him, while you get to make the payments and take the credit score hit. Don't do it!

LENDING MONEY TO OTHERS

Here is the rule when it comes to lending money:

Don't lend any money.

Whom would you be lending money to, anyway? Since you're probably not in the business of lending to the general public, we're talking about loans to friends and family. I'm not talking about the small stuff; friends and family members can routinely spot each other small amounts for short periods of time simply for convenience, without it ever becoming a problem. Instead, I'm talking about a situation where the amount is big enough to really get your attention, let's say 10% or more of your monthly budget. You are new enough in your financial life that you may not have had to face this yet, but sooner or later you probably will. When you are, it's likely to be accompanied with some kind of emotional appeal. I'm bringing this up now to give you some time to think about how you would respond ahead of time. If you say yes, these things are very likely to be the result:

1. You won't be repaid in full or on time.
2. You will be asked for yet another loan while the first one is still outstanding.
3. Your relationship with the friend or family member will be permanently damaged.

Why is this? If someone has a good credit score, a sound plan to repay, and a solid understanding that borrowing money involves repaying it along with a market-based rate of interest, then they can go to a bank for a loan if the need arises. So if someone is asking *you* for a loan, it must mean that this is someone who does *not* meet these conditions. If the person is asking for a loan, they almost certainly have several other creditors that they are trying to deal with. When they eventually come up with money to pay off some of their debts, guess who they'll pay *last*? If they get deeper into debt, guess who they'll come to *first*?

I am fully aware that simply saying no can be very difficult, so here are some alternatives: you can simply *give* a smaller amount, with no strings attached. (Just say, "I understand your situation, and I really want to do something. Here is something that I hope will help; don't worry about paying it back.") Or you can offer some other kind of way to help them deal with their situation other than simply loaning money. Or if you think that some or all of the reasons they need the money in the first place are that they've never really been taught how to manage their finances, well, then of course you can offer to teach them some of the many things we've been discussing in these pages. Saying no in one of these ways might actually be doing your friend or family member a bigger favor than saying yes.

If you decide to go ahead anyway, be very careful. Put absolutely everything in writing. See if you can agree on an amount less than what was initially requested. Agree on a very explicit repayment schedule, including consequences such as late charges. Charge a fair, market-based rate of interest. Explicitly state that the borrower is not, under any circumstances, to ask for any more until the current loan is completely paid off. If nothing else, maybe all this formality will cause the other person to reconsider borrowing from you. If it doesn't, at least you've done your best to make your expectations very clear.

Then prepare to lose the entire amount that you've loaned, because that is probably what will happen.

I've asked my colleague William Shakespeare his opinion on these first two sections on borrowing and lending, and he completely agrees. He summarizes them this way:

> *Neither a borrower nor a lender be,*
> *For loan oft loses both itself and friend,*
> *And borrowing dulls the edge of husbandry.*

In case your 17th-century English jargon is a little rusty, the second line can be paraphrased as "if you loan money to a friend, you are likely to lose both your money and your friend" and the third line means "anyone who borrows money is missing a valuable opportunity to learn how to control their spending better."

THE BEST WAY TO PAY FOR WHAT YOU BUY

In previous chapters we've talked about how to control your spending through budgeting and the importance of spending your money wisely by becoming a smart, well-informed consumer. But the one spending angle that we haven't talked about yet is this: once you've decided to buy something, how do you pay? I mean this in the simplest, most literal sense: you've decided to buy something, the seller wants their money, and you're willing to exchange money for whatever it is that they are selling—now what? Most of the time you have a choice, and the usual suspects are currency (bills and coins), check, debit card, or credit card. Does it matter which one you pick? Are there smart ways and not-so-smart ways to pay? Or does it simply not matter, since it all ends up coming out of your pocket in the end, one way or another?

Well, it *does* matter! This is a multiple-choice question that you'll face dozens if not hundreds of times a year, and many thousands of times over the course of your financial life. As you might suspect, if there is one best way to pay for what you buy, then you should always use it, every time you have a choice. Well, there *is* one best way, and here is your rule:

Always use a credit card to pay, but never use credit.

What? Isn't "using a credit card but not using credit" an oxymoron, like "jumbo shrimp" or "awfully nice"? No, it's not—and here's why: when you pay your monthly credit card bill, in full, before the balance is due, then you aren't charged any interest. So your strategy is to use a credit card but to pay the monthly balance each and every month without fail. If you do this, then using a credit card is perfectly safe and offers some critical advantages over all the other ways that you can pay. (It's even better if you arrange to have your complete credit card balance paid each month automatically; just be sure to examine every transaction during your budget cycle for fraudulent or inaccurate charges.) But if you *don't* pay the monthly balance in full, on time, each and every month, then credit cards are extremely dangerous to your financial health. Because this point is so vitally important, I am going to restate the rule in a little bit longer form so that when you look back to refer to the rule, you won't forget it:

Always use a credit card to pay; but always pay the monthly balance,
in full, on time, each and every month, without fail.

To understand why credit cards are the best choice in the first place, let's first summarize the problems with the other three choices. Currency is a bad choice, as you already learned in the budgeting chapter, because it leaves no trail and makes the compare and learn steps of the budget cycle a nightmare. Checks are better, but there can be a significant time lag between when you write the check and when the recipient cashes it, and this also complicates the budget cycle. In addition, checks are slow and inconvenient at the point of purchase.

Before we go on, let's make sure that you understand the difference between debit cards and credit cards: if you don't, that's okay—lots of people don't—and these cards are virtually identical to the naked eye. A *debit card* allows you to spend the money in your checking account, but not any more than that. Debit cards are like checks in this way; if you try to spend more than you have in your checking account, either the transaction will be declined or you'll be charged an overdraft fee. But a *credit card* is different: it allows you to spend any amount of money up to your preauthorized credit limit, whether you currently have that much in your account or not. Each month, you are billed for the balance. If you pay the balance in full, you aren't charged any interest, and then you go on to the next month. If you pay only part of the balance, then you are charged *interest* on the unpaid portion—usually at an extremely high rate. That's where the danger comes in!

So back to our comparisons: debit cards are great for convenience, but they have two disadvantages. First, they are subject to something called *blocks*: when you make certain purchases such as buying gas, paying for a hotel room, or renting a car, transactions are often recorded for a much higher amount than you actually spent. A few days later, the high charges are reversed and the actual ones substituted in, but in the meantime the block could cause you an overdraft problem. The second problem with debit cards is that they don't help you with your credit score.

But credit cards solve *all* these problems, and that's why they are the best choice. They are convenient at the point of purchase, and the budgeting cycle is a breeze because all of your transactions are conveniently summarized each month, online, in easily downloadable form. There are no timing differences to deal with, and no blocks. Best of all, responsibly using credit cards improves your credit score. And you already know what *responsibly* means—paying off the balance in full, each and every month, no matter what your right brain says. Using a credit card is like driving a car—safe and indispensable if you know what you are doing, and very dangerous if you don't.

While using credit cards without using credit is the best strategy for you *eventually*, it may not be the best strategy *immediately*. There are two reasons for this. First, you may not be able to qualify for a credit card yet (or the credit cards that you do qualify for don't meet our criteria, which we'll cover in the next section). Second, you may not yet have enough experience with controlling your spending through budgeting to trust yourself with a credit card. If either of these applies to you, then you can use a debit card as your interim strategy. Think of your debit card like training wheels when learning to ride a bike. As soon as you can qualify for a good credit card and you feel confident in your spending control skills, then switch over. Finally, if you're having trouble qualifying for a card because you don't have enough financial history, there is a special kind of card called a *secured* credit card that can be another excellent intermediate step—check it out.

SELECTING A CREDIT CARD

Are you being inundated with credit card offers coming to you through the mail? Have you had the "honor" of being "preselected" for a credit card? Have you ever had a checkout clerk at a chain discount store advise you how much you could save if you immediately apply for a card sponsored by that store? If you haven't yet experienced any of these treats, you soon will. Credit cards are among the most heavily and aggressively advertised products around, so I want to be very clear about the next point: advertising and promotions should have absolutely *nothing* to do with your credit card selection. The credit card features that get most of the attention in advertising are ones that you don't care about. You don't care about APR (the annual percentage rate, or the amount of interest that you'll be charged on unpaid balances), because you'll never have any unpaid balances. You don't care about easy balance transfer terms, because you'll never transfer any balances. You don't care about "reward" cards that offer airline miles or discounted trips and dining, because these are good deals only for very big spenders. (You might be one someday, but not in the 1st third of your financial life.) All credit cards are *not* the same—there are some good choices out there, and there are some really, really bad ones. Research matters!

Even if you manage your credit cards perfectly, switching credit cards (by canceling one card, then applying for a new one) will hurt your credit score. Therefore, applying for a credit card should never be spontaneous, experimental, or haphazard. You should only apply for a credit card after thoroughly reviewing all of your options and carefully selecting the few that best meet your needs. To start with, one primary card and one emergency card are all that you will need. Choose them wisely and then stick with your choices.

You want to center your research on information provided by objective, credible third parties. How do you find them? Use search terms like "credit card comparisons" and "best credit card." Weed out sites that are from the card providers themselves; those are just advertisements. Also in the mix are a variety of other sites that seem more interested in getting you to apply, right away, for one or more of the cards in their collection. These are third-party sales organizations, and they receive a commission from credit card providers if applications come through their site; avoid them, because they aren't objective. You won't be able to tell them by their names, but once you've taken a look at a few of them, it will be obvious. (Hint: look for the big "Apply Now!" pop-ups.) Finally, though, you'll find several sites from financial news organizations, financial periodicals, consumer advocacy groups, and so on, which are just what you're looking for.

Here are the nonnegotiable *musts* you're looking for: you want a card that guarantees zero interest charges if the balance is paid in full each month (no "minimum finance charge" or "activity fee" for completely paid-off balances). You want one that offers an online, downloadable monthly statement. You want to be sure that your account will have a specific credit limit and that the issuer reports both the limit and your monthly balances to the three major credit bureaus (more on them later). Finally, you want a reasonable grace period, which is the number of days after the statement date that you have to pay the balance before interest charges begin (look for at least 20 days; 25 or 30 is better). If a card doesn't feature all four of those items, cross it off your list. If you're not sure, play it safe by calling the issuer's customer service number and asking.

Beyond that, you'll want to balance the remaining features based on your individual situation. One key thing to consider is how widely accepted the card is; this is determined by the credit card brand (such as Visa, MasterCard, American Express, and Discover) and has nothing to do with the bank or other institution that issues it. You'll want the annual fee to be either zero or very modest. There are potentially lots of other fees; check them out compared to the competition. (You should never pay some types of fees, like an application fee; this is a signal that you are dealing with a particularly unappealing type of issuer known as a *fee harvester*.) Finally, some cards offer cash-back or rebate programs that can be excellent choices. Take all these things into consideration, make your selection, and apply. Then stick with your choices, unless the issuer changes the terms so dramatically afterward that you truly have no choice but to switch.

CREDIT SCORES

A credit score is a three-digit number that measures how good a credit risk you are at any point in time; the higher the number, the more creditworthy you are. Your credit score is based on your debt-and-repayment history. Contrary to the mistaken impression that many people have, it is not based on your overall financial condition, your income, your net worth, your job or how long you've had it, or anything else—it is based *only* on your debt-and-repayment history. This history is then run through some sophisticated statistical software, which is derived from a large database of other people with similar credit histories, and out pops your score. The score is then made available (for a fee) to anyone who is considering lending you money; they will use the score to determine whether or not to make the loan to you, and if so, what interest rate to charge. Since high scores indicate a lower risk to the lender, the higher your score, the lower the interest rate.

Credit scores are getting used more and more widely. The time when your score is most important is when you're in the market for a house mortgage, but that's not the only time. Landlords, cell phone companies, credit card issuers, insurers, and a growing list of others use credit scores to screen out potentially high-risk customers. Employers even sometimes use credit scores to screen out high-risk job applicants. Depending on your circumstances, your credit score can have a big impact on your financial life. And yet many people don't even know what a credit score is.

Here's a brief description: although many kinds of credit scores are available, the main one—and the only one you care about—is called the FICO score, which ranges from a minimum of 300 to a maximum of 850. FICO is the trade name for the Fair Isaac Corporation. (Although the name Fair Isaac conjures up an image of a wise and noble man with a long beard and flowing robes—no. Instead, the company was founded a few decades ago by Mr. Fair and Mr. Isaac.) FICO provides the sophisticated software and the math behind it, but it doesn't keep track of all the transactions. Instead, the transaction-by-transaction record keeping is done by *credit bureaus*. There are many such bureaus in the United States, but the three main ones are Equifax, TransUnion, and Experian. FICO is closely affiliated with these credit bureaus, since their work is so interconnected, but they are all separate and independent companies.

The three credit bureaus track each and every credit-related financial transaction that occurs in the United States every day—including yours. Then they apply FICO's algorithms to each individual's transactions, and everyone's FICO scores come out. Think of all the credit-related transactions as *inputs* and the FICO scores as *outputs*.

Now, here are four key points.

1. The actual FICO algorithm that turns your transactions into your score is proprietary, and you and I can't see it. But FICO's website (www.myfico.com) does an outstanding job of explaining the basics in general terms. I highly encourage you to learn all about this, so that you know what does and doesn't matter in the determination of your score.

2. A credit *report* is different from a credit *score*. Your credit report comes from the credit bureaus and is simply a listing of all the transactions that make up your credit history, but this listing of information does not contain your actual score. If you had your credit report in front of you, and some idea of how the FICO scores are generated, you could probably make a pretty good guess at the approximate range that your score will fall into, but you would not have the actual credit score number. The purpose of seeing your credit report is to make sure that all of the information on it is accurate and complete. Sometimes inaccuracies and omissions occur, and when they do, they will lower your credit score. It is in your interest to monitor this and to contact the credit bureaus immediately if you spot a problem. They are obligated by law to work with you to correct it.

3. You are entitled, by U.S. law, to see a copy of your credit report, for free, once per year. Not only that, since there are three primary U.S. credit bureaus, you are entitled to see a credit report once per year from each one of them. You can order these free credit reports directly from

the websites of each of the three bureaus, or from a single central site that has been set up. (The advertisers who try to pull in customers by offering free credit reports are hoping that viewers don't know they could get three free credit reports per year on their own. The purpose of pulling you in is to aggressively market lots of other financial services to you while you're on their websites.)

4. Even though you are entitled to three free credit reports per year, if you want to see your actual FICO *score*, you'll probably have to pay for it. You won't have to pay much, though, especially if all you want is the score. But you don't actually need to know your exact score very often. Since the scores are based on your debt-and-repayment history, the main thing you need to do is manage your payments very responsibly and then make sure that the credit bureaus' tracking of your transaction history is complete and accurate; that will ensure that the FICO score itself is accurate.

So how high a credit score is high enough? At some point, if you are going to buy a house, you are going to take out a mortgage. Mortgage lenders generally have a FICO "magic number." If your FICO score is *below* the magic number, you get a mortgage with a very high interest rate and unfavorable terms; this is called a *subprime* mortgage. I don't recommend that you ever take out a subprime mortgage, so this magic number is your bare minimum goal. If your FICO score is *above* the magic number, you qualify for a *prime* mortgage. (Even in prime mortgage territory, your interest rate will drop as your score increases—but only up to a point.) The catch is, the magic number varies from one week to the next based on economic conditions, and it varies from lender to lender. So for now, I encourage you to learn all about FICO scores in general and to do everything you possibly can to improve your score, but there isn't much point in paying to actually see and track the score until later. You definitely don't want to pay for anything like *real-time monitoring*, which means you get a text message or equivalent every time your score moves up or down by a point; services like these are expensive and only make sense for people with very serious debt problems. Manage the inputs carefully, and the output will take care of itself.

A SAFE AND EASY STRATEGY TO EARN A GREAT FICO SCORE

Since you aren't going to be borrowing any money, the primary way you can establish a credit history and improve your score is through the responsible use of credit cards. Following this strategy perfectly will not earn you a perfect score; scores near the maximum are possible only for those who successfully utilize a wide variety of different types of credit, such as mortgages (which you are not going to be doing for a while) and car loans (which you are not going to be doing at all). If you have student loans to repay, this can actually help your credit score, since it represents another type of credit; just be sure to make every payment on time. Nevertheless, it is still entirely possible to earn a great score—one high enough to qualify you for a prime mortgage—using only credit cards. Here is your seven-point strategy.

1. **First and foremost, take care of the basics by maintaining a spotless payment record.** This means paying all of your bills on time, every time. Automating the regularly occurring ones can really help. If you are incorrectly billed, or want to dispute any charges, address and resolve the situation promptly.
2. **Carefully select your credit cards, then stick with your choices; completely avoid all other forms of debt.**
3. **Add new cards slowly, until your credit utilization is 25% or lower.** Yes, you'll be adding cards that you don't intend to use very often. Think of them as backup or emergency cards. But you don't want to add cards too quickly, since that will hurt your score in other ways. Shoot for one per year or slower. Once you've gotten to 25% credit utilization, then stop adding cards. In any case, never have more than five cards. What is credit utilization? Your average monthly balance, divided by the total of all of your credit limits. (Go to the FICO website for a much more complete explanation.)
4. **Ask for credit limit increases.** This is easy to do; just call the customer service number on the back of any of your credit cards and ask for a limit increase. The worst thing that can happen is that you'll be told no, in which case you're no worse off. But you might be told yes, in which case you have just instantaneously raised your credit score.
5. **Keep your backup cards active.** Make sure that you know what the required minimum usage is for your backup cards, so that you don't risk cancellation. In any case, you should always use each card at least once a year.
6. **Review your credit report three times each year, using the 4-month-stagger approach, and promptly request corrections of any inaccurate or incomplete information.** On January 1 (for example) of each year, order a free credit report from one of the credit bureaus; then review and notify that credit bureau of any inaccuracies or incomplete information. Repeat this with a second credit bureau on May 1, and then again with the third on September 1. If

you repeat this cycle every year, you'll have covered all three credit bureaus, and you'll be virtually assured of having the right inputs to the generation of your credit score at any point in time—and none of this will cost you a cent.

7. **Order your actual FICO score from each credit bureau after you've gone through the annual credit report review cycle once; and again about 6 months before you anticipate buying a house.** You'll want to see your actual score for the first time after you've reviewed and corrected any problems in the credit bureaus' files, not before; that's why we wait until after you've gone through one annual review cycle. Why see it at all after a year? To establish a baseline. Yes, you'll probably have to pay for it, but the charge is reasonable. Assuming that you continue to follow the strategies we've discussed, this first FICO score won't be too bad at all—*and* it's probably the lowest one that you'll ever see. That's because as you continue to accumulate more and more good history with your credit, you'll be rewarded more and more in your score.

SUMMARY

1. *Don't borrow any money.* When you need or want something, pay in full at the time of purchase, saving up in advance if necessary. The only possible exception is a mortgage on a house, which we'll cover later.
2. *Don't lend any money.* If you feel that you absolutely must, be careful about it, and draw up a formal agreement detailing your expectations. Then be prepared to lose what you've loaned.
3. *Always use a credit card to pay, but never use credit.* The only way to use a credit card without using credit is to always pay your balance, in full, each and every month, *without fail,* automatically if possible. If you can't qualify for a credit card yet, or you aren't yet confident in your ability to consistently stay within your monthly budget, then use a debit card as an interim "training wheel" strategy until you can.
4. All credit cards are not the same; very good and very bad choices are available. Make your selection based on careful research of information provided by objective, credible third parties. Do *not* make your selection based on advertising, promotions, or preselection. Start with one primary card and one backup for emergencies.
5. Your FICO credit score is a three-digit number ranging from 300 to 850 that measures your creditworthiness. It is based on your debt-

and-repayment history and nothing else. Three primary credit bureaus (Equifax, TransUnion, and Experian) collect your credit-related transactions, and these are run through software from FICO to generate your score. You can request a credit report from each of the credit bureaus once a year for free, to review the transactions for completeness and accuracy. But if you want to see your actual score, you will probably have to pay.

6. Credit scores are used by lenders of all kinds, including mortgage lenders. This will become important if and when you are ready to buy a house. But increasingly, FICO scores are also being used by a variety of other parties, including landlords, cell phone companies, credit card issuers, insurers, and even prospective employers. Therefore, it is in your interest to understand how the score is calculated and to take steps to increase it.

7. Follow the seven-point strategy to safely and easily earn a great FICO score. Since you aren't going to be borrowing any money, the strategy is based on the responsible use of credit cards. Your goal isn't a perfect score; it is a score at least high enough to qualify for a prime loan.

Taxes, Risk Management, and Insurance

𝒯axes! Strong opinions abound on virtually every aspect of the subject—at least among taxpayers. Are taxes already too high, or are even higher taxes necessary to balance the budget? Is the burden fairly distributed, or are adjustments in order? Is the tax code complicated in order to ensure fairness across a wide variety of situations, or is the complication simply the result of privileged interests getting what they want? If you think of those as contemporary questions, they're really not—they have been brought up and debated for as long as there have been taxes.

If you are interested in pursuing those kinds of discussions, you'll have no trouble finding forums to do so. But we're not going to engage in any of that here. Instead we want to take a realistic look at the effect that taxes have on your financial life and offer some practical advice about how to deal with them successfully. In our discussion, we'll focus solely on the U.S. federal income tax. Even though that's not the only type of tax that you'll pay, it is likely to be the biggest, and many of the points that we'll discuss are adaptable across the tax landscape.

Since taxes are all about rules, that's the format we'll take. Below are eight rules that I recommend you follow in dealing with taxes. The first four are principles that you should adopt, and the next four are specific areas of competency that I recommend you develop.

THE EIGHT TAX RULES

1. **Pay your taxes in full, on time, every time**. Taxes are serious business, and they deserve your complete attention. A rule like this

might seem obvious, but I'm including it to emphasize that taking a casual, haphazard, or last-minute approach toward complying with tax laws is an extraordinarily bad idea. The consequences of ever getting on the wrong side of the IRS, or any other tax enforcement body, are significant.

2. **Pay the minimum legal amount of taxes that you owe and not a penny more**. Understanding rule #2 requires that you understand the difference between two similar-sounding, but vastly different, words: *evading* taxes and *avoiding* taxes. Tax *evasion* is a criminal offense. It refers to dishonestly or fraudulently misrepresenting your financial status to reduce tax payments. On the other hand, tax *avoidance* is perfectly legal. This refers to taxpayers making decisions explicitly to take advantage of specific rules in the tax code, to reduce their tax liability. The tax code is complex. Two taxpayers with identical financial situations can end up paying wildly different amounts, both perfectly legally. The taxpayer who pays less has done so by being more familiar with which specific elements of the tax code could be legally used to his or her advantage and then doing so. Legally and financially speaking, there is no virtue at all in paying more taxes than you are required to. Do not evade taxes, but avoid them to the greatest extent that you legally can.

3. **Commit to understanding the basics of the income tax and to keeping your understanding current.** This rule is a natural extension of rule #2. If you don't have a good working knowledge of the basics, or at least the basics that are most applicable to your own situation, you are very likely to end up paying more tax than you need to. To state it a little more forcefully—ignorance of the tax code is likely to be an expensive habit. You don't need to become an expert, and you don't need to build your knowledge overnight. But you can commit to improving your knowledge of the important basics, year after year.

4. **Have an effective record-keeping process**. There's no way around it—a fundamental part of financial responsibility is keeping good financial records. If you're already following the recommendations made in recent chapters—doing all your spending using either a debit or credit card featuring summarized, downloadable transaction details—then you've already got the most challenging part of this under control. Keep this, and all your other financial records, secure (and remotely backed up, if applicable), and your tax preparation process will be significantly simplified.

5. **Know your marginal tax rate (your tax bracket) and your average tax rate**. You probably know that tax rates are structured in a *graduated*, or *progressive*, way. This means that higher and higher levels of income are taxed at higher and higher rates. At the time of this writing, there are six brackets of income, with six progressively higher tax percentages levied on each one. The lowest bracket is 10%, ranging up to the highest rate of 35%. (I'm emphasizing "at the time of this writing" because the number of brackets, and the rates charged, can and do change from year to year. For example, the number of brackets has been as few as three and as many as fifteen. The U.S. Congress has proven very willing to adjust the structure in response to all kinds of economic and political forces and is likely to continue this practice.)

How do these progressive brackets work? Let's say that you earn just barely enough to put you into the highest tax bracket: 35%. (Congratulations!) That doesn't mean that your total tax bill is 35% of your income. Instead, you pay 10% on your first "chunk" of income, a higher rate on the next chunk, and so on; you only pay 35% on the very last chunk. In this example, by the time you add all that up, your total tax bill would average out to about 29% of your total income. In tax language, we say that your *marginal* tax rate is 35%, but your *average* tax rate is 29%. Both rates are important. The average tax rate is important because it determines your total tax bill. The marginal rate is also important because that's the rate you'll pay on any *additional* income you earn this year. For example, if you are considering earning some supplemental income, understand that you'll pay 35% on that extra income, not 29%.

6. **Have a deduction strategy.** Deductions are expenses that the tax code allows you to subtract from your income before your tax is figured. Examples of deductible expenses are mortgage interest paid on an owner-occupied house, charitable donations, a certain portion of your medical expenses, and a long list of others. The more deductions you have (in dollars), the lower your total tax bill is. The tax code gives you a choice: you can list all your deductions one by one and add them up (this is called *itemizing*) or you can take a single flat amount that the government offers everyone called the *standard deduction*—one or the other, but not both. Which do you take? Whichever is higher, because that's how you legally pay the least tax.

It is in your interest to know whether your deductible expenses in any given year are likely to be higher or lower than the standard deduction. Early in your financial life, before you own a house, it isn't unusual simply to take the standard deduction. But eventually your deductible expenses will probably begin to approach the standard deduction amount, and sooner or later it will make more sense to itemize. You don't want to miss that crossover point because each year you take the standard deduction when you could have itemized could cost you in unnecessary taxes.

7. **Have a withholding strategy**. Like most U.S. employees past and present, I am a veteran of many coffee-break debates about what the ideal tax-withholding strategy is. What is a withholding strategy? As Bobby Budget explained to Billy Bigshot, employees fill out a form with their employer called a W-4. Based on how it is filled out, the employer knows how much to withhold from your earnings toward your income tax. When you eventually file your return, if the amount withheld is greater than your actual tax bill, you get a refund check from the U.S. government. If your tax bill is higher than what has been withheld, you pay the government the difference.

Contrary to what a lot of the coffee-break debaters believe, getting a big refund check year after year is not an indication of financial genius—just the opposite! When you get a big refund check, it just means that the IRS has been holding your money on your behalf; and while they are holding it, they are earning interest on that refund money—and you're not! In other words, you've just generously provided the IRS with an interest-free loan. On the other hand, if your employer doesn't withhold enough, *you* get to earn interest on that difference, until you have to pay. In both cases, the amount of tax paid is identical—the only difference is who is earning interest.

So what is the ideal withholding strategy? It depends on your skill level at budgeting and tax bill estimation. If you are a rookie at both, then you should be conservative and aim for a zero difference between your tax bill and the amount withheld (zero refund, zero additional tax owed). Once your skill level is high, though, you can get more aggressive at reducing your withholding and earning interest on the money that you will eventually have to pay in taxes. The extra skill is required because you will have to be completely certain that when your tax bill is due, you will have the funds available to pay your taxes. How do you adjust your withholding? Work with your employer's payroll department, or any tax professional, who can advise you on perfectly legal ways to adjust your W-4 to your advantage.

8. **Know when to seek outside expertise, and what kind.** Here is a simple model, listed in the order of increasing expense to you:

Level 1: Do all taxes and tax research yourself, using readily available resources. You can buy or check out one or more books, search online, and so on.

Level 2: Use tax software, carefully researching which product best meets your needs and ensuring you only use the most up-to-date version. Often it is possible to use software that can also be used in automating your budgeting process.

Level 3: Engage a certified tax professional. Services can range from simply filing your return based on information that you provide to extensive consultation on tax planning for the current and future years.

When you are just starting out in your financial life, level 1 may be perfectly sufficient. Or you may be someone who is so comfortable with computing tools that you couldn't imagine filling out a tax form when you know there are simple applications available that can do the job better than you can; if that's the case, you might skip directly to level 2. Eventually, though, your financial life may get complicated enough that you'll want to go to level 3. Each level costs more than the preceding one; but each level also offers a greater chance of spotting potential tax savings. The more complex your situation becomes, the more likely it is that it makes sense to move to the next higher level.

RISK MANAGEMENT

Throughout our entire discussion, we have emphasized the importance of consistently and methodically improving your financial position, month by month and year by year. But even though that is the safest and surest way, the sobering truth is that you still face financial risks that have the potential to make a big dent in all of your hard-earned progress or even wipe it out completely. Worse still, this can happen suddenly, with little or no warning. So it is very important to understand just what you can, and can't, do about these kinds of risks.

When most people first start to think about financial risk, they think of it too narrowly. It's clear that investing your life savings in a single startup technology stock is a financial risk. But is driving over a crowded and snowy mountain pass in a car with bald tires a *financial* risk? It is if you end up causing damage and injuries to yourself and others that you are ultimately financially responsible for. Is getting so fed up with your boss that you punch him in the nose a *financial* risk? It is if he fires you—right before he sues you. The point is that financial risk should be thought of in the broadest sense: it is any situation that has the possibility of causing you direct financial harm.

An overall risk-management strategy is a fundamental part of being financially responsible. Now that you've begun thinking of financial risk in a broad way, it makes sense that you'll need multiple lines of defense, and that's just what I recommend. Here are the three lines of defense in your overall financial risk-management strategy.

1. **Avoid unnecessary risk.** All the financial recommendations in this book have been considered from the standpoint of avoiding unnecessary risk; following the advice presented, supplemented with your own research, will keep you protected. But the advice presented here is limited to purely financial situations. It is up to *you* to use your own common sense to avoid unnecessary risk in other areas of your life that may have financial ramifications. In other words, it's up to you to avoid driving over snowy mountain passes on bald tires and punching your boss in the nose!
2. **Insurance.** This is your second line of defense, and we'll cover it more thoroughly later in this chapter.
3. **Your cash bucket.** You're avoiding unnecessary financial risks, and you're insuring against the most common unavoidable risks, but even then some types of risk can sneak past these first two measures. That's where your cash bucket comes in—it's your third line of defense. We talked about it earlier, before risk avoidance and insurance, because it takes some time to fill the bucket up, and it was important to get you started as soon as possible.

INSURANCE

Insurance is a unique kind of expense; when you buy it, you are actually desperately hoping that you're wasting your money. However, if you end up needing it, you will wish that you'd bought even more. Despite this unusual aspect, the basic concept of insurance is simple enough; an insurer will assume financial risks on your behalf in exchange for a payment, called a *premium*, that you make to the insurer. This arrangement is called an insurance *policy*; the policy is a document that gives the specific details of what is covered, what isn't, and what the insurer promises to do in the event of a claim.

From your point of view, such an exchange makes sense if the probability of the risk is high enough, if the amount at risk is large enough, and/or if the premium is low enough. The insurer's point of view is a little different and relies on the law of large numbers. An insurer collects extensive historical statistics about the incidence of certain kinds of risk. The larger the pool of people that the insurer can include in the risk coverage, the more certain the insurer can be that the historical probabilities will hold. That's why premiums are lower for the most common types of risks and coverage and higher for more unusual ones.

For most types of insurance, the two basic policy elements that cause premiums to go up or down are the *amount* of coverage and the *deductible*. The amount of coverage is simple to understand; this is the *upper* limit of what the insurer will ever pay you in the event of a claim. If your coverage limit on damage to your car is $5,000, then that is all your insurer will pay; if you sustain more than $5,000 in damage, you're on your own for the difference. In contrast, the deductible is your insurer's *lower* limit. It is neither in your interest, nor the insurer's, for you to file numerous tiny claims, so for anything less than the deductible amount, you're on your own again. As you might expect, policies with high coverages and low deductibles carry high premiums; to lower your premiums, you can decrease coverage limits or increase deductibles.

When it comes to insurance, it is all about carefully considered, intelligent choices based on lots of diligent research. Insurance is an absolutely essential ingredient in your overall financial strategy, when properly utilized. What you want to do is to buy just enough of the right kinds of insurance and no more. This requires a clear-eyed and realistic understanding of the financial risks that you face, weighed against all of the true costs of insuring against those risks.

Visualize one of those old-time balance scales, the kind with a small platform for weighing on each side. On one side, you have the *possibility* of a large financial loss. On the other side, you have the *certainty* of a stream of premium expenses. The direction in which the scale tips depends on whether you're willing to assume the risk yourself or whether you want to pay the insurer to assume it for you. As Dirty Harry would say, "Do you feel lucky?" Now think of not just one of those scales, but one for each type of insurance: a scale for car insurance, another for life insurance, one for health insurance, for kidnap and ransom insurance, for meteor strike insurance—the list is long. If that starts to seem a little overwhelming, it gets worse. You'll need to use each scale not just once, but multiple times. For example, when you use the car insurance scale, you'll need to consider insuring against damage to your car, theft of your car, damage to other cars caused by your car, medical coverage for you in the event of an accident, medical coverage for others in the event of an accident, and so on. The point to take away is this: insurance isn't a simple yes/no decision, but a whole series of decisions. And the direction that each of these scales tips will change over time, as your circumstances change. This means that you'll be facing insurance decisions, large and small, throughout your financial life.

With so many decisions to make, it's not surprising that a lot of people don't make them very well. So what are the most common mistakes?

1. **Not understanding the choices.** Unfortunately, it is easy to get a little lost; the fine print can contain a lot of legalese. Some insurers, and some agents, are better than others when it comes to helping you break down the policy features and decisions into everyday language. Whatever you do, never buy any insurance unless you clearly understand exactly what you are and aren't buying. If that means taking extra time, or asking the agent to explain it to you again, or switching insurers or agents until you can find an explanation that makes solid sense to you—then that's what it means. It is tempting to give up trying to understand, especially when the agent that you're working with is pressuring you with ideas like "this is our most popular option" or "without question, this fits you like a glove!" Hold your ground and don't make any decisions until you clearly understand all the options.

2. **Buying more than you need.** One reason for overbuying is that insurance decisions are all about the risk of unpleasant things occurring. Imagining the worst can set your right brain into tailspin before your left brain can start sorting out the actual probabilities. Before you know it, you've signed up for the highest possible coverage amounts and the lowest possible deductibles. Although that's an understandable reaction, my not-so-gentle advice is this: get over it! Plain and simple, imagining worst-case scenarios and intelligently deciding how to guard against them is a *necessary financial skill* that you will need to master. Another reason for buying too much insurance is what is called *overlap* between policies; you may be paying two different insurers to cover you for the same risk. (Example: your car insurance might include coverage if you are injured in a car accident, while your health insurance covers medical treatment regardless of the reason.) There are so many different types of coverage and available options, potential overlaps are common. The trick is to learn to spot them and then buy only enough insurance to cover you once—and only once—for each type of risk.

3. **Buying less than you need.** The most common reason for underinsuring is that people are—understandably—trying to save on premium expense. As a general rule, if something is worth buying insurance to guard against, it is worth buying *enough* insurance to guard

against it. In general, raising your deductibles is a wiser way to reduce premiums than lowering your coverage amount.

4. **Not keeping up with your changing personal situation.** Once you've gone through the process of putting a policy in place, the insurer will notify you when it's time to consider renewing it. Very often, the default choice offered is simply to renew the same policy with the same levels of coverage and all the same options selected (sometimes with an upward premium adjustment). It's very easy to accept this default choice—just check a box and off you go—so that's what many people do, without thinking through whether the previous policy still meets their needs. People early in their financial lives are especially likely to experience bigger and more frequent changes in their circumstances, so make it a habit to really reevaluate your choices each time you renew.

5. **Falling into the subscription effect trap.** Not only is it important to review your coverage levels regularly, it is also important to review the prices that you pay for them regularly. The automatic monthly billing aspect, coupled with default renewals, exposes you to the danger of letting prices creep upward without your full attention. As always, the best defense is your budgeting process. If your insurer is raising your premiums past the point where they're competitive, then complain about it. If that doesn't get you anywhere, consider going to another insurer.

6. **Picking an insurer who doesn't meet their end of the bargain.** The whole reason for buying insurance in the first place is to be protected in the event that you have to file a claim, so this should be your primary consideration when selecting an insurer. Like so many other things in personal finance, there is no substitute for research. You want an insurer who will meet their end of the bargain when you need them to, without delays or surprises. Customers who have had great, not so great, and downright terrible claims experiences are more than willing to share their stories publicly if you look for them. The lowest-priced insurance might be that low because it is offered by an insurer that is efficiently run and careful about whom they insure; or the price is low because the insurer has a habit of holding back on fulfilling claims. As always, you can expect advertising to tell exactly one side of the story; the other side that you uncover may or may not match up. It is very much in your interest to know which is which.

There are many different kinds of insurance; virtually anything can be insured for a price. Instead of covering the entire menu, we'll just take a quick look at the most common types. Here is a typical progression for someone early in financial life: the first two types you are likely to encounter are health insurance (often subsidized to some degree by your employer) and renter's insurance. As soon as you get a car, you become a car insurance customer. Those three might be all for a while, but the next events are probably life insurance (if you add a financial dependent) and dropping renter's insurance in favor of homeowner's insurance (if you buy a house). You may or may not consider other types throughout your financial life depending on your circumstances, but those are the most common.

WORDS OF ADVICE—ON SELECTED INSURANCE AND RISK-MANAGEMENT TOPICS

A list of brief tips on some of the most common categories of insurance appears below, plus a few important items from the broader field of risk management. These are brief, so think of them as broad guidelines, not ironclad rules. You'll need to do lots more research on your own. Above all, keep in mind that these comments are specifically intended for a typical person in the 1st third of their financial life. If you're not in the 1st third—or if you're not typical when it comes to that subject—then consider the advice with caution.

1. **Health insurance.** People early in their financial life are famous for letting their right brains have complete and utter control of their health insurance decisions. Why? The choices are complicated, the costs are high, and the prospect of future illness or injury is unpleasant. Right-brain reaction: "I am young and healthy; in fact I'm downright indestructible. I don't need any health or medical insurance, or else just the bare minimum." Bad idea! Tell your right brain to have a seat and engage your left brain in truly understanding what your choices are. You are taking a big and unnecessary risk if you don't. If you want to save on premiums, go with very high deductibles, not with big gaps in coverage. And keep yourself healthy!

2. **Homeowner's and renter's insurance.** Whether you rent or own, you need it. And keep the list of valuables that you're insuring current; if you don't, you're not getting the value for your premiums that you think you are.

3. **Car insurance.** Car insurance is broken down into several subcategories. Each state requires that you carry some minimal level of car insurance in *certain* subcategories or you won't be allowed to operate

your car in that state. The specific requirements vary from state to state, but the basic idea is that if you cause an accident, you must have insurance to cover people that you injure or cars that you damage. But there is no requirement that forces you to cover injuries to yourself or damage to your own car in an accident that you cause. Here is the point: of course, you will carry whatever types of car insurance your state requires, but it is a big mistake if that's the *only* car insurance that you carry. You'll want yourself and your passengers, as well as your car, to be covered in the event of an accident. You'll also want your car to be covered if it is damaged in any other way not related to an accident (vandalism, storm damage, hit while parked, etc.). Save money by having high deductibles but not by skipping entire categories of coverage. And of course, drive safely!

4. **Life insurance.** Life insurance comes in two types: *term* and *permanent*. Here's the recommendation: *you want term life insurance*, not permanent. Permanent life insurance comes in many varieties; some of the more common types are *whole*, *universal*, and *variable*. But whatever names they go by, all forms of permanent life insurance have a long-term investment aspect. In part IV, we're going to discuss a completely different—and much superior—long-term investment strategy, so you're not interested in any of the permanent insurance–related investments.

    Even though your choice is term life insurance, you only need it during a very specific time during your financial life. That time *begins* as soon as you have any financial dependents, so don't buy any life insurance at all before then. The time for term life insurance *ends* when your net worth becomes large enough that you can provide for these dependents through the provisions in your will, or as soon as your dependents are no longer dependent on you. As soon as you meet either condition, don't renew your term life insurance policy when the current term expires.

5. **Private mortgage insurance (PMI).** If you buy a house, you'll probably be required to pay for this type of insurance if you pay less than 20% down. This isn't good news, because even though you pay the premiums, the insurance is for the benefit of your lender, not you. But as you'll learn in part III, you *will* pay 20% or more down, so you won't need PMI.

6. **Long-term care (LTC) insurance.** This type of insurance is increasingly advertised, so you may be curious about it. But LTC doesn't make sense to consider in the 1st third of your financial life; you can ignore it at least until your late 40s. (If you are financially

responsible for someone who is one or two generations older, though, you may need to investigate it.)

7. **Wills.** A will isn't insurance, but you can think of one as part of your overall risk-management strategy. You don't need a will if you have no dependents or if your net worth is less than $100,000. But as soon as you meet either of these conditions, you do need a will, no matter your age or health. Don't put it off—it's a must. Unless your situation is unusually complicated, you can do it yourself inexpensively.

8. **Living trusts.** These are often brought up along with wills. But it's unlikely that you'll need one in the 1st third of your financial life. Living trusts are important once your net worth becomes large (say, over $1 million), or if there is something unusually complex about your assets or about the way you want to distribute them after your death.

9. **Living wills.** Despite the similarity in names, a living will is completely different from a living trust, or a standard will, but a living will is very important in its own right. A living will allows you to express your wishes in advance, in the event that you become incapacitated and unable to communicate them for yourself. In particular, you can advise health-care professionals whether you do, or don't, want your life extended through artificial means if your chances for recovery are very limited or none. Yes, it is a grim prospect to think about, and it can evoke very strong feelings all around. But in the absence of a living will, you may be putting your loved ones, and/or the medical professionals caring for you in a very difficult position. Most people haven't spent much time thinking about this, but when they do, they come to the conclusion that filing a living will is a simple and inexpensive precaution that potentially can save a lot of heartache. The laws concerning living wills vary from state to state. I highly encourage you to at least investigate this in your own state and then decide for yourself.

SUMMARY

1. The Eight Tax Rules are:
   a. Pay your taxes in full, on time, every time.
   b. Pay the minimum legal amount of taxes that you owe and not a penny more.
   c. Commit to understanding the basics of the income tax and to keeping your understanding current.
   d. Have an effective record-keeping process.

     e. Know your marginal tax rate (your tax bracket) and your average tax rate.

     f. Have a deduction strategy.

     g. Have a withholding strategy.

     h. Know when to seek outside expertise, and what kind.

2. Your risk-management strategy is your means of guarding against financial risk, which is any situation that could result in direct financial harm. Your three lines of defense are (1) avoidance of unnecessary risk, (2) insurance, and (3) your cash bucket.

3. Insurance is an arrangement whereby an insurer will assume financial risks on your behalf in exchange for a payment called a premium. It makes sense for you if the probability of the risk is high enough, if the amount at risk is large enough, and/or if the premium is low enough.

4. The coverage amount is the upper limit of what an insurer will pay for a claim, and the deductible is the lower limit. For exposure above the coverage amount or below the deductible, you are on your own. Raising coverage amounts and lowering deductibles increases premiums and vice versa.

5. The most common mistakes that people make in the area of insurance are not understanding their choices, buying either too much or too little, not adjusting coverage as life circumstances change, failing to notice and evaluate premium increases, and selecting an insurer who doesn't pay claims reliably, fairly, and promptly.

6. A typical progression of insurance types for someone early in their financial life is health, renter's, and car insurance, followed by homeowner's and life insurance. Other types may or may not be considered based on individual circumstances.

7. Specific tips are offered for each of the most common types of insurance, as well as for wills, living trusts, and living wills.

Part III

BIG-TICKET ITEMS:
CARS AND HOUSES

• *11* •

Cars

$\mathcal{W}$elcome to part III! In the first two parts of the book, we've covered a broad variety of topics at a pretty fast pace. Now we'll slow down on the number of topics to go into more depth on some of the most important ones. Part III is devoted to *big-ticket items*—those purchases that are relatively few in number but large in dollars.

Most people get pretty excited when approaching the purchase of a big-ticket item. Chances are that you've spent a long time anticipating it and dreaming of the day that you'd finally be in a position to buy. It's also common to experience some first-timer's nervousness and apprehension. If you're thinking that excitement, anticipation, nervousness, and apprehension sound like the ideal set of conditions for your right brain to want to step in and take over—you're absolutely correct. If you are also thinking whoever is selling you the big-ticket item probably has more experience with these kinds of transactions than you do and just might be inclined to try to take advantage of your right brain—you're correct again. As you go through part III, I'll provide you with ample information and tools to ensure that you make a sound, financially successful choice—not an emotional one.

Before we zero in specifically on cars, though, I want to call your attention to one very specific pitfall that people stumble into when purchasing any big-ticket item: they tend to lose sight of the fact that they are going to have to *sell* that big-ticket item someday. It's easy to do. The buying process is exciting, and you can easily get caught up in comparing and selecting, and in evaluating all the various aspects of buying and owning. But some cars, houses, or other big-ticket items are much easier than others to sell later and will bring much better resale prices. It might seem a little counterintuitive to be focusing on how easy it will be to resell before you even buy, but it is critical that you do so if you want to make the soundest financial choice. *Future resale potential needs to be your primary concern in any big-ticket-item purchase.* Some people call this having an exit strategy before entering. Keep it in mind—it's one of the key lessons of part III.

FIRST THINGS FIRST

Warning: if there is going to be a paragraph in this chapter that you won't like, it will probably be this one. That's because before we even begin talking about car selection and buying, we have to address first things first: affordability. The time to get serious about buying a car isn't when you're convinced that you need one, it's when you need one *and can afford it.* At the risk of pouring cold water on your excitement, I'll remind you of some of our earlier lessons. You aren't going to borrow any money, so you'll be paying cash up front for whatever car you buy. And buying a car doesn't qualify as a financial emergency, so the cash can't come from your cash bucket. Instead the cash will come from money you save. There are two ways you can go about this.

1. First, completely fill your cash bucket. Then begin saving for a car and buy only when you've saved enough. This is the recommended way to go, but it means waiting quite a while until you can buy.
2. Save for a car at the same time that you're filling your cash bucket, as long as you always place at least 10% of everything you earn into your cash bucket while you're doing so. In other words, if you are saving 20% of your income, you could split it 10%–10% between car savings and cash-bucket savings; or you could put 5% toward your car fund and 15% toward your cash bucket. But however you split it, 10% is the bare minimum that goes into the cash bucket.

There is no third option that would let you stop filling your cash bucket temporarily while you save for a car. Your cash bucket is too important. And there is *definitely* not a fourth option of borrowing money.

In addition, the costs involved in owning and operating a car are substantial, and are *on top of* what you pay to buy it. So you'll need to be in a position to include these in your monthly budget and still continue following the First Rule—even after your cash bucket is filled. We'll talk more about what these costs are shortly, but here is the point: before you buy, you'll need to prepare a hypothetical monthly budget, which includes the costs of owning and operating a car. You may find that you'll have to cut back on some of your other expenses to continue meeting the First Rule. Make sure that you have identified a specific way to do this; you shouldn't buy a car until you're sure that you can afford these car-related costs and still continue saving.

At this point you may be asking, "So what am I supposed to do? I just got a job, and I don't have *any* car money saved up yet. If I don't borrow some money and buy a car, how am I supposed to get to work?" There are other options: Public transportation. Carpool. Bicycle. Move closer to work. Get a job closer to home. If you know someone with one or more cars that they use only occasionally, propose some kind of informal short-term rental. Investigate membership in a car-sharing cooperative. But whatever you do, don't take the easy way out by borrowing money or by dipping into your emergencies-only cash bucket. Keep exploring alternatives, be willing to make sacrifices in your budget, and adopt a mindset of "I *have to* find an answer to this!"—and you will. When you do ultimately buy a car, you'll have the satisfaction of knowing that it is completely paid for and that you can afford to operate it *while still* saving for the future. Instead of getting behind the wheel with a feeling of financial stress, you'll feel justifiably proud of your financially responsible approach and your growing financial skills. You will have a true, very well-deserved pride of ownership.

CARS—A FEW BASICS

For most of us, a car is one of the very first big-ticket items we'll ever buy, and we'll end up owning at least one car for as long as we're able to drive. When you are just starting out in your financial life, it's especially important to make a solid, sound decision. The rule of being a smart, well-informed consumer who does plenty of homework throughout the process of buying and owning is especially in force when it comes to cars. Lots of people make costly mistakes the first time around, and I don't want you to be one of those. Sometimes they keep making the same mistakes over and over with each car they buy, simply because nobody ever told them that there are much better ways to go. And I don't want you to be one of those, either.

I am using the word *cars* throughout this section just for convenience. Your situation, or preference, may lead you to consider vans, pickups, motorcycles, or whatever. Just substitute the vehicle type of your choice for *car*—the ideas are the same. But not everybody falls into the category of prospective car buyer. You may live somewhere where public transportation is affordable and convenient, and you can get wherever you need to without owning a car. Or you might live somewhere where parking is nearly impossible to either find or afford, or both, and a car just doesn't make sense. Maybe you can't qualify for a driver's license for some reason. If any of these describe your situation, you can just skip this chapter, knowing that you can come back if your circumstances ever change. For the rest of you, buckle up and read on!

Now for some basic terminology of car ownership. You probably already know these basics; but if not, I'd rather have you learn a few things here instead of in the middle of a conversation with someone who is selling you a car.

1. **VIN.** Every car has a *vehicle identification number,* or VIN, associated with it. The VIN is like the car's fingerprint; it stays with the car from the factory to the junkyard. The 17-digit VIN format was standardized in the United States in 1981, so cars manufactured before then may or may not have VINs, or may have VINs in any number of individual state formats that were in use before then. The VIN is actually assigned to the engine and transmission, so even if a car is rebuilt, or gets new parts inside or out, the same VIN goes along with the "guts" of the car. Tags showing a car's VIN appear in different places on different cars but are never too hard to find. VINs are invaluable in researching the history of any specific car that you're interested in buying.

2. **Title.** A title is a legal document issued by your state that establishes ownership of any specific car. A title says, "This specific car with this specific VIN is legally owned by this specific person or company." A title never expires; when you buy a car, the seller needs to legally transfer the title to you. Likewise, when you ultimately sell, you will in turn transfer the title to the new buyer. The title should *not* be kept in the car; you should keep it in a safe place at home or in a safety deposit box.

3. **Registration.** Once you have the title to a car, you can prove that you own it; but if you want to actually legally drive it on public roads, the next thing you need is a registration. A registration says, "This specific car, with this specific VIN, has up-to-date license plates, tabs, and stickers, and has met all of this state's legal requirements (such as emissions tests or safety checks) to be operated on this state's public roads." Unlike a title, though, a car's registration expires periodically (annually in most states) and must be renewed. The registration *should* stay in the car; if you're ever pulled over, you'll need to show it.

4. **Service schedule.** Every make and model of car comes with a recommended service schedule from its manufacturer, which details what types of maintenance should be performed at various mileage intervals. *Minor* services are more frequent and include things like oil and oil filter changes, checking and correcting tire air pressure, and brake inspection. *Major* services are at wider intervals, cost considerably more than minor services, and can vary quite a bit depending on the type of car.

THREE TYPES OF CAR KNOWLEDGE

When it comes to buying and owning cars, three distinct (but often related) areas of knowledge come into play.

1. **Automotive.** The automotive industry is constantly changing and evolving. In addition, cars are complex and increasingly sophisticated machines. Some people can pop open a hood and instantly diagnose and fix any problem or can ride down the freeway and identify each passing car's year, make, and model; if you're one of those people, then you have a high degree of this type of knowledge.
2. **Scam avoidance.** Unfortunately, the world of automotive scams is *also* constantly changing and evolving (although some of the tried-and-true scams are timeless). This is true both in buying cars and in keeping them maintained. Search the Internet for the kinds of commonly practiced scams that are out there; you'll be amazed. (Try a search term like "top car sales scams" and then step back!) I hasten to add that many experienced, qualified, and honest professionals in the automotive industry have worked hard to build their reputations, but you'll have to do some homework to identify them.
3. **Financial.** Just because someone can rebuild an engine or easily spot a forged title doesn't mean they know a thing about compound interest or resale values. It's common for people who are inexperienced with cars to assume that someone with high automotive and/or scam-avoidance knowledge is also well qualified to help with the financial aspects. Be careful about this; these are quite different types of knowledge.

To make a good buying decision, as well as the right financial decisions that come along with car ownership, you'll need knowledge in *all three* areas. You can study and research on your own to build up this kind of knowledge or you can seek it from others. The best strategy is to do plenty of both. If a friend, colleague, or family member has a high degree of knowledge and is willing to help you out from time to time, that can be a great benefit; but that collaboration will be even more productive if you do your part by researching as much as you can on your own. And if someone is going to be helping you, make sure that you understand which of the three types of knowledge that person is most qualified to help with, so that you can take other steps to fill in the gaps. Even if you know nothing at all about cars, it is neither responsible nor advisable to consciously choose to avoid learning anything at all about them. You don't need to become an expert, but if you intend to successfully own a car, it is in your interest to commit to learning at least some of the basics.

Naturally we're going to focus on the financial aspects for the remainder of this chapter. The point of detailing all three kinds of knowledge is to emphasize that when it comes to a big-ticket item like a car, a purely financial approach isn't enough to keep you out of trouble. On one hand, don't be afraid to ask for help in those areas where you need it—ideally from someone you already know and trust. On the other hand, don't completely abdicate *all* elements of decision making to the person or people helping you. The key is to take a balanced approach.

THE TOTAL COST OF OWNERSHIP MODEL

Some of the costs of purchasing and owning a car spring immediately to mind and are impossible to ignore, but others tend to hide in the background and can escape consideration. To make sure that *all* of the financial effects are included in any decision, we'll use what is called a Total Cost of Ownership model. Don't let the name intimidate you; it is a very simple approach, with just two categories of car costs. All you do is add them up for each car that you are considering, and all other things being equal, you'll select the car with the lowest total cost—that's it.

To calculate the costs, you'll need to make two assumptions: how long you'll own the car and how many miles you'll end up putting on it per year. If you're not used to this kind of cost planning, the requirement to make assumptions like these might stop you dead in your tracks. How are you supposed to look into the future and know how long you'll own your car or how much you'll drive it? Relax: the assumptions don't have to be completely accurate for the model to do its job perfectly well. Just make some rough, ballpark assumptions and you'll be fine. Whatever you end up assuming, the important thing to remember is to use the very same assumptions for each car that you're comparing.

Here are the two cost categories:

A. **Net price.** This is the complete price you'll pay to buy a given car, minus what you'll clear when you ultimately sell that same car.

B. **Costs to own and operate.** The main items are gas, maintenance, insurance, parking, and regulatory fees (such as tab or tag renewals and emissions tests).

MORE ABOUT NET PRICE

Looking at the net price *forces* you to avoid the most common mistake that we identified earlier; everybody knows that the price you pay to buy a car is important, but it is easy to lose sight of the fact that you'll be selling that same car someday, too. But how can you know what any particular car will sell for, years in the future? Well, you can't know exactly—but it is surprisingly easy to make a pretty close estimate. Here is the key: cars tend to depreciate at fairly predictable rates, and these rates vary considerably. The rates of depreciation depend on the make and model, age, mileage, and condition of any specific cars that you might be considering. It isn't too hard to tell the slow depreciators from the fast ones with a little research.

You'll notice from the paragraph above that I'm already assuming that the value of your car will decline during the time you own it. Some assets— like houses, which we'll discuss in the next chapters—stand a realistic chance of increasing in value while you own them. But unless you are a vintage car collector with a high degree of expertise, cars will nearly always depreciate. Since you know that some makes and models depreciate much more slowly than others, now you can see why we're focusing on net price. You want to select a car that will *depreciate the least* during the time you own it. Getting the best net price means selecting a car you can resell in the future for *only a little bit less* than you paid for it.

This idea of net price—price to buy minus price received when selling— is probably new to you. Since you are just starting out, everything that you've ever bought up to this point was probably something you used until you wore it out, lost it, or simply threw it away. You've probably never bought something of relatively high value that you knew you were going to resell someday. But take a minute to think about net price and how it is different from the initial price. Once this difference sinks in, it will change the way you think about car prices for the rest of your financial life.

So how do you go about finding the slowest-depreciating makes and models? This is where some well-focused Internet research comes in! I recommend either the *Kelley Blue Book* site (www.kbb.com) or the *NADA (National Automobile Dealers Association) Guides* site (www.nadaguides.com); at least at the time of this writing, these are the leading sources of a wide variety of information about the resale value of cars in the United States. When you go there, it may take a little while for you to get familiarized with how these sites work, but once you do, you will see everything you need.

It's easiest to explain by using an example. Let's say that you're trying to choose between two used cars, a Batmobile produced by the ABC Company and a Catmobile from rival XYZ. The Batmobile is a very impressive car, sure to draw lots of admiring looks from your friends. On the other hand, the Catmobile is regarded as dependable but far less prestigious. Each is 5 years old, each has 100,000 miles, each is in "good" condition, and gas mileage is identical. The higher-end Batmobile will cost you $9,000, while the Catmobile's cost is $5,000. Next, you need to make a couple of assumptions: how long do you think you'll own the car, and how many miles do you think you'll drive it in that period? Let's say your best rough guess is that you'll own the car for 5 years and that you'll drive it about 16,000 miles per year, or 80,000 miles, over the 5-year period. So we start with the Batmobile, and we look up the resale value (the Kelley website offers a choice called *Private Party Value*, which is the one you want) of a Batmobile that is *10* years old and has *180,000* miles (5 years older and 80,000 more miles—get it?), and we see that the resale price is $4,000. But just to be careful, we look up several other nearby years of Batmobiles; it is possible that there might have been some kind of major design change during that 5-year period that would throw off the comparison. For simplicity, we'll say that this additional research simply confirms that the $4,000 resale price is solid.

Now we repeat the process for the Catmobile. It turns out that 10-year-old Catmobiles with 180,000 miles resell for $3,000. Now you're ready to calculate the net prices of each. The net price of the Batmobile is $5,000 ($9,000 minus $4,000), but the Catmobile's net price is only $2,000 ($5,000 minus $3,000). Case closed! The Catmobile is a much better net price choice than the Batmobile; in fact, the net price of the Batmobile is more than twice that of the Catmobile. Think of it this way: you just earned $3,000 for an hour or so of Internet research.

Here is a very important point about the process. When you looked up the prices of 10-year-old Batmobiles and Catmobiles with 180,000 in mileage, it wasn't to find out *exactly* what you can expect when you sell yours. The real purpose was to compare Batmobiles and Catmobiles, so that you can get the general idea of the net price difference. When you ultimately sell your Catmobile, it may sell for more or less than $3,000—remember, it is a different model year than the one that you looked up. Instead, the point is that whatever price you end up selling your Catmobile for, you can be confident that your ultimate net price will be far lower than if you'd bought the Batmobile.

Before we leave this example, let's address a final point. I'll bet many of you are thinking, "But I'd rather be driving a Batmobile!" Fair enough. But now that you know how to work with net price, you can explore that possibility more intelligently. Instead of 5-year-old Batmobiles, check out the *net* prices of 10-year-old ones. Depending on what you find, a Batmobile may be in your future after all!

NEW VS. USED

Why did we focus on used cars in the example? Simple: *buying a new car is a net price loser*, every time. New cars are priced with a hefty premium (a lot of which probably is necessary to pay for advertising), and that premium vanishes the minute you drive your new car off the dealer's lot. It is gone forever; you will never recapture that premium on resale. Think of that new car smell as the smell of your net worth shrinking.

So here is your rule when it comes to deciding between a new or used car:

Never buy a new car. Clear enough?

After spending some time doing research on various makes and models, you'll notice a specific pattern in how nearly all cars depreciate. The two things that cause a car to decline in value are *age* and *mileage*—but these two factors behave very differently. When it comes to age, cars begin to depreciate very quickly right away. Resale value takes a big hit in the first few years, as buyers quickly move on to the newest styles. But then, as the car enters "middle age," *age-related* depreciation really slows down. But *mileage-related* depreciation works just the opposite! It is based on how long the engines in various types of cars will last before needing a major rebuild. So mileage-related depreciation starts slowly but then begins to pick up the closer the engine gets to the time when it will likely need extensive work. In short, age depreciation starts quickly and then slows down; mileage depreciation starts slowly and then speeds up.

What does this mean? Cars that are *older, but with relatively low mileage,* tend to be the biggest net price winners! The U.S. average for car mileage is roughly 15,000 to 18,000 miles per year, depending somewhat on the region of the country. So, for example, a 6-year-old car with 40,000 miles would be the type of car highly likely to be a net price *winner*, because it has been driven much less per year than average and has already experienced the worst of its age-related depreciation. A 2-year-old car with 90,000 miles would likely be a net price *loser* because it has been racking up miles much faster than average and is still subject to hefty age-related depreciation in the next few years.

SHOPPING FOR A USED CAR

Since we've ruled out new cars, you'll be focusing your search on the used-car market. Now that you're familiar with a couple of trusted websites on resale values, you'll be able to tell fair, competitive prices from ones that are too high. That is a great start, but I'd recommend getting some more consumer education before you start actually shopping. Many websites and publications can guide you through the steps, and pitfalls, involved in the actual used-car-buying process. How do I run a VIN report on a specific car? How do I check the title history of a car? What does it mean to sign an *as-is* agreement when I buy a used car? Will *Lemon Laws* protect me if I buy a nightmare car? Just a few hours of research should get you a good understanding of the answers to these questions, and many more. Please don't skip this step: a lot of money is at stake. Once you do that, you have a choice to make: should you buy from a dealer or from an individual selling a single car privately? There is no right answer; you can find what you're looking for in either place. The pros and cons vary, though, so let's take a look at each.

Dealers include new-car dealers who have an inventory of used cars that they've accepted as trade-ins, as well as other dealers who *only* carry used cars. An advantage of dealing with either is that you can go to one place and see a lot of choices in one trip. If you are still fairly open about what specific type of car you're after, a dealer's lot can be a good place to go to browse. Another advantage is that dealers can offer various kinds of warranties. The disadvantage is that you will be dealing with professional salespeople who are likely to want to explore your willingness to consider some of the higher-end items in their inventory. In addition, these professionals might tend to push to accelerate your decision time frame (as in, before you leave today!). If you hold firm on your price range and decision process, though, most salespeople will get the idea and let you take the lead. When buying from a dealer, be aware that the price marked on the car isn't necessarily the *whole* price. ("Well, it's X for the car, Y for such-and-such, Z for this-and-that, etc.") Make it clear that the only price that you want to talk about is the out-the-door price and that you're not interested in the various component pieces. Finally, re-member that everything is negotiable in a used-car lot. It doesn't hurt a thing to try offering a lower price. It may get you nowhere, but nothing ventured, nothing gained. Just remember, you can abandon the negotiation process at any point if you don't like where it is going; you are under no obligation of any kind until your signature finalizes the deal.

With private individuals, randomness prevails. You can find wonderfully honest people, sincerely willing to make a good deal fast; you can find hard-nosed hagglers looking for suckers; and you can find complete crackpots. You won't encounter many professional car salespeople, but you won't find many warranties, either. For this reason, it is imperative to supplement your VIN research with an inspection from an independent mechanic, even if it's at your expense. You can make great deals with private individuals, but there's a lot more legwork involved in finding them. Once you do, the "everything is negotiable" principle applies here as well.

MORE ABOUT COSTS TO OWN AND OPERATE

As noted earlier, the main items in this cost category are gas, maintenance, insurance, parking, and regulatory fees (tag renewals, emissions tests, etc.). We've spent the majority of this chapter talking about net price because that's where people tend to make the biggest mistakes. But don't let that mislead you into thinking that the costs to own and operate your car aren't important. In fact, the costs to own and operate your car will probably end up being *much more* than its net price. These costs are a very important part of the picture, and you'll need to research each one of them before you buy. Some of them (like parking and regulatory fees) will be almost the same regardless of what kind of car you buy, but others (like gas, maintenance, and even insurance) are highly dependent on your choice.

As a reminder, here is how you go about using the Total Cost of Ownership model. Start by making an assumption about how long you'll own whichever car you'll buy, and how many miles you'll drive it during that time. Then, for each make and model you're considering, calculate the most likely net price (using the *Kelley Blue Book* or *NADA Guides* websites), then add in the costs to own and operate. The car with the *lowest total cost* is your best financial choice. Here are some tips in considering the costs to own and operate.

1. **MPG.** As you become more familiar with the Total Cost of Ownership model and begin running through some actual examples, a key fact will jump out at you that surprises most people when they first realize it: *the single biggest element of total cost is the cost of gas.* Nearly always, you'll end up spending more on gas to operate your car than you will for the car itself. That means that the MPG ratings of the cars that you're considering matter—and they matter a lot. And if gas prices move up and stay high permanently, the net prices of virtually all cars will suffer, but those with relatively high MPG ratings will suffer *less*. It is always a good move to stick to the upper end of the MPG ratings for any category of car you're considering.

2. **Avoid unnecessary driving.** Gas is your biggest operating cost, but it is not the only cost that goes up with mileage. The more you drive, the faster you reach your car's service schedule milestones, the more you'll pay for insurance, and the faster your resale value

will fall. Miles matter! After you've used the total cost model a few times, try calculating the total costs again, but assuming 10% less mileage. You will be surprised by just how much even a modest reduction in mileage will save you.

3. **Follow the recommended service schedule for the car that you choose.** Trying to save money by stretching out or skipping service will usually cost you more in the long run. Make a habit of servicing your car on time and of keeping the paperwork for each service; when you resell, it will be to your advantage to demonstrate that you've done so.

ALTERNATIVE TECHNOLOGIES

At least at the time of this writing, many people are considering alternatives to traditional internal combustion engines. It's easy to see why: the gasoline used to power traditional cars is both limited in supply and increasingly blamed for a number of serious environmental problems. Auto manufacturers are offering more and more alternatives, and researchers are scrambling to further refine them and to develop still others. And as mentioned before, the price of gas has a tendency to spike upward from time to time, and many experts foresee a time when prices will jump upward and remain there. In that scenario, alternative technologies look very appealing.

New technologies have appeared throughout history in countless other markets beyond the automotive industry, and we can draw some lessons from them. When new technologies emerge to replace old ones, the progression usually follows a fairly predictable pattern. This pattern has an early, a middle, and a mature phase. When a new technology is first introduced, and it looks like there is enough initial interest that it may ultimately replace an existing one, many new players enter the market with their own versions. These can either be brand-new companies or companies that offer a version of the new technology in addition to their existing offerings of the old technology. This early phase is usually turbulent and exciting, with a great variety of offerings, each company eager to prove that its approach is not only viable but will soon become dominant. Buyers during this phase are referred to as *early adopters* and are willing to pay a premium price to be among the first to adopt some version of the new technology. The middle phase is characterized by market shakeout, where only those participants with the strongest products survive. To be among the survivors, a product not only has to be based on a sound technological approach but also must be capable of being produced at a low enough cost to be viable for a wide market. Finally, in the mature phase, only a few survive. The other companies go out of business or are bought out by the survivors.

The point is that in the early phase, there are many, many types of new technology, and approaches to using them, to choose from; but by the mature phase, there are only a few. The technologies (or platforms) that don't survive are called *orphan technologies*. When early adopters buy during the early phase, they run the risk of picking a particular approach that will later be abandoned, or orphaned. When that happens, the early adopters are usually stuck with an obsolete and unsupported product—which they paid a big premium for. Ouch.

I think you can see where this discussion is headed with regard to net price. If you opt for an alternative technology, your financial outcome will either be extremely good or extremely bad—but probably not anywhere in between. It will be extremely good if gas prices go up and stay high, and if you have chosen the particular alternative technology that emerges as dominant. But if either one of those conditions is *not* met, your losses on net price will wipe out any gains on gas savings. In particular, if you select a technology that eventually becomes orphaned, you'll not only pay a big premium when you buy, but your resale value will be minimal. The conclusion is that alternative technologies are financially risky; the key is to choose the *right* one.

ARE YOU READY?

Okay, time for a final check before you begin your car journey. Have you done thorough research? Check! Have you saved up enough for the initial purchase price *on top of* the 10% minimum First Rule requirement, and *outside* of your cash bucket? Check! Have you studied your monthly budget to make sure that you can afford the new costs of owning and operating the type of car that you've selected while still being able to maintain a minimum 10% savings rate? Check! If so, then full speed ahead toward buying your first car: *you are ready!*

SUMMARY

We'll use a "do's and don'ts" format for this chapter:

Car Do's:

1. Use the Total Cost of Ownership model to select a car, which will force you to consider net price (total cost to buy, minus the likely resale value).
2. Zero in on relatively older cars with relatively few miles.
3. Shoot for the makes and models with relatively higher MPG ratings.

4. Ask for help from others where you need it, remembering that automotive and scam-avoidance knowledge are necessary for a good financial outcome—not just financial knowledge.

5. Familiarize yourself with the *Kelley Blue Book* or *NADA Guides* websites to become knowledgeable about car prices and the factors that influence them.

6. Shop carefully, considering the pros and cons of dealers as well as private individual sellers. When you've made your final selection, pay in full at the time of purchase.

7. Follow the service schedule for your car and keep the records from each service.

8. If you are considering alternative technologies, be careful; the goal is to select the *right* alternative, the one most likely to survive.

9. The best way to save money on owning and operating a car is to minimize the number of miles that you drive it.

Car Don'ts:

1. Don't buy until you've saved enough *on top of* your regular 10% minimum savings and *outside* of your cash bucket.

2. Don't buy a new car.

3. Don't buy until you've verified that you can afford the new, ongoing costs within your monthly budget while still being able to maintain your savings rate.

4. Don't try to save money by skipping or stretching out service intervals.

• *12* •

Should You Buy a House?

*Y*ou've probably heard that paying rent is like throwing money away. But you've probably also heard some unnerving stories about bad financial outcomes that homeowners can experience, like foreclosure or selling at a big loss. Despite all that, one of your most basic needs is to put a roof over your head, as well as the heads of any dependents you may have—and that means that your basic choice is to either rent or buy. Financially speaking, which is better? It isn't a trivial question: whether you rent or buy, providing shelter for yourself and dependents will be a major part of your financial picture throughout your entire financial life. You are probably already well aware that the difference between getting this right and getting it wrong can be a very big deal. We haven't used a question as a chapter title at all so far—but we are now, because this particular question is so important. So what's the answer?

The short answer is, yes—financially speaking, you should buy rather than rent.

Here's why: renting is a pure expense, in the sense that it's an ongoing, unrelenting drain from your financial bathtub. The flow of water goes in only one direction—always out, never in. That's what people mean by "throwing money away." If you buy, you will *also* face an ongoing series of expenses, which are usually even bigger—but these come along with two big financial advantages. The first is that you will eventually be able to *recover* a big portion of those expenses when you ultimately sell. The second is that you'll be in a position to benefit from a couple of very significant income-tax advantages. Later we will cover exactly how the finances work when buying a house, but here is the bottom line: because of these two big advantages, buying a house is *almost always* better financially than renting. Buying allows you to turn a pure expense into the opportunity to purchase and then resell an asset, in a tax-advantaged way. *If you go about it in the right way*, the result is virtually always a very substantial boost to your net worth, which you won't get from renting.

But none of that is likely to happen unless you approach buying a house in the right way. Renting might be throwing money away, but buying in the wrong way can easily result in throwing away even more. There is no getting around the fact that buying a house necessarily involves some risk, and the stakes involved are probably bigger than in any other financial decision that you've made so far. That's why we're going to spend the entire rest of part III describing the *right* way to go about it. If you follow the path described here, you'll guard against the most common risks and you'll put yourself in an excellent position to realize the significant benefits of house ownership.

But before you start down the path of buying a house, first you have to make sure you are completely ready to do so. That's exactly what the rest of this chapter is about. We'll cover nine tests, specifically designed to ensure that you don't buy until you're completely ready. I recommend buying a house over renting for financial reasons, but there might be other, nonfinancial reasons why buying isn't for you. Or you might be someone who will be ready to buy eventually, but not anytime soon. But don't decide just yet. Read through the nine readiness tests first; these will give you a much better idea about the commitment necessary to move ahead, so that you'll be able to put yourself in an "as soon as possible," "later," or "never" category. But whatever you do, don't buy a house until you've passed all nine of these tests!

By the way, just as we used *car* as shorthand for any form of personal transportation, we'll use *house* as shorthand for any structure you legally own *and live in yourself most of the time*. The distinction is important, because the tax advantages we just mentioned can only be applied to the *one* structure that you designate as your primary residence. So for our purposes, a house can mean a stand-alone house (usually referred to in the industry as a *single-family home*), a townhome/townhouse, a condominium, a co-op, and so on—as long as you own it and live there primarily. We are not going to be discussing pure real estate investing, rental homes, or vacation properties. These are things that you might eventually become interested in, but I don't recommend them for the 1st third of your financial life.

So here are the nine tests you'll need to pass before buying a house. Passing means answering each of the questions with a definite yes. Some are simple checks you can perform quickly; others might take months or even years until you can put yourself in a position to pass. Some are strictly quantitative, and others are more qualitative. The first three are about you and your life situation, the next five are tests of your financial readiness, and the last one is a test of the market conditions in the area where you want to buy. After you've read them, we'll discuss how to proceed next.

1. THE 5-YEAR TEST

"Can I commit to staying in the house that I buy for at least 5 years?"

For buying to be a good financial choice, you have to be in a position to live in that particular house for at least 5 years. That's not realistic for everyone, and if it isn't realistic for you, then you should continue to rent until it is. Do you think that you're likely to change jobs within the next few years, and that the new job is likely to be relatively far away? How about if you're single, but you think there is a pretty good chance that you won't remain single over the next few years? What if you are relatively new to the area where you are living and want to try it out awhile before deciding if you want to remain permanently? Depending on your answers, any one of these might be good reasons to hold off on buying a house for now.

Think of it as a race—renter vs. buyer—with the winner being the one who has made the best financial choice. But the race is handicapped; the renter always has a head start because of the significant up-front costs of buying a house. The buyer will usually catch up and pass the renter, but it takes some time for that to happen. Once the buyer catches and passes the renter, the buyer will invariably extend the lead and eventually leave the renter in the dust. This will happen almost every time, unless the buyer sells early, before catching up. The key is to never buy a house unless you're sure that you can remain in it long enough to catch the renter. Most people call this the *break-even time*.

Break-even times vary from situation to situation, but to be safe, I recommend that you begin by assuming it will take at least 5 years. Yours might be even longer. To find out, you should visit one of the many web-based calculators available for just that purpose. (Search on a term like "rent vs. buy calculator" and you'll get several hits. Some are better than others; be sure to select one that takes income taxes into account. Calculators like these will ask you to input some key variables, then calculate and display the break-even time for your situation.)

What if the calculator produces a result less than 5 years? My advice is to use 5 years, or the calculated result, whichever is *longer*. That's because these calculations are based on rough guesses about certain important variables, and you want to play it safe. So if you are entirely willing to commit to staying in a house for at least 5 years—or the calculated break-even time, if that is longer—then you pass this test. But if this kind of commitment makes you hesitate, even a little bit, then you should continue to rent until your situation changes.

2. THE FINANCIAL PRIORITY TEST

"Am I ready to make the financial aspects of house buying my primary consideration?"

People buy houses for all sorts of reasons. Maybe they want their "piece of the American dream." Maybe they somehow feel inferior for renting while peers, colleagues, or other family members have already bought. Maybe they feel responsible for others in the household, or even pressure from them. Maybe they feel that owning a house is a reward of some kind, which they deserve. Or maybe a couple is newly married and thrilled at the prospect of finding their dream house. I'm sure you could add other examples to this list.

But let's be very clear about this. Buying a house is a very large financial transaction, almost certainly the largest you have ever made. The financial consequences, good or bad, are correspondingly large and will have a major impact on your financial position for many years to come. If you've been following all the advice presented so far, this will be the only time you'll borrow any money—and you'll be borrowing a lot. Therefore, it is vital that you recognize that *first and foremost, this is a financial decision.* In the process of selecting, financing, owning, and reselling your house, you'll face many key decision points. At any one of these, if you lose sight of the pure financial implications, then you are increasing your risk, and you may be heading for trouble. *All decisions about house ownership have a very big impact on your financial future.*

What about all those other reasons for which people buy, the ones we listed above? Are those good or bad reasons? Let's just group all of those non-financial reasons together and call them emotional reasons. I'm not here to judge whether any or all of them are good or bad; that's up to you. But I am here to tell you that it is an extraordinarily bad idea to buy a house for *primarily* emotional reasons. You can accommodate any of your emotional reasons all you want as long as you always remember to make the financial aspects the *central* consideration in any house-related decision. If you are certain you can do this, then you pass this test and can proceed.

3. THE VERY BIG COMMITMENT TEST

"Am I ready to commit a great deal of money, time, and effort over a long period of time?"

This test is similar to the one above but goes even further. Buying a house is a very big commitment, and it is important to understand up front what the nature of that commitment is. First of all, you'll be committing a great deal of money; most people understand that part right away. Saying yes to a house means saying no to a long list of other things that you could be doing with that money. On the other hand, if you've already been following the advice from the previous chapters and have established a habit of consistent financial discipline, this particular aspect of home ownership may not represent quite such an abrupt adjustment.

Another part of your commitment involves research and study. You should set your expectations right from the start that becoming a smart, well-informed house buyer is going to necessarily include an investment of your time doing research and getting educated far beyond just what you're reading here. And the commitment of time and effort isn't just during the buying process; once you've bought a house and are living in it, a different kind of commitment will be required. To protect your investment, your house has to be maintained and kept in good condition. If you've already developed some handy-around-the-house skills, then you're a step ahead—because you'll need them. If not, your choice will be to either develop these skills, resign yourself to paying for such expertise, or most likely some combination of the two. Electrical systems, plumbing, roofs, landscaping, heating and air conditioning, and what may seem like an endless list of other house-related items will call for your attention at various times.

So think it all the way through. Ask yourself honestly, "Am I ready to commit more money than I have ever committed to anything else, to commit to investing all the time required to do the necessary research and homework, and to commit to staying on top of all the house maintenance issues required to protect my investment?" You'll need to answer with a resounding yes to all of the above; otherwise, you're better off waiting.

4. THE INCOME TEST

"Is my income high enough for my local housing market?"

Now we move to the more quantitative financial tests. The first of these, the income test, has two parts. The goal is to find out whether your income will qualify you for a mortgage large enough to allow you to buy the kind of house that makes sense for you. We haven't even talked about mortgages and what it takes to qualify yet, nor have we covered the first thing about house hunting. But don't worry; we'll cover all that later, and you won't need a detailed understanding of those topics to perform this test. Here's how it works.

First, find the minimum acceptable price range for your market. The hardest part about this is keeping your right brain from turning this simple research into a full-blown house-hunting expedition! All you're doing is some basic Internet research about the current selling prices in the specific areas you're interested in. Find at least a few houses currently for sale that represent the bare minimum of what would meet your needs. That doesn't necessarily mean that this is the level of house you'll end up buying; what you're trying to find is the price range of the bare-minimum acceptable houses to you. Calculate an average of these prices and remember the number.

Now you need to find out roughly what interest rate levels are for a *30-year fixed-rate housing mortgage with 20% down.* (You'll learn all about what that means later.) An easy place to get that information is from the "Financial Help Center" tab on the FICO website (www.myfico.com), making sure to select your own state. Alternatively, you can contact local lending institutions and ask. Either way, you won't end up with a single rate but a fairly tightly bunched range. Just estimate an average rate from the bunch, and that will be good enough for this rough reality check.

From this interest rate, select a multiple from the house affordability table in figure 12.1.

Interest Rate %	Multiple
4	3.9
5	3.6
6	3.3
7	3.0
8	2.8
9	2.6
10	2.4
11	2.3
12	2.1
13	2.0
14	1.9
15	1.8

Figure 12.1.   House affordability table.

To determine the highest house price you are likely to comfortably qualify for, multiply your annual income by the appropriate multiple on the table. So if you make $50,000 per year and the rates for 30-year fixed-rate mortgages with 20% down are running at 7%, then the maximum house price that you should be looking at is $150,000. If you earlier determined that your bare-minimum acceptable houses cost *more* than that, you'll need to continue renting and work to improve your income. But if houses are available for less than that, you can proceed. In other words, if the maximum affordable house (from the table) is greater than the minimum acceptable houses (from your research), you pass.

This can get tricky if you have supplemental income in addition to your primary job (which I hope you do). The rule of thumb is that if the supplemental income is regular, predictable, and well documented, you'll probably be able to include it; otherwise, probably not. If this is your situation, and this is what makes the difference between passing this test or not, you should seek clarification from a lending professional before proceeding.

5. THE CASH-BUCKET TEST

"Is my cash bucket full?"

This is the simplest test of all to understand, but that doesn't make it easy! As a reminder, *full* means either 4, 6, or 8 months' average primary income, depending on the degree of risk you're facing, as described in chapter 8.

If your cash bucket is full, you pass. Just remember that house buying is not a financial emergency, so you won't be using anything from your cash bucket throughout the entire buying process. If it isn't yet full, continue saving until it is.

6. THE 27% TEST

"Have I saved up enough for down payment, closing costs, and move-in costs?"

Here is another simple test, but brace yourself: for most people, it is the toughest one to pass and the one that will almost certainly take you the most time. Here it is, plain and simple: *you will need to save up 27% of the selling price of whatever house you plan to buy before you buy it.* Where do these savings come from? From your own First Rule savings, over and above your already-full cash bucket. The 27% breaks down like this: 20% for a down payment, 5% for closing costs, and 2% for the costs of physically moving in and other first-time homeowner expenses. If you are thinking that this will require an extended period of sacrifice and a deep commitment to saving money through the budgeting process, you are completely correct. It will take a while, and it won't be easy.

Depending on the market conditions, you may run across real estate or mortgage professionals who will tell you that this requirement is too strict, and that you can get by with less. Remember that these professionals have a stake in getting you to take a shortcut, but you have an even bigger stake in holding firm! Buying only after you are able to meet this test puts the odds of financial success much more strongly in your favor. It will make affording your *next* house much easier. It will allow you to move from buying your first house to beginning your long-term investment program, which is where you can really begin to accelerate the growth of your net worth—immediately after you buy. In short, this may be the hard way to buy your first house, but it is the *right* way. So until you've saved up 27%, keep renting and keep saving.

7. THE CREDIT SCORE TEST

"Is my credit score high enough to get a prime loan?"

In chapter 9, we outlined a six-step strategy to maximize your credit score without borrowing any money. In that strategy, we described how it isn't necessary to pay to see your actual score on a regular basis, as long as you regularly monitor the inputs via free credit reports and promptly correct any inaccuracies. Well, now it *is* time to actually order your scores and take a look. You'll want the FICO scores from each of the three credit bureaus. (Lenders often throw out the high and low scores and take the one in the middle.) If you've been using the strategy outlined in that chapter, you should see credit scores higher than the baseline score you initially saw. If it's been a while, the scores may be *considerably* higher—congratulations!

Now the question is, how high is high enough? Earlier we explained that lenders use a magic-number FICO score to differentiate between *prime* and *subprime* loans. There isn't one single magic number; the cutoff may vary from lender to lender, from area to area, and from time to time. What you want to find is the FICO subprime cutoff, in *your* area, *right now*. Again, it won't be difficult to get a fairly tight range. Just do a search on "FICO score subprime cutoff" and you'll get a number of hits that will give you an idea of the current situation.

Your ironclad, unbreakable rule is this: *you aren't interested in a subprime loan under any circumstances.* This is true even if someone tells you that you can qualify for one—you simply aren't interested. Subprime loans are pro-hibitively expensive, and they substantially lower your chances of long-term financial success. So order your scores and compare them to the cutoff. If you are below—or even near—the cutoff, you will have more work to do to improve your score. Use the resources available on the FICO website to develop a strategy. But if your scores are above the cutoff—ideally well above—then you pass this test.

8. THE MORTGAGE AFFORDABILITY TEST

"Can I afford the monthly payments within my budget and still continue to save?"

Once you've saved up 27% of your target price, you'll need to make sure that after you move in, you can handle the monthly payments and other increased expenses and still be able to save at least 10% of everything that you earn. So the first thing you'll need to find out is what the approximate monthly pay-ment is going to be. There are many PITI calculators on the Internet you can use to help with this; the calculation is quite generic, so it doesn't matter which one you use. The inputs are the approximate price you are targeting, the down-payment amount (use 20% minimum), the type of loan (30-year fixed interest rate), and the current interest rate for that type of loan that you researched in the previous readiness test. You'll also need the property-tax rates for your area and an estimate for what homeowner's insurance will cost. These last two items will require a little more research, but aren't too hard to come up with after a little time on the Internet. Remember, at this point you're not going for precision, just a realistic estimate. The PITI calculator will then give you P (principal), I (interest), T (property taxes), and I (home-owner's insurance). You want the total of these four items, per month. (For now, don't worry about what each of these items is; much more on all of them is coming up later in part III.)

Next, break out your current monthly budget; you're going to do some removing and adding, create a hypothetical budget, and then see how things stack up. First, *remove* your monthly rent and then add in the PITI amount. Next, you'll need to deal with utilities, like power, water, and garbage re-moval. Depending on what you're paying as a renter, these will likely be higher than your current rates. Finally, you'll need to add in something for house maintenance, which is probably something you didn't spend much, if anything, on as a renter. A good estimate might be 0.5% to 2% of the house's value per year, and then one-twelfth of that per month. (So if your target price is $300,000, start by using somewhere between $150 and $600 per month in your hypothetical budget.) Now you've got it all in front of you, and the question is, can you afford a PITI payment of this size, *and* the higher utility bills, *and* the house maintenance expenses, and still manage to continue saving at least 10% of everything you earn? If not, try cutting back on any discretionary items like vacations and entertainment. Now can it fit? Once you've managed to find a way to make everything fit inside your hypothetical budget, and you're confident that you can sustain the plan, then you've passed this test.

9. THE MARKET CONDITIONS TEST

"Is it advisable to buy in my local market right now?"

Congratulations! You've met the first eight readiness tests, proving that you're ready, at long last, for the housing market. Now the question is this: is the housing market ready for you? As in many things in life, timing is everything.

The first thing to emphasize is that housing markets are famously *local*. National averages receive a lot of media attention because the housing market has a big effect on the overall U.S. economy, but national averages may or may not have anything to do with what is happening where *you* are buying. The average temperature on Earth is 57 degrees Fahrenheit on any given day, but knowing that doesn't help you decide whether to reach for your sunblock or your parka. The only market conditions that you want to pay attention to in this readiness test are the ones in your own local market.

Like most other markets, housing markets run in up-and-down cycles. As soon as you start spending any time researching house prices, you'll start hearing the terms *buyer's market* (lots of houses available for sale and relatively few buyers seeking them) and *seller's market* (lots of eager buyers searching but relatively few houses to choose from). Obviously, all other things being equal, you'd prefer to buy at the height of a buyer's market and sell in a seller's market. But even though that would be ideal, I'm not going to advise you to wait for the perfect time to buy. For one thing, it's impossible to know when any market cycle is at its height until well afterward. For another, it's not free for you to wait—you're paying rent, which you'll never get back, for each month that you choose to wait for the market to come around to an ideal buying condition.

So my advice is, as long as you've met the other eight buying conditions, go ahead and buy as soon as you are ready—*with one very important exception*. It doesn't happen often, but occasionally housing prices will move in a downward trend. I'm not talking about typical seller's market cycles, nor am I talking about a long period of flat prices—I'm talking about a sustained period where housing prices are *literally declining* month by month. If you are unfortunate enough to find yourself in a local market experiencing this, you'll be better off keeping your money in savings and waiting out the decline. It won't last forever; sooner or later, prices will hit bottom, stabilize, and then start back upward. When that signal becomes clear (which will probably be just about the time when everyone has told you that you've waited too long to get the best prices), then you are safe in resuming the buying process. At any time other than absolute price declines, though, give yourself a green light on this test.

DECISION TIME

Now that you've seen the nine readiness tests, you might be thinking that they're pretty demanding—and they are. *Can* you buy a house without answering yes to all of them? Absolutely. In fact, it might seem like the pressure to do so is coming from all sides: from real estate agents and mortgage brokers, from well-meaning friends and family, and even from government programs designed to "get you into a house" with a tiny down payment. Some or all of these might add fuel to the most persuasive voice of all—your own right brain. But *should* you ever buy a house without answering yes to all nine of these questions? No! Remember: *you* are in charge of your financial future, and nobody else.

Let's return to the question posed by this chapter's title: should you buy a house? Now that you've seen the readiness tests, you've got a much better idea about what is involved. The 5-year test might have been a deal breaker for some of you, at least for now. Or the 27% test may have caused you to put the brakes on your expected timetable. But whatever your reaction, now you're in a better position to put yourself in one of these three categories.

1. "I want to buy a house as soon as possible." In that case, now you know exactly what to do next—do whatever is necessary to pass the nine readiness tests. It's likely to take a while to pass them all, especially the 27% test. You can shorten the time required by increasing your savings rate, using your budget process. You might want to go back and reread the Ultimate Acceleration Strategy in chapter 5 and the section on supplemental and passive income to get some ideas that may help you shorten the time required even further.

2. "I want to buy someday, but not in the foreseeable future." For you, the nine readiness tests have been a preview of coming attractions that you'll need to deal with someday, but not today. The preview has been valuable, though, because you can still choose to work on many of the readiness tests in advance, so that when your situation does allow you to buy, you can do so right away. I'd recommend saving the 27% just as urgently *as if* you were going to buy soon. The money will wait patiently until you are ready, earning interest all the while.

3. "I never want to buy a house." That's fine; if buying truly isn't *ever* going to be for you, then the sooner you come to that conclusion, the sooner you can shift your attention to long-term investing. Even though most people who have achieved financial success have typically chosen to buy, it isn't a hard-and-fast requirement. In any case, if you fall into this category, you can now skip the rest of the chapters on house buying and proceed directly to part IV.

Notice that in all three cases, renting is still part of your financial future, at least temporarily. But no matter whether you'll be renting for a relatively short interim period or for the rest of your financial life, my advice on renting is the same: your approach should be to rent in the cheapest way that you safely can. I emphasize *cheapest* because rent is an expense that is gone from your financial bathtub forever; it is simply a pure expense, and it isn't coming back. If you are in category #1 or #2, the more you can save on rent, the faster you can meet the 27% test. If you are in category #3, the more you can save on rent, the more you'll be able to direct into your long-term investment program. No matter what your situation is, it *never* makes financial sense to spend any more on rent than you absolutely have to. But I also emphasize *safely*, because the very lowest rents are often associated with high risks (proximity to environmental, natural, or structural hazards, high crime areas, etc.), and it simply isn't worth putting yourself or your dependents at risk just to save a little bit of rent expense.

Buying your first house is a very important move. Getting it right will put you on a path to a bright financial future. Once you've passed all of these tests, you can move forward with great confidence. Good luck!

SUMMARY

1. Buying is almost always a better financial choice than renting because of the opportunity to recover a big portion of your expenses on resale and because of significant tax advantages.
2. In this book, a *house* means any structure that you legally own and live in most of the time—which allows you to designate it as your primary residence for tax purposes.
3. Even though buying a house is almost always the best financial choice, many risks are involved. One of the biggest risks is buying before you

are completely prepared to do so. Completely prepared means passing the nine readiness tests shown below. You pass if you can answer with a clear yes to each of the nine questions.

4. You will need to continue renting until you pass the readiness tests. Your approach to renting should always be to rent just as cheaply as you safely can.

5. It is often very possible to buy a house without passing all of these tests, and you are likely to encounter some pressure to do so. But remember that *you* are in charge of your financial future; resist this pressure until you are completely prepared to buy.

The Nine House-Buying Readiness Tests

1. The 5-Year Test: *"Can I commit to staying in the house that I buy for at least 5 years?"*
2. The Financial Priority Test: *"Am I ready to make the financial aspects of house buying my primary consideration?"*
3. The Very Big Commitment Test: *"Am I ready to commit a great deal of money, time, and effort over a long period of time?"*
4. The Income Test: *"Is my income high enough for my local housing market?"*
5. The Cash-Bucket Test: *"Is my cash bucket full?"*
6. The 27% Test: *"Have I saved up enough for down payment, closing costs, and move-in costs?"*
7. The Credit Score Test: *"Is my credit score high enough to get a prime loan?"*
8. The Mortgage Affordability Test: *"Can I afford the monthly payments in my budget and still continue to save?"*
9. The Market Conditions Test: *"Is it advisable to buy in my local market right now?"*

• *13* •

Buying a House: How the Money Works

$\mathcal{T}$ime for a warning: we have a lot to cover in this chapter, and much of it may be new to you. This is definitely a cornerstone chapter in the book; we're going to describe the real financial nuts and bolts of house ownership. It probably won't be an easy read; this chapter will likely be of more value to you as a reference that you'll keep coming back to, rather than one where a lot of lightbulbs go off the first time you read it. But don't let this discourage you—jump right in and get the most that you can out of it. The next chapter will be a more entertaining case study, designed to reinforce the key points in this one. One by one, the ideas will become more familiar to you and begin to really stick.

Residential real estate is a very big business, which of course has its own jargon, conventions, standards, and rules. These can be a little imposing, especially the first time you come across them. The purpose of this chapter is to explain the financial basics of buying a house. Even though we won't come close to getting you to the expert level, the goal is to provide you with a working knowledge of the fundamentals that is solid enough to allow you to proceed with confidence. By the time you finish this chapter, it might surprise you how much better you now understand some concepts, terms, and ideas that you've been hearing and wondering about your whole life.

First, we'll cover some of the house-buying jargon, but we'll do it in five rounds of related topics. In each of the rounds, we'll introduce and define key terms that are important for you to understand. These terms will be italicized. After you finish each round, go back and scan through all of the italicized terms and make sure that you are clear on each one. As we go through each round, we'll also include a discussion of some of the most important points about that aspect of house buying. After the five rounds comes an explanation of the two big tax advantages of house ownership, followed by a high-level financial time line of buying, owning, and selling a house.

JARGON EXPLAINED, ROUND 1: YOUR MORTGAGE

Very few people can afford to pay the full price of a house up front; nearly all of you will need to borrow to have enough money to buy. This is the one and only exception to the rule that you learned in part II about never borrowing any money. Because of the dangers of borrowing, you want to approach it very carefully; this is one of the main reasons why we stressed the readiness tests in the previous chapter.

When you borrow money to buy a house, you don't borrow the entire amount. Instead, you first pay some portion, usually (but not always) somewhere between 3% and 20% of the price of the house, in one lump payment up front; this is called the *down payment*. Then you borrow the *remaining* amount, and this loan is called a *mortgage*. Mortgages can be structured in a variety of different ways, but they nearly always call for repayment of the mortgage over a specific period of time, called the *term*. The most common term for a house mortgage in the United States is 30 years, but several other (mostly shorter) terms are also available. *The recommendation for you is a 30-year term.* Most mortgages call for repayments to be made monthly; so, for example, if you have a 30-year mortgage, you will need to make 360 monthly payments (30 × 12 = 360) before it is completely paid off.

Your mortgage is a very formal arrangement between you and the lending institution. Finalizing your mortgage agreement is called *closing*. Closing is a single event, which happens at a prearranged time and place, where you sign a series of formal documents. Before closing, you aren't obligated to follow through and buy the house, and many of the elements of the purchase may still be negotiable; but after closing, everything is final. In addition to the down payment, you will need to pay another amount at closing: *buyer's closing costs*. These costs aren't part of the mortgage; they are simply out-of-pocket expenses. We won't go into the entire list of closing cost items, but they include things like broker's commissions, title searches, and various inspections. The list of items can number as high as 20. These add up to between 2% and 5% of the selling price. Buyer's closing costs are not optional and generally not negotiable; they are simply required in order to close the transaction.

After all of the closing documents are processed, you become the legal owner of the house. The legal proof of this is that your name will be placed on a certificate called a *title*, which is kept on file at a local government office. Even though you are the legal owner, this ownership is conditional on your repaying the mortgage. As protection, the lending institution places a claim on your house, which says that if you fail to repay under the terms of the mortgage, the ownership of the house will revert back to the lender. The term for this arrangement is that your house serves as *collateral* for the mortgage.

Why do lending institutions require a down payment in the first place? Why can't you just borrow the entire amount? The lending institutions require a down payment for their own protection. The bigger the down payment, the more protection they have. If individual lenders had their choice, they would all choose to require large down payments, but competitive pressures sometimes push down-payment requirements down to very low levels. The key point is this: a big down payment protects you too. *You are going to insist on paying at least 20% down,* even if the lender doesn't require that much. That keeps both you and the lender safer; more on why this is true a little later. Once in a great while, lenders may require even more than 20%. If that's the case, you'll have to save even more than our 27% test required, but you'll be even safer when you finally do buy.

JARGON EXPLAINED, ROUND 2: YOUR MONTHLY PAYMENTS

Throughout the term of your mortgage, you are required to repay the lender in a series of monthly payments, which are often called *installments.* Each monthly payment has two components: *principal* and *interest.* The term *principal and interest* often just goes by *P&I.* Principal refers to the unpaid balance of your mortgage, so the principal component of your monthly payment goes toward reducing this balance; every dollar you pay toward principal reduces your remaining mortgage balance by a dollar. The interest component is how you compensate the lending institution for the use of their money. Interest rates, or the price that you pay to borrow money, tend to move up and down in response to a variety of economic variables and business conditions. Over the past several decades, annualized rates for 30-year mortgages have ranged from roughly 4% to 15%.

Interest can be structured into your monthly payments in a variety of different ways, but the two main options that you face are *fixed rate* and *variable rate.* A fixed-rate mortgage specifies the exact rate of interest that will be in force for the entire term of the loan, while a variable-rate mortgage allows for the rate to move up or down, usually formally tied to some specific measure of prevailing market interest rates. When you have a fixed-rate mortgage, your monthly P&I payment remains exactly the same, to the penny, payment after payment, for the entire term of the loan. When you have a variable-rate mortgage, the monthly payment can change at intervals specified in the mortgage, such as every 6 months; if prevailing interest rates go up or down in the overall market, so will your monthly payment. Because of the inherent uncertainty of a variable-rate mortgage, you are only interested in the *fixed-rate* option. (If interest rates drop substantially compared to what they were when you took out your initial mortgage, you can take advantage of that by getting a *new* fixed-rate mortgage.)

How much do interest rates matter? What I'm about to tell you may or may not shock you; it depends on how much respect you've begun to gain for the amazing power of compounding. Let's take a 30-year, fixed-rate mortgage to use as an example. Now let's say that you were very lucky in your timing and that your mortgage is at the very bottom of the 4% to 15% range given above—in other words, if you were fortunate enough to get your loan at a time when the very best rate of 4% happened to be available. Finally, let's say you keep that house for the entire 30-year term of your mortgage, faithfully making all monthly payments. If you add up all 360 monthly payments and compare that amount to the beginning mortgage balance, how much have you ended up paying? Almost *double* the principal, that's how much. Stated differently, even if you get the best interest rate historically possible, you will still end up paying 172% of the value of your original mortgage—that's 100% for principal repayment and 72% for interest. You might have mixed feelings after 30 years. ("The good news is that I've finally paid off my house. The bad news is that I had to pay for it *twice*.") By the way, it doesn't matter if we're talking about a $50,000 mortgage, or $5 million—whatever the beginning balance of your mortgage is, you'll end up paying it almost twice over on a 30-year fixed mortgage at 4% interest.

But remember—4% is as good as it ever gets. What if you're not so lucky in your timing and the best interest rate that you can get is more in the mid-point of the range, at 10%. In that case, you'll end up paying your principal back well over *three* times over the full term of your mortgage! What about the top of the range, at 15% interest? You'll pay your mortgage back over *four and a half times*! So to answer the question directly: interest rates matter a lot.

But your P&I mortgage payments aren't the only monthly payments that go along with owning a house. You'll need to make two other types of payments on top of those: *property taxes* and *homeowner's insurance*. Property taxes are required by law; these are the main way that cities, counties, and school districts get their funding. Property taxes are usually expressed as a percentage of the current resale value of your house and vary widely depending on where the house is. The rates can be as low as 0.2% per year or as high as 2% per year. That means that for a house with a resale value of $300,000, the property tax bill can range from $600 per year all the way up to $6,000. (If you're looking at houses on a city or county boundary line, buying on one side of the street or the other can make a difference.) Homeowner's insurance is required by your lender, but that's okay because *you* should insist on it, too. Homeowner's insurance rates vary widely also; the difference depends upon where the house is located, how old it is, and the type of coverage you select. The lender will usually specify a minimum level of coverage before they will approve the mortgage. You should plan on paying between 0.3% and 1.5% of the value of the house per year.

So each month you will need to pay your lender (P&I), your local government (for property taxes), and your insurer (for homeowner's insurance). Sometimes, though, the lender will act as a collector for your property taxes and homeowner's insurance. When this is the case, you just make one big payment to your lender; the lender keeps the P&I and then pays the local government and your insurer on your behalf. The benefit for you is the convenience of making one single payment to one party each month; this is called your *PITI* (principal, interest, taxes, and insurance) payment. Does your lender do this on your behalf just to do you a neighborly favor? Well—not exactly. It is in your lender's interest to make sure that you stay current on both property taxes and homeowner's insurance. If you fall behind on either, it can have the effect of reducing the value of your house, and your lender is counting on the value of your house as collateral. You pay the same amount either way, and you aren't going to fall behind on any of these payments; so you really don't care if you make one PITI payment or pay each party directly.

Some people have yet another kind of insurance, called *PMI*—private mortgage insurance. This protects the lender—not you—in the event that you can't make your monthly P&I payments. Even though it's for the benefit of the lender, *you* have to pay the premiums. Fortunately, PMI is only required when buyers make a low down payment. But since you will be making a down payment of at least 20%, you won't have to buy PMI. We're including it here only because you're likely to run across this term when you start talking with lenders.

JARGON EXPLAINED, ROUND 3: YOUR EQUITY

The *equity* you have in the house you own is the amount that would result if you sold that house right now at today's fair market value and then paid off the remaining principal balance to your lender. In other words, equity is the house's current selling price, minus the balance remaining on your mortgage. The price that your house could sell for today is simply based on the conditions in your local real estate market, but the remaining principal balance on your mortgage is a little bit trickier to understand.

If you have a 30-year fixed-rate mortgage, you might think that after 10 years, one-third of the term has gone by, so your principal balance should be one-third less, too. It makes sense, right? But that's not how it works. As you might have suspected, compounding is at work here. Compounding doesn't work in straight lines; it starts out very slowly, begins to pick up steam, and then really takes off—remember? Principal is drawn down very, very slowly in the early years of a mortgage, then catches up only in the very late years.

Take a look at the graph in figure 13.1. The horizontal axis is time, and it covers the entire term of a 30-year mortgage. The vertical axis shows what *percentage* of the original mortgage amount remains to be paid. The graph assumes that all monthly payments are made on time.

If there were such a thing as zero percent interest on a mortgage, then the graph would show a completely straight line, going from 100% on the vertical axis straight to the 30-year point of the horizontal axis. But because of interest, the line is curved *outward*. Earlier we said that interest rates on mortgages have historically ranged between 4% and 15%; for the graph, we've chosen a midpoint of that range—10%. A graph showing 4% interest would have less of an outward curve, and one showing a 15% rate would have more of an outward curve; but no matter the interest rate, the line will curve outward.

What this means is that you're going to have to be patient! In the beginning years of your mortgage, the principal will decline at an agonizingly slow rate. So back to our question: after 10 years of dutifully making monthly

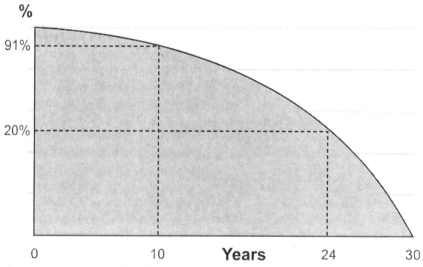

Figure 13.1. Percent principal remaining on a 30-year mortgage at 10% interest.

payments on your 10% mortgage, will the principal be reduced by one-third? Far from it—after 10 full years, you've only paid off 9% of the principal, with 91% to go. You have to keep paying until you are 24 years into the mortgage before you're even halfway paid off. Then the pace picks up significantly later in the life of the mortgage. For people who have never been exposed to how compounding works, this can come as a big surprise—and not a pleasant one.

JARGON EXPLAINED, ROUND 4: WORST-CASE SCENARIOS

Before we sketch out some of the worst-case scenarios, let's go back to the concept of equity: your house's current selling price minus the balance remaining on your mortgage. Normally, we think of selling prices going continually upward. Meanwhile, as you keep making monthly P&I payments, your principal balance keeps going downward. (Yes, very slowly at first—but in a downward direction nevertheless.) What this means is that equity is typically a positive number, and it grows into a larger and larger positive number the longer you own the house. So get ready for this: after a while, if your equity gets large enough, your lender will undoubtedly call your attention to their willingness to *loan you some more money*, using your ever-growing equity as collateral. This is called a *home equity loan*, and you're not interested, no matter how eagerly the lender tries to entice you with the possibility. This is one worst-case scenario that you'll never face, because you simply won't borrow any money beyond your original mortgage.

But what happens if the selling price of your house goes *down* while you own it? Historically, this is rare, but recent events prove that it can certainly happen. If it goes down by enough, your house's selling price can actually get lower than your principal balance—and that means that your equity would be a negative value. There are a couple of special terms for this: a mortgage with negative equity can be called either *upside down* or *underwater*. Having an underwater mortgage is a worst-case scenario for you—and for your lender, too. Hold that thought: we'll come right back to it.

What happens if you don't make your monthly payments to the lender on time or in full, or if you stop making them altogether? If this situation goes on long enough, you are contractually and legally considered to be in *default* on the mortgage, and the lender is entitled to assume full ownership of the house. This event is called a *foreclosure*. If that happens, you forfeit the down payment that you'd initially made, all the payments that you made before the default, and any claim whatsoever on the proceeds that the lender will receive from selling the house. Oh, and by the way, you must leave the house—the lender has the right to engage local law enforcement to force you to leave, if necessary.

Obviously, this is a worst-case scenario for you, and several of the readiness tests from the previous chapter are specifically designed to prevent you from getting into such a situation. But it isn't *necessarily* a bad scenario for the lender. When the lender forecloses, they forfeit the principal remaining on your mortgage, because the act of foreclosure guarantees that you'll never pay it off. But they now completely own the house and can immediately sell it at the current market price. When equity is positive, they come out ahead on the sale. But when the mortgage is underwater, the lender takes a loss when they foreclose. *That's why lenders require down payments.* A 10% down payment, for example, gives the lender a 10% cushion of protection against a possible drop in the value of the house. The bigger the down payment, the more protection the lender has against the possibility of the mortgage ever getting underwater.

So that's why the *lender* likes big down payments—but why do *you* care? As long as you know that you'll keep on making your monthly payments no matter what, you shouldn't care if your mortgage is underwater or not—right? Not quite. Lots of things can occur in life that you don't plan on, and some of them might require you to sell earlier than you thought. Maybe you have a fantastic but unexpected job opportunity in another city. Maybe you incur a big financial emergency like an uncovered hospitalization, which threatens you with expenses even beyond what your cash bucket can cover. Maybe another member of your family becomes disabled and you decide that living near them is necessary so that you can provide care. There are countless other examples, but these are enough to give you an idea. If you need to sell unexpectedly and your mortgage is underwater, then you're at risk of selling at a loss. The position that you always want to be in is to owe less on your house than its current resale value. That way, if you have to sell unexpectedly, you may not gain as much as you'd originally planned, but at least you won't be facing a loss.

To sum it up: your lender never wants your mortgage to be underwater, and you never want your mortgage to be underwater. That's why *both* of you like big down payments. You're going to insist on paying at least 20% down—and your lender will love you for it.

JARGON EXPLAINED, ROUND 5: SELLING YOUR HOUSE

I've got good news and bad news. The bad news is that when you sell your house, you'll pay closing costs *again*, and this time they'll be even higher. *Seller's closing costs* average about 6% to 7%, and since your house will (we hope) be selling for a lot more than you originally bought it for, these percentages will be applied against a higher value than your buyer's closing costs were. Just like buyer's closing costs, these are simply out-of-pocket expenses required to close the transaction. These hefty closing costs, which you face every time you either buy or sell a house, are the main reason why it doesn't make financial sense to move from one house to another any more frequently than you absolutely have to. Select a house that will meet your needs for at least 5 years—*and stick with it.*

Now the good news: when you sell, the entire selling price comes to you in the form of a check. For most people, selling their first house means getting the biggest check they've ever received in their entire life. Of course, unless you have completely paid off the mortgage, you'll have to do that now; and that means writing a check for the entire unpaid balance (which is usually another record, this time for the biggest check you have ever *written*). So to sum it up—you receive a check for the full selling price, but then you divert 6% to 7% of that money to seller's closing costs and you divert another portion of it to pay off your principal. Whatever is left is the cash amount that you walk away with after the sale. If your house has appreciated enough, often this amount is enough for some, or even all, of the down payment on your *next* house.

When it comes to income taxes, though, your gain is calculated differently than the cash that you walk away with after the sale. For income tax purposes, the price that you sell your house for, minus the price that you bought it for, is called your *capital gain*. The price you originally paid for the house is given a special term, called your *basis*. Neither the buyer's nor the seller's closing costs enter into this; your capital gain is simply the difference between the buying and selling prices. But before you begin to worry about the income taxes you'll pay on the profit you've made—read the next section!

THE TWO MAJOR TAX ADVANTAGES OF HOUSE OWNERSHIP

Over the past several decades, the U.S. Congress has taken steps to encourage home ownership. The most important of these are two major income tax incentives. Earlier we emphasized that tax laws can change frequently; but these two tax advantages have been in place for a long time and are unlikely to be removed. Remember, though, both of these tax advantages apply only to your primary residence.

Tax advantage #1 is the *deductibility* of the interest portion of your mortgage payments. U.S. income tax rules allow you to claim the interest portion of your mortgage payments as tax deductions, as long as these payments are for a house that is your primary residence. Remember in chapter 10 we talked about the difference between taking a standard deduction vs. itemizing your deductions? Well, if you weren't itemizing before, you probably will be after you buy a house, so that you can take full advantage of this. How important is this deduction? If you are in the 25% tax bracket, for example, it means that the U.S. government subsidizes 25% of the interest portion of your mortgage payment by lowering your income taxes by that amount. Deductibility becomes slowly less important in the later years of a mortgage, as the "P" in your P&I payment gets bigger and bigger and the "I" gets smaller and smaller. But over the full 30-year term of a mortgage, deductibility really adds up to a very substantial benefit.

Tax advantage #2 can be even more important; it is called *exclusion*. Simply put, this means that if your house appreciates in value during the time you own it and you end up selling it at a profit, then you don't have to pay *any* income taxes on that profit. That's right—the capital gain on a primary residence is *excluded* from income tax. This is a major benefit because you will pay income taxes on almost any other kind of capital gain. There are limits to this exclusion, but they are high enough that they rarely apply to first-time house buyers. Right now, the limits are $250,000 for single people and $500,000 for couples. The more your house appreciates, the more valuable this tax exclusion is to you.

HOUSE OWNERSHIP: THE FINANCIAL TIME LINE

One way to summarize logically all the financial effects of buying a house is to group them chronologically into three phases: buying, owning, and selling.

Buying: First, you make a down payment of at least 20% of the selling price of the house. Then you add in another 2% to 5% for buyer's closing costs. On top of that, you should plan on roughly another 2% for the costs of physically moving in and other first-time homeowner expenses. None of these costs are tax deductible. (If we take the top end of the closing-cost range, these add up to the now-familiar 27% from the readiness tests.)

Owning: Each month, since you'll be taking out a fixed-rate mortgage, your P&I payments are literally fixed—the amount you pay per month is identical down to the penny. On top of that, you'll make monthly payments for property taxes and homeowner's insurance, and the amounts you pay for these expenses can change from time to time, usually upward, as the value of your house increases. Finally, throughout the time you own, you'll pay for various maintenance and repairs to keep your house in good working condition; these costs don't tend to appear as true *monthly* expenses—they occur on an as-needed basis. For budgeting purposes, though, you should plan on 0.5% to 2% of the house's value, per year. You'll keep paying P&I for as long you own your house, or until the end of your term, whichever comes first. But you'll keep paying for property tax, homeowner's insurance, and maintenance for as long as you own your house. The interest portion of your P&I payment is tax deductible each year. Certain maintenance items (energy-saving improvements, for example) may receive special tax treatment too, but the rules for these change frequently.

Selling: When you sell, you will receive a check for the entire selling price of your house. But you'll need to pay 6% to 7% in seller's closing costs, and then, unless you have already paid off your mortgage, you'll need to pay off the remaining principal. Unless your capital gain is over the very high limits, you won't have to pay *any* income taxes on the profit you make from selling the house.

PAYBACK TIME: THE BIG REBATE

We can summarize this process in an even simpler way: first, through sacrifice and discipline, you save up a big chunk of money as the price of admission for house ownership. Then, through even more sacrifice and discipline, you make a series of big monthly payments. This is no financial picnic so far! No wonder renting looks like a better way to go at first. But when you ultimately sell the house, you'll finally be in a position to realize some financial gain for all the sacrifice and discipline that you've practiced. *This* is when the house owner shoots way past the renter in the financial race. *This* is payback time. You could describe this sequence of events as "first you pay and pay and pay, but when you finally sell, you get a really big tax-free rebate."

This big rebate allows you to recover at least some of the expenses that you've paid out during ownership. You might even be able to recover *most* of them, and in some very rare, truly exceptional cases, it is possible to recover *even more* than you've ever paid out! The size of your rebate depends on how much the price of your house has appreciated during the time you own it. Even though the mortgage interest rate is very important, it isn't the single most important factor in ensuring a financially successful house-ownership experience, although most people think it is. Overwhelmingly, the most important factor is your house's price appreciation during the time you own it.

When we discussed cars earlier, we emphasized the importance of selecting a car based on resale value. The same principle applies to houses. When you buy a big-ticket item, remember that you want to put yourself in a position to sell that big-ticket item later at the highest possible price. The financial difference between cars and houses is this: when selecting a car, the goal is to choose the one whose resale value will *decline the slowest;* but when selecting a house, the goal is the one whose resale value will *increase the fastest.*

SUMMARY

1. The following terms were defined and discussed:

   Round 1: down payment, mortgage, term, closing, buyer's closing costs, title, collateral

   Round 2: installments, principal, interest, P&I, fixed rate, variable rate, property taxes, homeowner's insurance, PITI, PMI

   Round 3: equity

   Round 4: home equity loan, upside down, underwater, default, foreclosure

   Round 5: seller's closing costs, capital gain, basis

2. A mortgage for the purpose of buying a house is the one and only exception to the "don't borrow money" rule. Borrowing money is always risky, so it is critical to approach mortgages carefully.

3. The higher the down payment, the smaller the chance of your mortgage ever going underwater, which *both you and your lender* want to avoid. Even if the lender is forced by competitive pressures to offer low down payments, you aren't interested because you prefer the safety of a 20% or greater down payment.

4. Interest rates for primary-residence mortgages have historically ranged from roughly 4% to 15%. On a 30-year fixed-rate mortgage at 4%, you will end up paying back your principal almost *twice over* by the end of the 30-year term. At 15%, you'll end up paying your principal back *four and a half times over.* Interest rates matter a lot!

5. If you fail to make your monthly payments on time or in full, or if you stop making them altogether, you will be considered in default on your mortgage. If you default, the lender can foreclose on the house, which means that the lender assumes ownership, you forfeit all payments made up to that point, and you legally must leave the house.

6. The monthly P&I (principal and interest) payments will be the same each month, down to the penny, for a fixed-rate mortgage; but the *portions* designated for principal and interest will change. Initially, the payments will be mostly interest, with only a small portion going toward the reduction of principal; only much later in the mortgage will the rate of principal reduction pick up steam.

7. In addition to P&I, house owners pay property tax (0.2% to 2% of your house's value per year) and homeowner's insurance (0.3% to 1.5% per year) monthly. When these two items are added to P&I, the resulting term is PITI. On top of that, you should plan on various

maintenance expenses. These don't occur as a regular monthly bill; instead, you pay them as needed. You should plan on spending 0.5% to 2% of your house's value each year, and include one-twelfth of that in each month's budget.

8. When you buy or sell a house, you must pay closing costs. When you buy, these range from 2% to 5%, and when you sell, they range from 6% to 7%. These costs are *on top of* everything else, aren't tax deductible, and you won't get them back. That is a primary reason that it doesn't make sense to buy and sell a primary residence very often; pick one that you can stay in for at least 5 years.

9. There are two very favorable tax advantages of home ownership. The first one allows you to deduct the interest portion of your mortgage payments each year. The second one, called *exclusion*, allows you to pay no tax at all on the gain you make when you ultimately sell your house (unless the gain exceeds some very high limits). In both cases, these advantages apply only to your primary residence.

10. The negative financial effects of buying a house occur *when you buy* and *as you own*; the positive effects occur *when you sell*. Think of it as a very large purchase, followed by a stream of ongoing payments— but when you sell you are eligible for a potentially very large rebate.

11. How big the rebate is—and therefore how financially favorable the purchase of your house has turned out to be—depends on a very critical factor: *price appreciation*. Every percentage point of appreciation that occurs while you own your house makes a huge difference in the final financial picture.

12. Throughout the chapter, I've made several recommendations about exactly what type of mortgage makes the most sense for you. Summarizing all of these into one recommendation:

   You should buy rather than rent, but only if—and not until—you meet all nine of the readiness tests. When you buy a house as a primary residence, you will make a down payment of at least 20%, which you will pay from money that you've saved, outside of your cash bucket. You will take out a 30-year fixed-rate mortgage for the remaining amount. In the 1st third of your financial life, a primary residence is the only kind of real estate that you will buy, and the mortgage that you take out to buy it will be the only money that you will borrow.

· *14* ·

Case Study: Mortgageville

"*O*pposites attract." That's what everyone in Mortgageville said when Gary and Vicki got married. You see, even though they were both very bright, Vicki and Gary were almost completely opposite in their learning styles. Vicki Verbal was a classic verbal learner; she picked things up very quickly by reading about them or by hearing someone explain them. Meanwhile, Gary Graphic was a skilled visual learner; he preferred diagrams, flow charts, and graphs. If Gary was given a verbal description, his approach was to summarize everything onto a spreadsheet, stare at it for a while, and then see if he could translate everything into a visual form. It usually took Gary a little longer this way, but he often came up with valuable insights as a result of his efforts to represent ideas visually. When Vicki saw these pictures, she usually wanted to summarize them verbally to confirm her understanding.

Their friends laughed at the way they communicated with each other. When Vicki tried to explain something to Gary, she would always start with, "*Listen*, Gary. Let me *explain* . . . ." When it was Gary's turn, he'd say, "*Look*, Vicki. Here's what I'm trying to get you to *see* . . . ." As they got to know each other, they learned—each in their own way, of course—how to combine their approaches in a complementary way. As a result, they became quite a skilled learning team.

After their marriage, Vicki and Gary knew that they eventually wanted to buy a house. As attentive students of personal financial management, they understood that first they had to be able to pass all nine readiness tests. So that's what they set out to do. After a few years of sacrifice and discipline, they succeeded in meeting all of the tests and then realized their dream of buying their first house. They were even more excited to learn that their closest friends, Rhonda and Ronald Renter, were moving in at the same time—right next door!

The house that Gary and Vicki bought cost $300,000. They paid 20% down, leaving them with a mortgage of $240,000 to be paid over a term of 30 years. The interest rate on their fixed-rate mortgage ended up at 10%, just about in the middle of the historical 4% to 15% range. Their closing costs were 3.5% of the sale price, the annual premium on their homeowner's insurance turned out to be 0.7%, and their property-tax rate ended up at about 1%—all these are within the typical range for Mortgageville. Gary and Vicki make a fairly typical combined income and are in the 25% tax bracket. Finally, housing prices in Mortgageville have historically appreciated at about 4% per year, and most experts saw nothing on the horizon that indicated that this would change much in the foreseeable future. And even though Gary and Vicki were thrilled with every aspect of their new house, they had to admit that there was nothing about it that would cause it to appreciate any more or any less than the other houses in town.

Meanwhile, Rhonda and Ronald's house was identical in every way to Gary and Vicki's; the only difference was that Rhonda and Ronald were renting, while Gary and Vicki had bought. The rent for the Renters' house was $1,500 per month. They had signed a 1-year lease, and they were aware that after the lease expired, their rent would probably go up if they wanted to stay another year. In Mortgageville, rents tend to increase at about the same 4%-per-year rate that housing prices do.

The differences between buying and renting are best understood over a long period of time. So let's check in on our friends at three different points in time.

ONE MONTH

Both couples have just enjoyed the very first month in their new homes. Gary and Vicki have just gotten three bills in their e-mail: a mortgage statement, a property-tax bill, and a homeowner's insurance premium payment notice. Since this was the first time they'd gotten those kinds of bills, they printed them out to make sure that they understood each one.

The mortgage statement called for a monthly payment of $2,106. This wasn't a surprise; the amount was familiar to them from the paperwork they'd signed when they closed on their house. In fact, they knew that because they had a fixed-rate mortgage, the monthly payment for principal and interest (P&I) was going to stay at exactly $2,106 each and every month for as long as they stayed in the house and kept the same mortgage. In fact, they knew that if they stayed in the house for the entire 30-year term, the statement they were looking at would be the first of 360 monthly bills for exactly $2,106.

When they looked at the details on the statement, though, Gary noticed that the $2,106 was divided into two parts: $2,000 for interest and $106 for principal. "This must be a mistake!" he exclaimed. "Almost the whole payment is going toward interest." Vicki replied, "Listen, Gary, don't you remember the lender's explanation about that? Our monthly payments are fixed, but they start out heavy on the interest and finish up heavy on the principal. He said that if we wanted to know what to expect, we could look it all up on something he called a *P&I calculator* on the web."

That was all Gary needed to hear. For the next several minutes, keys were clicking as Gary found a P&I calculator and entered some key information about their mortgage. A few minutes later, he emerged in a familiar pose: graph in hand. "Look at this, Vicki," he said. "Our payment is broken down just the way this calculator says it ought to be. You weren't kidding about it starting out heavy on the interest. But what surprises me is how long it *stays* that way. It looks like our payments will be interest-heavy for *most* of the mortgage term. Our payments won't get principal-heavy until the 24th year of our 30-year mortgage!" (See figure 14.1.)

Vicki studied the graph and said, "I never realized that it worked quite like that, but it's definitely nice to know now exactly what's going to be on our next 359 monthly mortgage statements." Then they turned their attention to their monthly property-tax bill, which called for a payment of $250, and then to the $175 homeowner's insurance monthly premium notice. "Every month, we'll pay $2,106 plus $250 plus $175, which comes to $2,531.

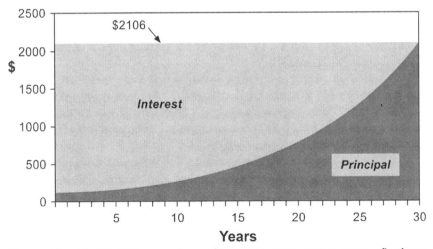

Figure 14.1. Monthly P&I payments on a $240,000 mortgage (30-year term, fixed-rate of 10%).

That's what they call *PITI*," explained Vicki. Just then, Rhonda and Ronald knocked on the door, and the neighbors spent some time comparing notes on their housing expenses.

Finally Rhonda spoke up. "The two of you pay $2,531 a month? We pay only $1,500. On top of that, every time anything needs to be fixed, replaced, or repainted, we can just call the landlord, but you have to pay for all that on your own."

"There's more," said Ronald. "It took you a really long time to save up the down payment of $60,000, plus another $10,500 for closing costs. We didn't have to go through all that sacrifice and discipline like you did. We just paid 1 month's damage deposit and moved right in. Are the two of you really sure you did the right thing by buying?"

TEN YEARS

Ten years have now gone by, and the two Mortgageville couples are still the best of friends, and more to the point—still neighbors. Gary and Vicki are still paying off the same 30-year fixed-rate mortgage, while Rhonda and Ronald are now on their 10th consecutive 1-year lease. Vicki and Gary invited their neighbors over to celebrate their mutual 10-year milestones. Eventually the discussion turned to their respective financial situations.

"At first we were paying $1,500 a month," Rhonda began. "But since then, our rent has gone steadily up, by 4% a year. That doesn't sound like much, but believe it or not, we pay over $2,200 a month now. I guess it's that *power of compounding* that you two are always talking about. Meanwhile, *your* monthly payment is still frozen where it was at the beginning. Since your PITI is over $2,500 a month, I guess we're still coming out ahead, but I admit that it's gotten a lot closer."

"I added up all the monthly payments we've made these past 10 years, and it's a pretty big number," added Ronald. "Are you ready? We've paid over $220,000 in rent since we moved in. That comes to an average of over $1,800 a month. But your PITI is over $2,500! That means it was smarter of us to remain renters all this time—right?"

"Well, not exactly," Vicki responded. "Let me try to explain this. If all you compare is the monthly payment amount, then renting will *always* seem to be the better choice. But there are other things to consider, too. Like the deductibility of our interest payments, for example. And even more important, even though we've been paying more per month than you have, we've been building up our equity at the same time. And any profit we'd make if we sold is excludable from our income taxes."

Rhonda and Ronald just stared back blankly—as if Vicki were speaking a foreign language.

"Here, let me show you," offered Gary. "I thought this might come up, so I whipped up a couple of spreadsheets ahead of time. First, though, let me point out that you're quite right—we really have paid out a lot more than you have over these past 10 years. You've paid out $220,000 so far, but we've paid over $353,000. Here, take a look." (See figure 14.2.)

ALREADY PAID

At closing:

Down Payment	60,000
Closing Cost	10,500

Ten Years Worth of:

Principal	21,749
Interest	230,992
Property Taxes	36,674
Homeowner's Insurance	21,000
Maintenance and Repairs	30,000
Tax Savings (Deductibility)	-57,748
Total	**353,167**

Figure 14.2.   Actual 10-year house costs.

"Here's where you can see how I got $353,000. First, there was the down payment and closing costs that we had to save up for. Now, take a look at the 10 years of PITI, and all the maintenance and repairs that we've had to pay for. But since we're in the 25% tax bracket, and the interest paid on a primary residence can be *deducted*, we've saved over $57,000 in taxes. That's like getting the U.S. government to make two of our monthly payments every year."

"But listen, there is another whole side to this," Vicki continued. "When you decide to leave your rental, that's it—you just leave—with nothing. But when we decide to leave, we can *sell*. We originally bought for $300,000, but housing prices have been going up by about 4% per year. The best we can tell, if we were to sell our house today, we could sell it for over $442,000. Compounding has been working *for* us all this time. Our principal has been dropping at the speed of a glacier, but that high selling price still leaves us with a nice equity of about $224,000."

"Everything Vicki just described is based on what would only happen *if* we chose to sell right now," Gary pointed out. "Of course, we aren't planning to sell anytime soon. But still, we legally own this house, and it is worth much more today than when we bought it—so the equity actually *adds to our net worth*. I thought it would be easier to see if I included all that alongside the spreadsheet that I already showed you. See what you think of this." (See figure 14.3.)

"The money we've already paid out, just as I showed you before, is on the left," Gary went on. "But the right side shows what would happen if we chose to sell today. After paying off the principal and paying for closing costs, we'd end up with over $195,000 in our pockets. If you combine that with what's on the left, it brings our total cost for owning the house for 10 years down to a much lower number. It comes to about $1,300 per month, which is even lower than the monthly rent you started out with.

"To sum it all up: if you include what would happen if we sold today, then we're actually in a *better* financial position than if we'd rented, even though we've paid out more so far. And it's all because the value of our house has appreciated."

"I like to explain it a little differently," said Vicki. "This is how my parents always talked about it. With renting, you pay—and that's it. With buying, you pay more—but then you get a *rebate* when you sell. How big the rebate is depends on how long you've owned the house, how much it has appreciated, and the interest rate on your mortgage—plus a few other things."

"So if you use the numbers from this spreadsheet," Gary continued, after clicking a few calculator keys, "it breaks down like this. For every dollar you've spent, we've spent about $1.60. But if we sold our house right now, we'd get 88 cents back, which comes out to be a 55% rebate. So $1.60 minus 88 cents gives us a net cost of 72 cents—compared to your dollar. Understand?"

Figure 14.3. Ten-year house costs with hypothetical sale.

Rhonda and Ronald took it all in with great interest. "Ronald, are you thinking what I'm thinking?" asked Rhonda. "You bet I am," replied Ronald. "Let's go figure out how long it would take us to save up for a down payment on a house of our own!"

THIRTY YEARS

The mood was festive at Vicki and Gary's house; they had just made their 360th—and *final*—mortgage payment. Of course Ronald and Rhonda were there too, to help with the celebration. But their mood was a little more subdued. You see, despite what they'd spoken about years earlier, they were still renting and were just about to sign their 31st yearly lease on their rental house.

"Well, congratulations! It took 30 years, but now you own this house free and clear." said Rhonda. "From now on, you live here *for free*." Vicki and Gary knew that she wasn't completely right about the *free* part; they understood that the property tax bills, homeowner's insurance premiums, and various maintenance expenses weren't going to stop just because the mortgage was finally paid. But still, there was no denying that paying the last of their monthly $2,106 P&I payments felt great!

Ronald spoke up: "Gary, I've known you long enough to know that you've probably got a nice spreadsheet that summarizes the financial difference between 30 years of owning and renting. Rhonda and I are well aware that we blew it by never buying, but we can't help wondering just how big a mistake it really was. So go ahead and give it to us straight—we'd rather learn our lesson late than not at all."

"Well, as a matter of fact, I do have a little something," replied Gary, "but it's a graph, not a spreadsheet (see figure 14.4.). Here, have a look.

"First, even though we've both been here for 30 years, I used a time frame of 35. Neither of us is planning on moving anytime soon, and I wanted to be able to look ahead a few years. I put a vertical line in at the 10-year mark, because that's when we last looked at the numbers together, remember? That's when your total cost was about $220,000, and our net cost, if we had sold then, was about $158,000."

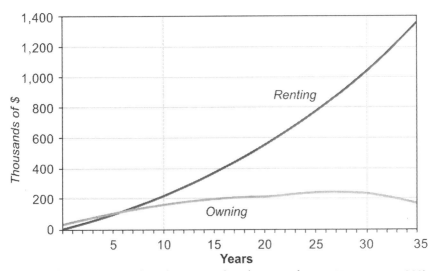

Figure 14.4. Total cost of renting vs. owning ($300,000 house, 30-year term, 20% down, 10% fixed rate).

"Yes, we remember," sighed Rhonda. "And I can see where those numbers are on this graph. But that was in the 10th year, and the difference wasn't really that big. Look at it now—the difference between owning and renting has gotten huge! What happened?"

"Compounding takes time to really kick in," explained Vicki. "But now it's had 30 years to work. And compounding works *for* an owner and *against* a renter."

"No kidding," said Ronald. "Our rent started at $1,500 a month. Today it's up to $4,850."

"And this house that we paid $300,000 for would sell today for about $970,000," added Vicki.

Gary added, "Remember during year 10, when I showed you that we'd get a 55% rebate if we sold? If we sold now, we'd get a 77% rebate—*more than three-quarters of everything that we've ever paid to live here would come back to us* as soon as we closed."

"The renting line is smooth," noted Rhonda. "That makes sense. Our rent has gone up steadily at 4% per year. But the owning line looks like it has a few 'bumps' in it. Is that a mistake?"

"There are actually reasons for those bumps," replied Gary. "Remember when we explained that any profit you make on reselling a primary residence can be excluded from your income tax? Well, that's true—but there are limits. After about the 22nd year, our profit if we resold finally reached the exclusion limit of $500,000 for a married couple. So any gains *over* that are taxed, which makes a bump in the graph there. And the other bump is right now, in year 30, because that's when our P&I payments finally go away!"

"Okay, I get it," replied Rhonda. "But here's another question. It is really great how well you've done financially. But is the main reason for your success that you've stayed in the same house all this time? If you'd sold at some time during the 30 years, and then bought another house, would you have to start all over again at year zero on the graph?"

"The reason that we did well was appreciation," replied Gary. "We owned an asset that went up in value at 4% per year for 30 years. We would have done *almost* as well if we had owned a series of two or three houses instead of just one—*as long as they would have appreciated at 4% while we owned them.* There's nothing magic about owning just one house, but it does make it easier. That's because there is just one set of closing costs to pay. If we'd split the 30 years among three houses, we'd have *three* sets of buyer's and seller's closing costs to pay, and you never get that money back; that closing cost money would just add to the costs. But except for the extra closing costs, we could have done just as well."

Ronald was still staring at the graph—shocked. "I knew this had to be adding up, especially the way our rent kept going up and up. But look at the renter line—we've now paid over *a million dollars* in rent over 30 years, without *anything at all* to show for it. Meanwhile, your costs have more or less flattened out, and now they're actually about to start going *down*."

"Ronald, we thought you understood all that the last time we went through the numbers and that the two of you had decided to buy a house of your own," said Vicki, with diplomatic gentleness. "If you had, you'd be in a much better position. We couldn't understand why you never did."

"I can explain that," said Rhonda. "We waited too long to get serious about it. We'd already been renting for 10 years when we learned about the real advantages of buying, and we were all set to start saving for a down payment. But we learned that it's really hard to change spending habits after 10 years. Every time we resolved that *'this would be the year'* to reduce spending and really start saving, there always seemed to be some really good reason why we needed to make an exception and put it off. So I hate to admit it, but in hindsight I guess the explanation is that we just never got around to it because it was just too hard to change our spending habits once we'd gotten so used to them."

"Well, now I can see that we were right about renting in order to keep our monthly costs down—*dead* right," said Ronald. "But you two were really smart, right from the start. You started early, so you never got into the habit of spending a lot on other things. I really wish we knew then what we know now. Now I can see just how smart the two of you were."

"Well, I'm really glad we bought," replied Gary. "But to tell the truth, I'm not feeling too smart at the moment. When Vicki and I bought, we knew that housing prices in Mortgageville were going up at about 4% per year on average and were expected to continue at that rate. That sounded pretty good to us, so we were happy to buy a house that seemed like it would appreciate at that rate. But since then we've learned a lot more about appreciation. Even though the average is 4%, some neighborhoods go up more, and some go up less. And some houses in a neighborhood will go up by more than others, and some less. What we've learned is that with just a little bit more research, we probably could have done a better job of picking out a house that would have appreciated by *more* than 4%."

"A few extra points couldn't make that big a difference, could they?" asked Rhonda. "Is it really that big a deal?" In response, Gary showed them the graph in figure 14.5.

"Let me try to explain this," said Vicki. "The 4% line is exactly the same line that was on the other graph. That's the line that explains the financial position that Gary and I are in right now. The other two lines are 'what if' lines. The 0% line shows what our position would be if Gary and I had bought a house that didn't appreciate at all. Every other assumption is exactly the same—the *only* difference is the rate of appreciation. Look at how much

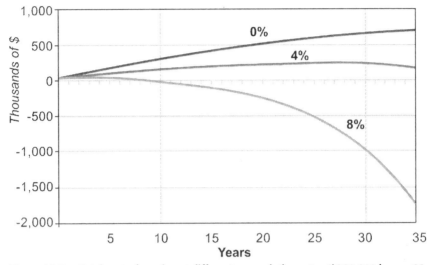

Figure 14.5. Total cost of owning at different appreciation rates ($300,000 house, 30-year term, 20% down, 10% fixed rate).

higher the costs are on the 0% line! Buying a house that doesn't appreciate at all is only a little bit better than renting!

"But the 8% line shows the other side of the coin; that's where we'd be if we'd found a house that appreciated by four points *more* than the Mortgageville average—a real *resale winner*. The costs actually *go negative* sometime around year nine."

"Wow!" exclaimed Rhonda. "The difference that appreciation makes is enormous. But is that the *most* important thing? Doesn't the interest rate on your mortgage make just as big a difference?"

"Gary spent some time graphing that, too," replied Vicki. "And yes, interest rates matter quite a lot, but not as much as appreciation. A percentage point of difference in appreciation matters *much* more than a point of difference in interest rate—it's not even close."

"When the line goes below zero, does that mean what I think it does?" asked Ronald.

"Absolutely," replied Gary. "If we'd bought a house 30 years ago that appreciated at 8% instead of 4%, we wouldn't have ended up paying a cent for a roof over our heads for 30 years. Instead, we would have *made* a lot of money! Even after taxes, we would have made a net profit of almost a million dollars by living in it and then reselling it. Our rebate after selling would be *over 100%*. You're not going to believe this, but our rebate would be 181%!"

"Let me get this straight," said Ronald. "If you'd bought a house that appreciated at 8%, you would have *made* a million dollars by living in it and then reselling it after 30 years. Meanwhile, we've *paid* a million dollars for renting for 30 years. That's a $2 million difference in our net worths!"

"Exactly right," said Gary. "Look—we know that it might not be realistic to shoot for a house that will appreciate by four more points than the local average, but you can tell by looking at the graph that *even one or two points would make a huge difference*. So now we feel a little bit like the two of you do—if only we knew then what we know now!"

"Hey, here's an idea," said Vicki. "We've each learned something really important that we wish we'd known when we were just starting out, when it could have done us some good. Let's write down the most important things that we've learned, and put them in a book for young people."

"I know the most important thing that *we've* learned," said Rhonda. "Financially, buying is way better than renting. And it's best to start planning for it as early as possible."

"And I can see what *our* number-one lesson has been," added Gary. "The rate of resale price appreciation is the single most important thing to pay attention to when you buy. Even a little bit of extra appreciation makes a *huge* difference in your financial outcome."

SUMMARY

Financially, buying is way better than renting. It's best to start planning for it as early as possible. The rate of resale price appreciation is the single most important thing to pay attention to when you buy. Even a little bit of extra appreciation makes a *huge* difference in your financial outcome.

• *15* •

Buying a House: Let's Do It!

*T*he last three chapters were intended to give you an overall understanding of the financial aspects of buying a house. Now that you're armed with all of that knowledge, it's time to get more specific about exactly *how* to go about buying.

This chapter consists of just two lists. As Gary and Vicki just learned, a few extra points of appreciation can make a *huge* difference in the financial outcome when you buy a house. As you begin talking with real estate professionals, the term they use for appreciation is usually *resale value*, or just *resale* for short. So the first list is all about how to find the resale winners. The second list describes the steps in the house-buying process, as well as a couple of financial tips for after you buy. Each step includes some key do's and don'ts, which will allow you to successfully navigate your way from renter to owner.

SIX TIPS FOR FINDING THE RESALE WINNERS

Only some buyers really make a point of buying for resale. Even fewer first-time buyers know the importance of this, *but you are going to be one of them.* This list will serve as your guide about how to find the resale winners.

1. **Broaden your thinking.** The housing market in Mortgageville (4% appreciation each and every year) wasn't too realistic. In real life, housing markets *generally* go upward, but not smoothly and not always. Instead, like most other markets, they experience up and down cycles, which are not easy to predict. Despite these cycles, *certain parts* of the market always fare better than average. When the housing

markets go up, these resale winner subsets of the market consistently appreciate more than average; when the housing markets are flat, or even depreciate, these subsets are consistently more successful at resisting the downward pressure.

More specifically, housing prices in some *countries* consistently outperform the global average; some U.S. *regions* seem to always do better than the national average; some *cities* within each region are usually strongest; some *neighborhoods* are frequent resale winners; and finally, certain *houses* are always going to fare better than others. Up until now, your choice of where to live has been mainly about convenience. Now you need to change your thinking, with resale value as your very top priority. Do some research! Okay, maybe you're not going to pick which *country* to live in based on house appreciation potential, but before you automatically choose to live in the region, city, or neighborhood where you've lived before, give some careful thought to how your current location stacks up relative to others. Remember, this is a longer-term decision than you've been used to making; once you buy, you're probably locked in for a fairly long time. Make sure that you're comfortable with the house appreciation future of the region, city, and neighborhood that you're locking yourself into.

2. **The three L's.** Ask almost any real estate professional how to find a house with great resale value, and you'll get one consistent response. They'll look you in the eye, making sure that they have your full attention, and say, "There are three keys to resale: location, location, and location." (The fact that virtually all of them will tell you this, and in just this way, makes me wonder if it isn't some kind of a license requirement. A good reply is, "That's fine, but could you give those to me again, in alphabetical order?")

Well, it *is* true that location matters a lot in determining resale value. Some of the reasons for this just make good common sense: locations good for resale are, all other things being equal, those in outstanding school districts; or with ready access to workplaces, retail centers, and/or public transportation; or with terrific views. Also good is being surrounded by houses that are more valuable; this condition gives your house's resale value plenty of "room to grow." Conversely, locations along airport flight paths, on busy streets, or in a neighborhood where lots of new construction is planned will hurt resale, as will owning the most expensive house on the block.

3. **Find an agent with high local expertise.** Earlier we emphasized that real estate markets are famously local in nature. It only helps a

little for me to give general examples about good and bad locations; the real key is to compare the attributes of the houses that you're considering in your specific area to all the other houses in that area. That's where a good real estate agent, with lots of local knowledge, is indispensable. Not only that, but a good agent can also tell you that plenty of other factors go into determining resale value besides location: quality of construction, floor plan, size and shape of the lot, and a host of others. Later in this chapter, we'll talk more about how to find a good agent; make sure that whomever you select is an expert at spotting high-resale-potential houses in your local area; and then trust their advice.

As a reminder, we're using *house* as shorthand for any type of residence, not just single-family homes—and location is a critical consideration for *all* of these different types of houses. For example, if you're considering a condo, the location of the complex is important, but so is the location of the unit within the complex. Continuing with the condo example, location is usually the most important factor, but it isn't the only one: a perfectly located condo complex may have insufficient reserves or pending lawsuits, which in turn spell resale disaster. The point is that an agent with expertise in the particular *type* of housing you're looking for, as well as experience in the local area, is a must to uncover the resale winners.

4. **Avoid very new and very old.** Think of this as the Goldilocks strategy; not too new, not too old, but in between is just right! As a general rule, if your target house were a person, you'd want to avoid those below preschool age and above retirement age. Your reaction to the first part of this might be, "This is just like cars! New houses lose value right away, just like new cars do." Not quite: new houses do not really carry a newness premium like cars do, but they have a different problem; they tend to be located near lots and lots of *other* new houses, often in full-blown developments. Lots of new houses in one concentrated area create a supply and demand problem. Specifically, an influx of supply creates a downward pressure on price (or a resistance to an upward movement in price). By the way, this line of thinking applies not only to brand-new houses, but also to existing houses in neighborhoods near areas that are, or might be, scheduled for new development.

What about the other end of the scale? Although the listings might use terms like *character*, *vintage*, or *seasoned*, the houses that I'm talking about are just plain old. The thinking goes like this: to start with, old houses can be really inexpensive relative to the newer ones in the same general area. And since we're emphasizing the importance of location, some of these old houses might be in really outstanding locations. On top of that, some may qualify as fixer-uppers. So you buy an old house in a great location, surrounded by more expensive houses, launch into some carefully selected repair or remodel projects; then 5 or more years later, you sell at big profit. What's wrong with that plan? Nothing at all—for people who have built up the craftsmanship know-how, supplier contacts, knowledge of local building codes, and experience to pull off a financially successful fix-up. I do not recommend this approach for a first-time house buyer. In fact, I don't recommend houses over about 50 years old *at all* for the first-timer. The types of repair and maintenance issues that can occur in older homes tend to be more complicated—and expensive. If your agent has a specific and compelling reason to override this advice for a particular house, then you are probably safe, as long as you fully understand and agree with the reason; otherwise, steer clear of older houses for your first purchase.

5. **Think like the masses.** Nothing is more personal than your house; it's where you *live*. So you want it to reflect your individuality, style, and flair, right? You want a house that sets you apart from the crowd, right? You want something that is as unique and different as you are, right? Wrong, wrong, and wrong! *Your goal is to select a house that will be of interest to the maximum number of buyers when you are ready to sell.* Unique and different is bad for resale value, because unique and different will rule out too many future buyers. Likewise, something that represents the very latest in style and fashion may be just as quick to go out of favor 5 or 30 years from now when you sell; you want to look for a style that has *always* been popular, year in and year out. One very experienced agent that I know summed it up by saying that "the trick is to learn to think like the masses." People can have all sorts of different reactions to various styles, colors, and shapes of houses, but it is much easier to find general agreement when it comes to desirable locations. There are many wonderful ways to express your individuality *besides* your house selection. Instead, stick to types, styles, and locations likely to be popular with "the masses" in the future.

6. **Be wary of bargains.** The goal is to buy low and sell high, right? Absolutely. So to hit a home run with the buy-low part, you want to find a house with a big, deep discount from what the normal price would be, right? The answer is maybe yes, maybe no. Beware—a deeply discounted price might be a big danger sign, so you'd want to investigate very thoroughly before proceeding. Often this is a signal

that the seller is having (or is anticipating having) a lot of difficulty selling the house at the normal price. Until you understand exactly why this is true, such a purchase can be very risky. Sometimes there may be some legitimate reason for an unusually low price; I'm not saying that it *never* happens. But I am saying that a fantastic price might turn out to be step one in a buy-low-and-sell-lower outcome. Don't begin your search with the idea that buying a house is all about bargain hunting. You might come across a legitimate bargain in your search, but there is absolutely nothing wrong with buying a carefully selected house, with excellent resale potential, at a normal price. You can probably guess what my parting comment is going to be on bargain prices: rely on your agent's experience to help you find out what's really behind an apparent bargain.

Does all this mean that your *dream house* is out of the question? Maybe. It depends on what you've been dreaming about. Let's be really clear, though: this is your very first house. You want one that will sell easily, quickly, and for a great price when the time comes. You will definitely need the help of a good, experienced real estate agent to help you determine exactly what that means in your area and for the type of house you're considering. Given everything that's at stake with this decision—your very first house—make your dream house the one that gives you the best opportunity to have a truly successful *financial* outcome. That way, you'll be in a position to realize even bigger dreams later.

THE TEN STEPS TO SUCCESSFULLY BUYING AND OWNING A HOUSE

Okay, enough talk about *what* to buy; let's get right into the steps of *how* to buy. Because of everything that you've learned, as well as what you've done to meet the readiness tests, you're much, much better prepared than the typical first-time house buyer. So take a deep breath, get ready, and let's get started!

1. **Make sure the time is right.** The right time has two separate elements. First, this process is going to take your full attention and availability for at least a few weeks and probably longer, depending on the market. So make sure you're going to be in a position to give it just that. If you're facing more than usual stress, pressure, or time demands from other areas of your life, including your job, you're better off

waiting until you can start the process with a relatively open frame of mind and calendar. Whatever you do, you don't want to be racing against some kind of deadline (such as a lease running out) and find yourself having to make a series of time-pressured decisions. Second, all other things being equal, you want to start the process at a time of year when most other buyers aren't also starting theirs. In most markets, that means avoiding the late spring and summer rush, when many people are looking to buy during a school break. (Some agents say that the best time of year to buy is when the weather is worst.)

2. **Get prequalified.** This means selecting a lender and going through the process of having your financial position put under a microscope. But don't worry about it—as long as you've passed all the readiness tests, prospective lenders will love you. The key to selecting a lender is (no surprise) research. A good place to start is with referrals from people you know who have bought, but you should deeply research even the most enthusiastic referrals. The type of lender that you're looking for is one that is well established and trusted in your area and offers competitive interest rates on 30-year fixed mortgages and associated fees.

After you've supplied the required information and passed the lender's tests, you'll be supplied with prequalification documentation that specifically states the size of the mortgage that you've prequalified for. This will put you in a much better position to act quickly and be taken seriously when it's time to make an offer. This does *not* obligate you to select that particular lender for your mortgage, but it will save needed time and energy if you start out with a lender you'd be comfortable doing business with in the first place.

During the prequalification process, you might be offered all kinds of other mortgages besides 30-year fixed rate to consider; if so, *you're not interested.* (One you'll probably be shown is a 15-year fixed rate. In fact, you might later decide to pay off your mortgage more quickly than the 30-year fixed schedule calls for, but it's better to *choose* that strategy later than to *commit* to it now.) You might also be asked to consider *bundling in* some or all of the closing costs into your loan amount. This means paying less in up-front costs in return for a higher monthly mortgage payment. You're not interested in that, either; this is equivalent to lowering your down payment and adding to the mortgage amount, and you *want* your down payment amount to be at least 20%.

There's still another option that you may be asked to consider when talking with lenders, and that is buying *points* (which are sometimes called *discount points*). Here's what that means: the lender will lower your interest rate in exchange for some additional up-front cash from you. This *might* make sense for you—especially if your actual closing costs look like they'll be less than the very conservative 5% that you've already saved up. In general, the greater the reduction per point in the mortgage interest rate, and the longer you intend to stay in the house, the more likely it is that buying points is a good deal for you. To find out, you have to do the math. Fortunately, the math is pretty generic, and lots and lots of online calculators will do the arithmetic for you once you supply the key inputs. (Search on "discount points calculator" or any similar variation, and there they are.) These calculators usually take your inputs and then come back with a *break-even time*. If the break-even time is 5.7 years, for example, that means that if you sell before 5.7 years, buying the points isn't wise, but if you stay longer than 5.7 years, it's a good deal.

The readiness tests were all designed somewhat conservatively, and since you meet all of them, you may be surprised to find that the lender is willing to lend you quite a bit more than the amount you'd had in mind. This might cause you to think that you've been setting your sights too low, and now that you've found a lender willing to qualify you for a higher amount, this is your big chance to start considering a higher price range. This is a common trap that lots of people fall into: *don't do it*. In part IV, we'll discuss long-term investing opportunities that are far safer places to put your money than a more expensive house. Stick with your original price range, even if you've found a lender that will qualify you for more.

3. **Set a firm and final upper price limit.** You already established an upper and lower limit in readiness test #4 in chapter 12, but that was before prequalifying. Now that you have more information, it's time to make a firm and final decision on the absolute maximum amount that you'd be willing to spend on a house. Once you've established this, set a more comfortable target price of 5% or 10% less than the maximum. Don't make this upper limit decision lightly, because once you set it, you should treat this limit as sacred.

    Of course you're going to come across one or more "absolutely perfect" houses that are priced above your absolute maximum; you can count on it. It happens almost every time, so don't be surprised when it happens to you. Your only defense against this kind of upward price creep is your own determination. Promise yourself that you're going to stay under the maximum, no matter what. You can't depend on your agent, your lender, or the other members of your household to help you hold the line; *you* have to do it. When members of your household inevitably test how firm you really are about your limit, kindly but firmly explain to them the definition of the word *maximum*. Remember this above all: *you* are in charge of how much you ultimately end up spending on a house, and nobody else.

4. **Do an intense Internet search within your price range.** You've already done some preliminary searching; now it's time to do some thorough, systematic homework. By completely familiarizing yourself with the available and affordable listings in your area, you'll be able to determine what combination of your wish-list features are realistic, and in which specific neighborhoods. Your goal is to come up with a list of features, in prioritized order, that you're looking for in a house. Doing this in advance, before you start working with an agent, has two advantages. First, it saves you lots of time; it's a lot easier to get educated on what's available by clicking around than by driving around. Second, the more knowledgeable you are about the marketplace, the better job you'll be able to do in selecting an agent.

5. **Get a buyer's real estate agent.** Do not, repeat, *do not* try to buy your first house without a real estate agent! This is your first time through the process, and you need an experienced, knowledgeable professional representing your best interests in all of the steps that follow. You're looking for someone who has lots of successful experience helping people buy houses in the price range and areas that you're considering. Just like looking for a lender, referrals can be a good place to start—but once again, even the most enthusiastic referrals should be thoroughly researched. Lots of websites will give you tips on what to look for in a real estate agent. You'll be working closely with this agent through the biggest decisions of your financial life so far; you want someone whom you are comfortable and confident working with. Even if an agent is highly recommended, if you get a sense that that agent would rather not be working with a first-time buyer or seems to be the type who would rush you more than you're comfortable with, or who wants to keep steering you in directions that don't match what you're looking for—then pass and keep looking.

   One way to test for personal chemistry is to meet in person with a prospective agent and make a short speech like this: "I'm a first-time house buyer, so I am looking for an agent who will take the time to explain to me in detail any parts of the process that I don't understand and who will do everything possible to make sure that I buy the house that's right for me. Even though I'm a first timer, I have done a lot of homework ahead of time. I am already prequalified; here is the documentation. My target price is X, and my absolute maximum is Y. I will immediately stop working with any agent who shows me a house priced higher than Y. My very top priority is resale value. The features that I'm looking for are A, B, and C. The neighborhoods that I've identified so far that have those kinds of houses available are D, E, and F. Do you think that you'd be able to help me with this?"

You're looking for something more than an enthusiastic "yes!" because that's the response you'll hear from virtually every prospective agent you give the speech to. Instead, you're looking for the kind of yes that really convinces you that you can form a successful partnership with this agent. Listen for *specific* ways that the agent believes that he or she can help you. You might need to talk with several agents until you find the right one for you. Chemistry is personal and subjective, not something measurable, so it's perfectly okay to simply trust your instincts. As long as you select from those with the right credentials, based on your own previous research, you'll make a great choice.

6. **Search and select.** Okay, this is the part of the process that you've probably been envisioning from the first time you began thinking about buying a house. You're no longer doing an Internet search; this is the part where you and your agent get in the car and start visiting *actual available houses.* There is no right or wrong answer when it comes to how many houses to look at or how long the search should take. Work this out with your agent; a lot may depend on market conditions. It may seem like overkill, but I advise taking pictures of the key features at each house you visit. In addition, take extensive notes at each house. A good approach is to list all of the criteria that you're looking for and then score (or make some kind of note about) each house, for each of the criteria. Most first-time buyers are surprised to learn that it is really tough to keep everything straight at the end of the day, let alone several days later when you're trying to compare and contrast your top few finalists. If you have one or two sheets of paper (literally or digitally) on each house, summarizing all of your notes on it, scoring each house on all of your key criteria, with photos for each house, you'll be way ahead.

You're now very close to making your final selection. Warning: don't be surprised when your right brain kicks into overdrive as soon as you start walking through houses. It's perfectly understandable; just don't let this lead to a hasty or emotional decision. House hunting is the ultimate example of a decision involving a mix of financial and nonfinancial factors that we talked about in part I. Remember what we said then: stick to a structured decision-making process, such as the one we just described. Your right brain can get involved, as long it waits its turn and cooperates with your process instead of derailing it. Remember all of your criteria, *especially resale value*. If you're feeling more pressured or rushed than you're comfortable with, then hold off until you do feel comfortable—even if it means potentially losing out on your top choice.

7. **Offer and negotiate.** Once you've made your selection, it's time to begin the negotiation process, and the first step is to make a formal offer. What the negotiation process consists of, and how long it takes, can vary tremendously, depending on market conditions in general and your competitive situation with the particular house that you've selected. You've been relying heavily upon your agent's experience and advice up until now; well, that goes double during negotiations!

    Many offers contain *contingencies*. For example: "I am making a firm offer to buy your house at 96% of the listed value, contingent upon the successful passage of X and Y inspections" or "I offer to buy your house at full price, contingent upon the sale of the house that I currently own." There are many advantages and disadvantages to using contingencies in an offer. By now you know what I'm going to say about the subject: talk it over with your agent and trust their advice. Your first offer may not be accepted, and you'll find yourself in a multistep negotiation process. You may be outbid by another buyer on the first house you make an offer on and have to go to your second or third choices. But eventually, with the help of your agent, you'll make an offer on a house that is accepted, and then you'll be ready for the final step in the buying process.

8. **Close.** At last—you're ready to close the deal! Stand by to be overwhelmed by just *how many* elements there are in the closing process. I won't go through all of the pieces and parts here, because the process varies considerably from place to place and from time to time. You'll need the help of your lender and your agent to describe the entire closing process and to help you prepare. A specific time and date is selected (generally determined by your lender), and your job is to show up, on time, with a rather large check in hand. How large? You'll be informed well in advance of the amount, down to the penny. Remember when we estimated that you'd need to save up something

like 27% of the purchase price of whatever house that you buy? Well, closing day is when you turn over the largest portion of that amount in exchange for ownership of your new house.

You'll also be required to sign some documents: lots and lots of documents! (On the day of my first closing, I set two personal records: one, for the biggest personal check that I'd ever written, and the other for the most times that I'd signed my own name in any one day.) Even though there are many documents to sign, the key is to be prepared for each one of them. As previously mentioned, you'll need lots of help well in advance, starting with your agent and your lender, to understand each and every document that will be signed at closing. *Do not sign anything that you do not fully understand and agree to,* even if it means a short delay in closing to get properly informed and advised.

9. **Protect and enhance your investment.** After you've moved in, the *protect* part is a must; the *enhance* part is optional. Protecting your investment means staying on top of all of the maintenance and repair activity required to keep it in good working order. This makes it sound like it will be obvious what you need to do, but sometimes it isn't. On one hand, it is possible to go overboard by insisting on more fancy or elaborate approaches, on more maintenance items, and/or more frequent maintenance than is really necessary. But you can also go overboard in the opposite direction by delaying, ignoring, or skimping on repairs just to save money. If you do that, you might allow a small problem to grow into a big one. Common sense should be your guide, and if you're unsure, consult with other homeowners that you know, or do some Internet research. You're the owner now, you're in charge, it's your investment, and it's in your interest to protect it. The last thing you want is for the price appreciation that you sought out so carefully to be gobbled up by some sort of house damage that you could have prevented by being more diligent.

There are lots of ways to enhance the investment in your house, which is another way of saying making improvements that allow you to ultimately resell it for a higher price. You can remodel one or more rooms, add some landscaping, improve your energy efficiency, or build an addition that adds square footage, to name just a few of the options. The key on these kinds of enhancements is to do the math. You'll want to compare the cost of the enhancement with the expected increase in your house's resale value. On one end of the scale, remodeling a kitchen (by bringing cabinets, counters, and appliances up to date, or by changing the layout to better utilize the space) has a very good chance of being a resale winner, which means that it will improve your house's resale value by more than the cost of remodeling. On the other end of the scale, enhancements that are designed with your own individual desires primarily in mind are likely to appeal to far fewer potential buyers. For example, adding a swimming pool in an area where the climate is swimming-friendly for only a few months of the year has an excellent chance of being a resale loser. My advice for a first-time house owner would be to keep these kinds of enhancements to a minimum, limiting yourself to only a very few, surefire resale winners.

10. **Watch interest rates and refinance if appropriate.** The good thing about a fixed-rate mortgage is that your interest rate can never go up. Once you've gone through the closing process, if prevailing interest rates go up, you don't have to worry about it—your rate is frozen for the next 30 years. But if prevailing interest rates go *down*, can you take advantage of it? Yes, you can—but it will cost you another set of closing costs. So the rates have to go down *far enough* for it to be worth your while. On top of that, if you reset your interest rate, you have to reset the clock on the 5-year test, too. The way it works: if rates go down far enough, you take out a brand-new mortgage and use it to pay off your old one. This is called *refinancing*. Many web calculators are available to help you do the math to see if this makes sense for you; just search on "refinance calculator." Just remember: limit your new mortgage to only the principal amount of your old mortgage, and no more. Your lender might encourage you to borrow even more, especially now that you've proven yourself to be a reliable monthly P&I payer. But you aren't interested in pulling any *extra* money out of your house, because that would be just another form of borrowing.

That's it—you've done it! Through savings, sacrifice, discipline, and research, you've transformed yourself from a renter to a house owner. Not only that, but because of the *way* you've done it, you're a house owner with plenty of money in the bank, with a mortgage that is affordable without undue sacrifice, with no other debts, with a new deductible expense that will lower your income taxes, and with an outstanding chance to realize a significant tax-free financial gain when you ultimately resell. If you hadn't done this, providing a place to live for you and the members of your household would have been a continual drain on your financial bathtub. But you've done the smart thing, and you've done it the right way. Only one word will do in this situation: *congratulations!*

SUMMARY

The Six Tips for Finding the Resale Winners

1. Broaden your thinking. *Do some homework on resale value before making a long-term decision about which region, city, and/or neighborhood to buy in.*
2. The three L's. *Location is the single biggest factor in determining resale value. But location is also important, as is location.*
3. Find an agent with high local expertise. *General tips only go so far; finding an expert with specific local knowledge is imperative to finding resale winners.*
4. Avoid very new and very old. *Brand new or relatively new houses often appreciate more slowly at first because of their proximity to lots of other new houses; very old houses appreciate more slowly because buyers suspect that heavy repair and maintenance costs are probable.*
5. Think like the masses. *Your goal is to select a house that will be of interest to the maximum number of buyers when you are ready to sell. That means that unique, different, and stylish are not resale-enhancing qualities.*
6. Be wary of bargains. *Bargains might be warning signs. Rely on your agent's experience to help you find out what's really behind an apparent bargain.*

The Ten Steps to Successfully Buying and Owning a House

1. Make sure the time is right. *Don't start until your calendar and your emotions are ready for an intense, potentially stressful multiweek process. Avoid times of the year when most other buyers are starting their searches.*
2. Get prequalified. *This means selecting a lender to supply you with documentation identifying you as having prequalified for a specific loan amount.*
3. Set a firm and final upper price limit. *Decide on your absolute upper limit and set it in stone. It is certain that you'll be tempted by yourself and others to stretch this upward—it is up to you, and you alone, to hold your ground.*
4. Do an intense Internet search within your price range. *Your goal is to come up with a prioritized list of the house features that you want by familiarizing yourself with what is currently available in the market.*
5. Get a buyer's real estate agent. *Select someone with strong experience and credentials, who is willing to work with a first-time buyer, and with whom you feel a good personal chemistry.*
6. Search and select. *Don't select until you've done a thorough, methodical set of walk-throughs with your agent and you're completely comfortable from all angles. Of course, your primary selection criterion is front and center—resale value!*

7. Offer and negotiate. *Here is where a strong agent really pays off; when it comes to how much to offer, whether or not to include contingencies, and all other aspects—listen to your agent and trust his or her advice.*

8. Close. *On closing day, you will sign many documents and you will hand over a big check. Work with your lender and your agent in advance to fully understand everything that you're going to be asked to sign, and don't sign anything until you fully understand and agree to it.*

9. Protect and enhance your investment. *Stay on top of all the required maintenance to keep your house in good working order; in addition, you may or may not want to make a few selected enhancements that will increase the resale value by more than they will cost.*

10. Watch interest rates and refinance if appropriate. *After you buy, if interest rates drop far enough, it may make sense for you to take out a new mortgage; use a web refinance calculator to help you do the math.*

Part IV

LONG-TERM INVESTING

· *16* ·

Long-Term Investing: Introduction

*I*magine yourself just entering the last third of your financial life, inheriting a remarkably large amount of money. You're inheriting this money from a close relative, one who has always had your best long-term interests in mind. Even more remarkable, this relative wasn't even considered wealthy. Instead, your relative put this inheritance together slowly over many years of careful planning, closely watching spending to consistently save money through good times and bad and then wisely and methodically investing those savings—all for your benefit. Better still, this inheritance was no surprise: you've known it was coming all along. Even though you were tempted from time to time to dip into it early, you successfully resisted that temptation because you liked the peace of mind of long-term financial security far more than the temporary excitement that any kind of immediate gratification might bring. Because of that, as your friends and colleagues sweated through every up and down of the economy, you've instead been able to focus your attention on other, more fulfilling things.

Imagine the choices you have in front of you now! You've inherited enough that you no longer have to continue working—unless you want to. Maybe there is some other calling that you've always wanted to pursue, but you haven't been able to afford the uncertain or even zero level of income that would result from it. If you do choose to continue working, you can use your income any way that you want. You can use it to help others—friends, family, or any cause you find worthy—or you can just splurge! You can simply relax and enjoy life, or if some new challenge inspires you, you can pursue it. As you contemplate this newly available freedom, imagine how very grateful you would be to this wise, generous relative for the wonderful gift that has been given to you. You'd be so grateful that you'd want to prominently display that

215

relative's portrait in your home for the rest of your life, and maybe even name *all* your children and grandchildren after your wise and generous benefactor.

Now I'll tell you who this relative has turned out to be.

You.

It's true. (So maybe you should hold off on the portrait.) Seriously, everything that's been presented so far has been designed to make this idea of inheriting money from yourself a reality. If you've been following along carefully and are committed to putting each of the ideas we've discussed into consistent practice, then you *can* make it happen. Long-term investing is the final piece of the puzzle that makes it all possible.

So why have we waited until the fourth and final part of the book to begin discussing investing? It must be because the best time to invest is late in your financial life, right? Wrong! In fact, as our friends from Compound University learned the hard way, *the sooner you begin investing, the better.* We've waited until now to discuss it because we had to make completely sure that the stage was properly set first. Now that it is, it is time to turn our complete attention to this final, and most powerful, means of growing your net worth— and we're devoting the entirety of part IV to it.

You'll notice that I'm calling it long-term investing instead of retirement planning, or investing for retirement, as most writers do. That's because the investing part of it is required, the long-term part of it is required—but the retirement part of it is purely optional! The point is to put yourself in a position of flexibility and choice, and retirement is just one of the many choices you'll have in front of you as a reward for successfully investing over a long period of time. Technically you've already begun investing because the money in your cash bucket is earning a small return. But this is *short-term* investing; what we're going to spend all of part IV discussing is *long-term* investing. How long is long-term?

> *The idea is for you to establish a long-term investment strategy and make a substantial start on it during the 1st third of your financial life, continue it nonstop throughout your 2nd third, and then not touch a penny of it until you arrive in your 3rd, and final, third.*

Remember: the idea of dividing your financial life into thirds is just a way to help you understand the differences in the three phases. Don't worry about exactly when each third is likely to begin and end—the phases are more conceptual than literal. At this point, it's best to concentrate on understanding how financial decisions that you make *now* are likely to affect you much *later.* Remember, in part I we talked about the importance of getting used to thinking in very long time frames. That kind of thinking is absolutely required when it comes to long-term investing. To begin exploring this in more depth, it's time to—you guessed it—meet a few more new friends.

MINI CASE STUDY: BUCK AND PENNY

Everybody liked Buck and Penny Cash. They were an optimistic and friendly couple and were especially devoted parents to their three, now fully grown children: Lenny, Denny, and Jenny. Their neighbors viewed Buck and Penny as having few financial worries, since both of them had good jobs. Buck was an assistant manager at a local bank branch, and Penny worked as an independent contractor doing computer programming work.

Buck and Penny were in their mid-50s and had lived in the same house for nearly 30 years. The Cash couple prided themselves on being financially conservative; they were especially leery of taking on any debt beyond their current mortgage. Fortunately there was rarely any need to, since they were able to afford most of what they wanted out of their two-earner income. They noticed that many of their friends and neighbors their age were in various stages of credit card debt, and they were happy that they'd been able to avoid that situation.

Buck and Penny were big believers in college educations for their children, which they viewed as investing in their children's futures. Lenny, Denny, and Jenny all were admitted to various colleges and eventually completed their degrees. The resulting expenses were far beyond what Buck and Penny's income could handle, but they wanted to pay without taking on any new debt. What to do? They decided to tap into their equity and refinance their house—all three times—which was just enough to get all three through college. Buck and Penny didn't consider this to be taking on any *additional* debt. Their only debt was their mortgage, so they rationalized that all they were doing was *extending* their current debt, not adding anything more.

Lately, though, Buck and Penny had begun to contemplate their financial future. They were proud of their no-debt status, which hadn't always been easy. But they also had to face up to the fact that they had no savings (not even a cash bucket!) or investments. Still, as always, Buck and Penny remained optimistic and dreamed of the day when they would no longer have to work. Their goal was to retire in less than 10 years, in their mid-60s. Their plans for how to pay for their retirements were based on two things: Buck's pension plan at the bank and Social Security. (Penny had no pension plan because she had always been self-employed as an independent contractor.) They'd always thought that additional savings before retirement would be icing on the cake of the pension and Social Security, but college expenses had precluded any savings from being possible. Still, Buck and Penny reasoned that the pension and Social Security ought to be plenty; after all, both Buck's and Penny's parents had enjoyed long and happy retirements with similar strategies.

Because Buck and Penny were content with their strategy, they didn't pay any attention to trends that had been occurring throughout the United States over the past few decades. They were unaware that fewer and fewer employers were offering pension-type retirement plans, switching instead to *defined contribution* plans such as 401(k)'s that were dependent on employee contributions to a portfolio of employee-selected investments. They changed the channel on the TV whenever discussions about Social Security came on; if they'd stayed tuned, they would have learned that there is serious and growing concern about the future viability of Social Security unless significant changes are made. Instead they just dreamed about the happy day, not too far off now, when they could walk away from their jobs and enjoy life.

All of that came to a crashing halt one afternoon when Buck learned that the bank where he worked had been purchased by a much larger bank. He came to understand that he was now an employee of a very different institution, and that this institution had a very different—and far less generous—idea of retirement benefits. The amount that he'd built up in his previous pension account was still available to him, but not as a pension; instead, he was offered the "opportunity" to transfer that amount to a 401(k). Buck was concerned about this because his balance was quite small. As with most of these plans, the pension amounts didn't start getting big until the last decade of work, which Buck was just entering now. Worse, his new employer seemed to be planning to eventually eliminate assistant managers at most branches. Meanwhile, Penny's situation was also getting more worrisome. Increasingly, new technology was enabling contract programming to be done overseas, where skills were increasing and costs were much lower. As a result, she was having a harder and harder time finding programming contracts locally; she estimated that in a few years, she'd be lucky to have half as much work as she currently had.

Shaken, Buck and Penny came to the conclusion that they needed to completely rethink their ideas about retirement. Eventually they generated a plan with the help of a professional financial planner. The good news was that they still could see a way that they could retire. But there was lots of bad news, too; and the worst news of all was that it now looked like they'd both be working a lot longer than they'd hoped. And at least one of them would have to completely change careers—maybe even both of them. Adding to the bad news: they would need to dramatically scale back their monthly spending in order to begin saving and investing, which meant selling their treasured family home and relocating to a smaller, less expensive place, with greater chances of appreciation. Their retirement timetable would now be dependent on the performance of their investments, including Buck's new 401(k). They were already disheartened to realize that they'd both be working longer; it was even tougher to swallow the fact that the exact timetable was now "at the mercy of the stock market" and beyond their control.

Buck and Penny learned from their experience and became much more knowledgeable about what makes for a good—and a bad—retirement strategy. They were determined to pass their newfound enlightenment along to their children, so that at least *they'd* be prepared for their financial futures. Buck and Penny contacted Lenny, Denny, and Jenny and arranged a family meeting. "Here's the thing," Penny began, once the children had assembled in the family kitchen. "We'll be okay, but only because of Buck's original pension plan and some pretty healthy Social Security payments. But the way things are going, I don't think that either of those things will be around to help you kids."

"Let me put it this way," Buck said. "You should never count on anybody else's help for your retirement. Don't depend on your employer helping you, the government helping you, or your mother and me helping you any more than we already have. If any of them does, then it's a bonus, not something you should expect. Instead you're going to have to provide for your own retirements. The only way to do that is by saving and investing, and the time to begin is right now."

Lenny, Denny, and Jenny took it all in, completely silent. Finally Lenny said meekly, "I see your point, but I just don't have much money to invest right now." Denny added, "My career is just so demanding right now, I don't see how I'd have enough time to learn all about something as complicated as investing." And Jenny's observation was, "Hey, I just graduated! Isn't it a little early to start thinking about retiring?"

IT'S UP TO YOU

You might be thinking that the story of Buck and Penny is a little grim. Maybe so, but their story is all too typical. In reality, there are lots of Bucks and Pennys out there, and there are countless others who are in much worse shape financially. I've emphasized that your financial life is not your whole life. But as the story illustrates, difficulties in your financial life can severely limit your choices and negatively affect your circumstances in ways that extend to other parts of your life, too.

Lenny, Denny, and Jenny reacted unenthusiastically—and this isn't unusual. Maybe you've thought that way yourself. The suggestion to begin a lifelong program of saving and investing at an early age can sound a little extreme. After all, you've worked hard and sacrificed in school and on the job to generate your current income, and now somebody is suggesting that you set some of that aside for some super-conservative, decades-in-the-future reason? No, thanks!

But it has never been truer than it is now: the only party you can depend on to financially provide for your own future is *you*. Others may make promises or may have been able to help in earlier generations, but you're taking far too great a risk if you rely on help from other sources by the time you reach your later years. *It is squarely up to you* to take steps to ensure that you are provided for when you reach the age when your ability, or willingness, to earn an income begins to decline. Buck had it exactly right when he said that "the only way to do that is by saving and investing, and the time to begin is right now." It may feel like a sacrifice to get started, but compare that with the sacrifices facing Buck and Penny. The choice is yours: sacrifice a little early in your financial life or sacrifice a lot later on.

WHAT'S THE OBJECTIVE?

One way to begin thinking about the ultimate objective of your long-term investment program is to use a milestones format, similar to what we did in part I, when we were exploring the wonderful possibilities of passive income. Before considering the milestones, you'll need to understand a key point first: investments can be structured for either *growth* or *income*. When you start investing, and for the next few decades, you'll keep your investments structured for growth. That means just what it sounds like: your objective is to grow your investment account balance without ever withdrawing anything from it. Once you've entered retirement, though, your investments can be restructured to provide *portfolio income* for you, to replace some or all of your active income. Of course, as soon as you do that, you'll be sacrificing growth; but if your balance has become high enough during the growth phase, that's just fine. Keeping that in mind, here are some selected long-term savings and investment milestones:

Milestone 1: Savings program begun—at least 10% of everything you ever earn, paying yourself first

Milestone 2: Cash bucket filled and remains full (except in the case of a true financial emergency)

Milestone 3: House purchased (or decision made not to, at least for the foreseeable future)

Milestone 4: Long-term investment program begun

Milestone 5: Investment balance exceeds 1 year's average income

Milestone 6: Investment balance becomes the single largest element of your net worth

Milestone 7: Investment balance reaches a point where it can be converted to portfolio income that can last for the rest of your life, but at a *bare minimum* lifestyle. You can stop earning active income at this point or continue earning and go on to . . .

Milestone 8: Investment balance reaches a point where it can be converted to portfolio income that can last for the rest of your life at a lifestyle level *similar to your current one.* You can stop earning active income at this point or continue earning and go on to . . .

Milestone 9: Investment balance reaches a point where it can be converted to portfolio income that can last for the rest of your life at a *dream lifestyle* level

Take a minute to contemplate these milestones—it's fun to think about, isn't it? It probably puts you in a frame of mind to start thinking about what sort of goal you'd like to set for yourself. But you don't need a specific objective right now; instead, *your objective should be to begin your investment program just as soon as you can*, because compounding rewards an early start so greatly. The sooner you start, and the more you save and invest, the greater the chances that you can achieve the highest milestones. But for now, it is better *not* to get too specific about your ultimate objectives. At this point, it is very hard to know what will be most important in your life several years, or even decades, from now.

Think of it like this: it's easier to steer a ship when it is already moving. You may not know precisely where you want to take your ship, but you do know the general direction, which is enough for now. The best course of action is to get your ship provisioned, untied from the dock, out of the harbor, and heading in the right direction at a safe but steady speed. Once you're under way, you'll have plenty of time to consider various destinations, and you can start navigating directly toward the ones that interest you. But if you keep your ship in port, waiting for inspiration, motivation, or education, it will be too late to make it to most of the best destinations. Getting started as soon as you can gives you the maximum choice and flexibility later in your financial life—and *that* is a worthy objective in and of itself.

Buck and Penny got an early start, too—or that's what they thought. They each started their careers in their very early 20s. It is true that they began *earning* from an early age, but they never did any *saving*. From a financial point of view, that's not an early start at all. It doesn't really matter how long the faucet has been running if the all the water just goes down the drain. What does matter is getting an early start saving and investing—*that's* what gets your ship out of port and moving in the right direction.

It should be noted that there is some variability in the exact order of the milestones. As you might expect, the timing needs to be considered in the context of everything else that is going on in your life. For example, you might begin your long-term investment program long before buying a house, simply because you're not in a position to commit to staying in one place for 5 years. Or you might choose to begin your long-term investment program at the same time that you're saving up for a down payment on a house because you're uncertain about the commitment required to buy a house, and you want to keep your options open. There's nothing at all wrong with those kinds of variations. There is even one circumstance when I will advise you to begin your investment program before your cash bucket is full—but that is a *very specific* exception that we'll discuss in detail later.

What about the later milestones? Some financial experts or writers refer to milestones 8 and/or 9 as critical mass, escape velocity, or financial freedom. I like to think of these milestone levels as simply "enough." By that, I mean enough financial resources to have plenty of freedom, choice, and flexibility. Buck and Penny found out, late in their financial lives, that they didn't have enough. This greatly reduced their options and forced them to make sacrifices in almost every other aspect of their lives. Similarly, having enough won't make you happy all by itself. But it can free you up to find happiness and fulfillment in the other areas of your life; *that's* the objective.

YOUR ALL-IMPORTANT ADVANTAGE

Before we go any further, a particular point is vitally important for you to understand and keep in mind throughout our entire discussion of long-term investing. That vital point is this: *you are different from almost every other financial investor.* I don't mean that in the every-snowflake-is-unique sense; I mean that something very specific about your *situation* sets you apart from nearly all other investors, and this difference gives you a huge, all-important advantage. This difference means that you have every opportunity to be dealt a winning hand. All you have to do is get in the game and play your cards right.

The length of time that you intend to hold an investment before selling is called your *investment horizon.* Five years or even 10 years is considered by most investors to be quite a long horizon. But you are going to be holding your investments for decades. *That's what makes you so different, and that's what gives you such an overwhelming advantage!* We've already learned that the power of compounding is truly amazing, and we've already learned that its power grows exponentially with more time to work its magic. Since you are young and just starting out, you have an *ultra-long* investment horizon. And since you are going to structure your investments for growth, this means that the challenge you're facing is substantially different, and much easier, than the one almost all other investors face.

I can't stress enough just how different this makes you. Very few regular investors are as young as you are, so that already puts you in a small minority. But investing isn't a "one person, one vote" democracy; it's a "one *dollar*, one vote" marketplace. And since the few people like you who are investing aren't investing in large amounts (by market standards), that puts you in an even tinier minority. What this means is that nearly all of what the ever-present financial media have to say, nearly all of the advertising put out by investment firms, and nearly all of the folk wisdom, hot tips, and investing gossip that you might ever have heard *isn't intended for you and probably doesn't apply to you*. Most of the information out there is intended for the majority, who are investing in the vastly riskier and more challenging world of short and medium investment horizons. Plenty of very valuable information does apply to you, and you will need it—but you'll have to search it out.

THE FIVE MAJOR OBSTACLES TO INVESTMENT SUCCESS

Now that you fully appreciate that compounding is your tremendously powerful ally, it's time to meet the opposition. The five major obstacles to investment success are listed below. The first two are capable of striking quickly and causing you sudden and disastrous problems. The remaining three are a little more insidious; you can think that you're doing just fine and that everything is proceeding according to plan, but behind the scenes, like termites at a beach house, these three can be patiently and systematically eating away at the foundations of your investment success.

1. **Risk.** Probably the most famous foe of all, this enemy represents the very real chance that whatever you invest in will go *down* in value—the exact opposite of what we're intending. Given this danger, we have three very well-established and complementary tools to use to guard us against risk.
2. **Human nature.** "Uh-oh—you mean I'm my own worst enemy?" It's true. Our own right brains can compel us, sometimes very powerfully, to buy high and sell low. Human nature is probably the least famous—but most dangerous—of all of the obstacles to success. How to beat it? One word: *discipline.* We're going to be steadfastly sticking

to a simple and specific plan, in good times and in bad, which we know will always work in the long run.

3. **Inflation.** This obstacle relentlessly uses compounding *against* the investor, reducing the value of the investment returns. We'll overcome inflation by brute force, by tapping into the power of compounding more deeply than anything inflation can muster against us.

4. **Taxes.** Taxes are a constant and significant drain on investment returns unless, of course, you manage to obtain VIP status, in which case the tax bite can be very significantly reduced. Fortunately, this is extremely easy to do; the only challenge is choosing which of the many VIP options is the most advantageous to you.

5. **Frictional costs.** These are the costs of doing business when investing, somewhat like closing costs when buying or selling a house, and include fees and commissions. These frictional costs can be deceptive; they have a way of seeming harmlessly small. But if you don't pay close attention, these costs can have a death-by-a-thousand-cuts effect on your returns. Fortunately there are easy ways to keep these to a bare minimum without making any sacrifices in investment return.

YOUR LONG-TERM INVESTMENT STRATEGY IN A NUTSHELL

I'm convinced that when it comes to investing, most people can't stand the suspense; they want to hear the conclusion first before taking in all of the supporting rationale. So instead of forcing you to wait all the way until the end of part IV, we'll close this chapter with a sneak-preview version of exactly what we're recommending for your long-term investment strategy. During the balance of this part of the book, we'll cover certain parts of it in more depth. Finally we'll close part IV with a "Let's Do It" chapter, detailing how to go about implementing each step of the strategy. So here is our strategy, using a Q&A format.

1. **When do you begin your long-term investment program?** You should begin *as soon as possible* after you meet the two basic requirements. First, you'll need to be financially ready: you already have a First Rule savings program, a full cash bucket, and no debt. (There is one exception to these requirements that we'll cover in detail later.) Second, you'll need to have resolved your housing situation one way or the other, either by successfully buying or by deciding that buying is not for you, at least for now.

2. **How much do you invest, and how often?** Now that your cash bucket is full and your up-front house costs are paid, your savings (which are always a First Rule minimum of 10%) go directly into your investment account. So you will be investing just like you save—a relatively constant amount on a fixed schedule (every time you get paid). You do this whether the market is up, down, or flat.

3. **What do you invest in?** You buy the exact same set of investments every time you invest: a broad mix of very low-cost equity index funds that we'll get much more specific about in a later chapter. The investment mix in your account is called your *portfolio*.

4. **When do you sell these investments?** You won't sell *any* of these investments for a long, long, long time—not for decades, until you are in the 3rd third of your financial life. For the time being, though, you should think of the answer to this question as being "never!" This strategy is called *buy and hold*.

   By the way, the combination of #2, #3, and #4 is called *dollar cost averaging* or DCA. It entails investing a relatively constant dollar amount on a fixed schedule, buying the same mix of investments over and over again regardless of market conditions, and then holding for a relatively long time. The term isn't particularly descriptive of the strategy, but it is well known, so we'll use it from now on.

5. **Whom do you buy these investments from, and where do you hold your investment account?** You will buy from, and hold with, the seller with the very lowest frictional costs. If your employer offers a tax-sheltered retirement savings program, then you'll probably buy from the administrator that your employer has selected and hold your account there. Otherwise, after researching tax-sheltered options, fund availability, and frictional costs, you'll probably end up doing business with one of the many online brokerages.

6. **From whom will you get ongoing advice?** The answer to this question varies more than the answers to the others and is based on your own situation. You'll probably get at least some advice from your employer's fund administrator or your online broker. It's usually a good idea to supplement this with advice from an independent, fee-based financial planner. If you already have a relationship with a tax professional, this can be a good place to get help *with the income tax aspect* of your investment strategy. Finally, it is a must to have someone you respect and trust who can be called in case of a 911 investment emergency to talk you out of the "good ideas" that your right brain will undoubtedly suggest from time to time. In short, you'll get advice from a virtual team of people that you'll assemble based on your own circumstances.

SUMMARY

1. Providing for your own retirement is like inheriting money from yourself. Everything that we've covered up until now can be thought of as setting the stage for investing, which is the primary means of building up your self-inheritance.
2. The era of retirement being completely paid for by employer pensions and/or public programs like Social Security is coming to a close. The only way to be truly assured of a financially healthy retirement is to assume full responsibility for it yourself.
3. The idea is for you to establish a long-term investment strategy and make a substantial start on it during the 1st third of your financial life, continue it nonstop throughout your 2nd third, and then not touch a penny of it until you arrive in your 3rd and final third.
4. Investments can be structured for either growth or income. Yours should be structured for growth in the 1st and 2nd third of your financial life; in the 3rd third you can begin structuring some of your investment balance into portfolio income to fund your living expenses. The higher your investment balance, the higher level of retirement lifestyle you can afford.
5. It isn't necessary to have a highly specific retirement objective (dates, ages, or amounts) right away; instead it is best to simply *begin investing* as soon as you can, to allow yourself the maximum amount of choice and flexibility in defining your objectives later.
6. The real objective of investing is to achieve "enough" investment income to support freedom from the requirement to work and "enough" financial security to seek fulfillment and happiness in the other areas of your life.
7. Your decades-long investment horizon makes you a rarity in the marketplace; nearly all other investors are operating in the much more challenging and risky world of short- and midrange investment horizons. Your ultra-long horizon allows you to take much deeper advantage of compounding's later, jaw-droppingly powerful stages.
8. Because of your unusually long investment horizon, most of the financial news and advice, advertising, and informal information that you have ever seen before, or will run across during your investing career, isn't intended for you and probably doesn't apply to you. To get the information that you really need, you'll have to seek it.
9. The five major obstacles to long-term investment success are risk, human nature (your own right brain–driven emotions and instincts),

inflation, taxes, and frictional costs. Our recommended long-term investment strategy is designed to squarely address and overcome each of these.

10. Our recommended long-term investment strategy calls for you to (a) begin as soon as possible after you've met the basic requirements; (b) invest relatively constant investment amounts at regular intervals (payday) regardless of market conditions; (c) buy the same broad mix of very low-cost equity index funds every time, again regardless of market conditions; (d) hold these investments without selling any until the 3rd third of your financial life (b, c, and d together are often called *dollar cost averaging*); (e) buy from, and hold with, the fund seller who has the very lowest frictional cost available in a tax-sheltered account; and (f) get advice from a virtual team of people that will differ based on your own situation.

· 17 ·

Simple but Not Easy

$\mathcal{T}$he long-term investment strategy that I'm recommending for you is really pretty simple. Keep investing roughly the same dollar amount, at regular intervals, buying the same mix of funds every time, and *hold on to them* in a tax-sheltered account with a low frictional cost. There are some more details, of course, and we'll cover them thoroughly before we finish part IV. But those details aren't too hard to understand, and your left brain won't have much trouble taking them all in. As noted earlier, the strategy is based on time-tested, commonsense principles: nothing new, revolutionary, or risky. All in all, it really is simple.

But it isn't always easy to *follow* the strategy—maybe partly *because* it is so simple. You see, once you've mastered the details, your left brain isn't the problem. Your right brain is.

Let's say that I offered you a very simple deal. I'll pay you $1,000 if you clap your hands once and only once, per hour, over a 24-hour period. You can use any kind of tool you want to prompt you—alarm, cell phone, anything at all—but there must be one, and only one, clap per hour. Simple, right? And pretty easy, too. Most of you would probably take the deal, and most of you that did would probably succeed and happily accept your $1,000 payoff.

Now let's change the conditions a little bit. This time, the task is exactly the same, but I'm going to surround you with dozens of people for the entire 24 hours, and all of them are going to try every way that they can think of to talk you out of your plan to clap once per hour. Some of them will be people you know—friends, colleagues, and loved ones—who will beg you to please, please refrain from clapping. Others will be very skilled salespeople, offering you much *more* money, right away, but only if you immediately start clapping as fast as you can. Still others will offer compelling proof that I have no intention of paying you at all, that I'm a clap scam artist, and that if you were smart, you'd walk away from the whole thing right now. These people will be telling you all these things continuously, loudly, and simultaneously, throughout the entire 24-hour period. The task is just as simple as before, but now it isn't nearly as easy. Even the most strong-willed of you would be repeatedly tempted to give it up. The only way for you to succeed would be by adopting an attitude of strict, consistent discipline.

It comes down to this: your investment strategy absolutely will work in the long term, *but only if you follow it.* You won't be required to perform a task once per hour for a day; instead, it's probably just once a month—but for decades. The task isn't necessarily as simple as clapping your hands, but after you've got it down, you can automate it, in which case you won't have to do a *thing* except let it happen. It really is that simple! What makes it hard is the steady stream of right-brain appeals that you'll be faced with. We'll describe some of these as we go through the chapter, to give a better idea of what to expect. It's simple—but not always easy.

THE MINDSET OF THE SUCCESSFUL LONG-TERM INVESTOR

Before you began reading this book, you may have had a mental picture of what a successful investor looked like. Maybe you envisioned a professional investor in an impressive Wall Street office, a field-general executive type in an impeccably tailored power suit barking orders to a highly trained staff, surrounded by an array of computer monitors constantly refreshing up-to-the-minute graphs of every conceivable market statistic. Or maybe your image was influenced by some of the many TV commercials for investment firms. I especially like the ones featuring a rugged outdoorsy type, standing straight and tall on a mountaintop somewhere, intently gazing with confident determination toward a distant horizon, the wind ruffling his hair as an eagle soars overhead, while the voiceover tells us, "You're not one to follow the crowd; you blaze your own trail! You expect uncommon excellence from yourself—*and* your investment firm. Here at Fiercely Independent Investments, we understand blah blah . . . ."

No. Put all of these mental images aside.

None of this nonsense about rugged individualism, rapid-fire decisiveness, or "winning" through some kind of uniquely inspired insight has anything to do with the kind of mindset that you'll need to invest successfully. The mindset that's most helpful for the type of investing you'll be doing is one of *patience, consistency, and rationality.* Our strategy is based on sound, proven principles, so you don't stray from it. Your attitude is one of calm, assured discipline. You might sum it up by declaring, "My investment strategy and the process I follow to execute it are simple, methodical, and, frankly, boring. But in the end, the results will be very, very solid—and anything but boring."

If you're like me, analogies can help to bring ideas like this to life. One of my favorites is the hunters and farmers analogy. Not just any hunters, though—big-game hunters! The big-game hunter ventures into the wild, counting only on his wits, courage, and split-second reactions for success. (Well . . . and probably a really big gun, too.) In contrast, the farmer succeeds through careful planning, consistently sound and well-reasoned decisions, and unerring, methodical execution of the plan year after year after year. You're going to invest with the mindset of a farmer, not a hunter.

One successful long-term investor I discussed this with felt that even the farmer analogy was flawed. "Farmers have to work too hard at it," he explained. "Farmers have to carefully prepare the fields in advance, plant only under certain ideal conditions, and then vigilantly care for their crops as they grow. Think of it more like planting trees. The tree planter plants tree after tree and then simply walks away. He just keeps doing it, year after year, planting trees in lots of different places. The tree planter doesn't stick around watching and worrying, measuring how much each tree has grown every month and looking at weather forecasts. He just plants, moves on, and then plants some more in a different place. Decades later, he returns and finds a huge, healthy forest—just as he knew he would if he gave it enough time."

Want still more analogies? If you prefer Aesop's fables, you're the tortoise, not the hare. If you like sports analogies, you're more interested in winning the batting-average crown than in being the home-run king. How about a *Star Trek* analogy: your model is the coolly logical Mr. Spock, not the heroic Captain Kirk. For that matter, you won't need a Starship *Enterprise* whisking you to your destination at warp speed. Instead, your investment strategy is more like a big, reliable bus. When the bus arrives at your stop, just get on board, take a seat, and make yourself comfortable. All you have to do is patiently stay on the bus, and you know for sure that you'll eventually arrive at your destination. And it doesn't matter whether you're the only passenger or if the bus is packed with others—*everyone* who is patient enough to remain on board will arrive at the same highly rewarding place, eventually.

Perhaps the person who summed it up best was the famous 19th-century Russian investor Leo Tolstoy. Okay, I don't even know if he was an investor, but he was certainly famous and respected as a moral thinker, philosopher, and author of such masterpieces as *War and Peace*. Maybe, though, he was thinking about long-term investing when he wrote, *"The strongest of all warriors are these two—Time and Patience."*

FEAR AND GREED

Time and patience are definitely not your right brain's strong suits—*emotions* are. And the two emotions that are most famous for leading long-term investors astray are fear and greed. You are almost guaranteed to get a good dose of both throughout your investing career, and you're particularly susceptible when you're just beginning. Let's start with fear and describe what a typical fear scenario looks like. Imagine that you've begun systematically acquiring shares of very low-cost equity index funds, a little bit at a time, at regular, frequent intervals. So far, so good!

But after a few months, the market starts going down—sharply. This causes all of the funds in your account to go down sharply, too. As the situation continues to worsen, the financial media are all over the story in full force. Around the clock, you're bombarded with opinions about what's causing the downturn and who is to blame. Words like *crisis* and *meltdown* are increasingly heard. Every time there seems to be slight rebound, it doesn't last long, and the downward trend continues. Eventually the media start talking about recession.

Your investment balance continues to deteriorate and *is now worth far less than the total you've put into it.* Everybody else is selling. A talking head on TV says, "I've got all my clients' money in good, solid cash until this market settles down. We'll get back in at the bottom, and we'll get some very good prices when we do." Friends ask you, incredulously, "You're not still in the market, are you? Not now, of all times!" Your tax professional tells you that unless you sell before the end of the year, you won't even get a tax break out of this mess. The evidence is mounting, and it's very one-sided. Every instinct you have is telling you the same thing. Soon you're in a panic and thinking, "Let me out of here! Sell!"

Well, it's a crisis all right, but it's a right-brain crisis. Fear has crept in and taken over, but it's disguised itself as wisdom. After all, isn't it a wise idea to cut your losses before things get even worse? No—it isn't a good idea at all. Children in elementary school know that the idea is to buy low and sell high, but fear has convinced you that it is somehow "wise" to buy low and sell even lower. Your attention is riveted on what might happen in the next few weeks or months, even though your investment strategy is based on holding on to these shares for decades. You have mountains of evidence showing that every single time the markets have gone down previously, patience is always rewarded and sooner or later new highs are reached. Still, you desperately want to sell. Investment professionals have a technical term for selling at times like this: it's called jumping out the basement window.

The right thing to do is to stick with the plan. The hysteria to sell is being whipped up by those with a short investment horizon, and it doesn't apply to you. For you, what's really happening is that this is a truly wonderful opportunity to buy shares in funds that you've chosen at extremely low prices. The shares in these funds have gone on sale and are temporarily *incredible bargains*. A few decades from now, you'll look at the purchases you made during these "dark" times and smile as you realize that these are some of the very best returns you've ever gotten. But *only* if you stick to the plan.

Now let's look at the greed scenario; it's every bit as dangerous. Suppose the market is very good and has been for an extended period. You comfortably watch your investment balance climb month after month and congratulate yourself on your superior investment skills. In your relatively short time in the market, you've been experiencing at least double the rates of return that you'd hoped for. You start to think, "This is easy." A few months later, you start to think something even more dangerous: "I'm *so* smart. In fact, I'm so smart that you'd have to be really smart yourself to even understand how smart I am." (Uh-oh . . .)

Your confidence is reaffirmed every time you tune in to the financial media. With each new milestone the market reaches, the main discussion is about how quickly the next record high will be attained. Experts increasingly describe how the economy has been fundamentally and permanently restructured, as if by magic, in such a way that makes future downturns almost impossible. The only thing that bothers you is the growing realization that there are lots and lots of other investors out there who seem to be profiting from these ideal conditions even more than you are. The more you think about it, the more you begin to believe that your slow and steady approach is foolishly short-sighted in light of the "unprecedented opportunities that characterize today's market," which you keep hearing about.

At this point, one of several ideas might occur to you. You might decide to sell all of your boring index funds and replace them with much more aggressive choices. You might decide to *borrow* some money to be able to buy even more of these can't-miss investments; one form of this is called *margining* your investment account. You might even decide that since your returns have been so good and the future is so bright, you can afford to take some money out of your investment account early and begin enjoying the good life now.

The right thing to do is to stick with the plan! As wonderful as the market has been lately, these conditions are temporary. What's really going on for long-term investors like you is that you're temporarily paying a little more than you'd like to for your shares, but over the long term, you'll still get a positive return even on these premium-priced shares. The market will inevitably turn down, probably abruptly and steeply. When it does, you'll be very glad that your portfolio has remained balanced, that your account balance reduction won't be magnified by any borrowed money, and that you didn't fall for the illusion that you can afford early withdrawals.

The bottom line is this: *you just keep buying the same broad mix of very low-cost equity index funds, on a frequent, regular, predetermined schedule, over a very long period of time, no matter what.* You do this no matter what the market conditions are and no matter what the financial media have to say. Sometimes the funds will go on sale (this is called a recession, or an extended *bear* market), and sometimes you'll pay a premium (boom times, or *bull* market). But over a long period of time, the funds you've systematically bought will collectively turn out to be worth enough to buy you long-term financial security—safely and surely.

THE WORST THING THAT CAN POSSIBLY HAPPEN

Most investors think that the worst thing that can possibly happen is that the market goes down sharply. That might be true for investors with a short horizon, but as we just discussed, for very long-term investors like you, a down market is *good*—that's when you get the biggest discounts. Instead, for you, the worst thing that can possibly happen is this: fear or greed puts some very bad ideas into your head, and you act on them—and the bad ideas actually *work*. (Or they seem to work in the short term.) Here is a very short case study, which vividly illustrates the point.

A man jumps off a 90-story office building. The workers on the 80th floor see him go by and notice that he's smiling! Astonished, one of them calls a friend on the 70th floor and says, "Ask him why he's smiling." So the fast-moving friend hurries to the window and calls out, "Why are you smiling?" as the man falls by. People on the 60th floor hear the man yell, "Because this is fun!" On the 50th floor, workers hear him call out, "The view is great!" The 40th-floor people hear, "And the best part is . . . ," while those on the 30th hear him yell, " . . . it doesn't hurt a bit!" Those on the 20th floor have to strain a little harder to hear him, because he is no longer exuberantly shouting. But some are sure that they hear him say, " . . . yet." The people on the 10th floor can only report that the man is no longer smiling.

Sometimes impulsive acts that seem like really good ideas at first don't turn out so well after all. Emotionally driven investment decisions are virtually guaranteed to end badly—whether they start out that way or not.

NO NEWS IS GOOD NEWS

In both the fear and greed scenarios outlined above, the financial media played a starring role in encouraging you to do exactly the wrong things. Don't blame them: they're just doing their job. Remember, the majority of investors have a short investment horizon, and they are dependent upon up-to-the-minute information and analysis. Remember, too, that the financial media are highly competitive, and they're each trying to shout loud enough to be heard above the din. If a financial TV show's anchor began the broadcast by serenely saying, "Well, I'm not really sure what happened today, but whatever it was, you'll be sure to get some of the opposite if you just wait long enough . . . ," it wouldn't exactly be a ratings grabber, even though that anchor would be absolutely right.

We've seen that paying attention to financial news during market downswings and upswings can trigger fear and greed. What about when the market is flat? In 2004 the Dow Jones Industrial Average (sometimes known as the DJIA, the most commonly watched barometer of stock market performance) closed the year within 1% of where it opened. In other words, from the standpoint of a long-term investor in the DJIA, almost nothing at all changed during this year. It wasn't an up year, and it wasn't a down year; it was an "almost nothing" year.

So were the financial media quiet all during that almost-nothing year? You already know the answer: of course not! On each one of the 252 trading days in 2004, the market was either up or it was down, and each of the many financial commentators was obliged to tell you by exactly how much, and why, and what we might expect tomorrow—each one more urgently and breathlessly than the last. Remember: their whole job is to capture your attention whether your attention is warranted or not. If you had read or listened to every single word in the financial media during that year, how much would it have helped you decide what to do with your investment strategy? You know the answer to this one, too: not at all. You're investing the same amount, at the same frequency, into the same mix of funds *no matter what* the financial media have to say.

Watching the market every day is like checking the thermometer around the clock during February to find out whether spring is really coming. It's not strong enough to say that the financial media are irrelevant to your long-term investment strategy; *they are potentially harmful to it*. The only possible effect that paying frequent attention to the perpetual stream of reports, analyses, predictions, and drama can have on you is to give you some really bad ideas, so my advice is to avoid it altogether. It might be of some use to certain other types of investors, but it doesn't apply to you. So change the channel, click to a different site, or turn the page. You'll learn everything that you need to learn about the performance of your investments by looking at your account balance once a year or so. You're far better off paying daily attention to other important parts of your life.

So—you don't need any news about the markets; but high-quality *education* about investing is another story. For some of you, what you've read in these pages may have sparked an interest. If so, there are many outstanding ways to further your knowledge. Here are a few recommended book titles to start you off: *The Little Book of Common Sense Investing* by John C. Bogle; *The Elements of Investing* by Malkiel and Ellis; *The Four Pillars of Investing* by William J. Bernstein; *The Bogleheads' Guide to Investing* by Larimore, Lindauer, and LeBoeuf; and *Stocks for the Long Run* by Jeremy J. Siegel. Beware, though, that many forms of investing education do not meet the criterion of high quality. Be especially wary of any education designed to sell you something.

The final point on this topic: some years the market goes up, some years it goes down, and some years—like 2004—it does almost nothing. Well, that's one way to look at it, but that's not the way that *you* look at it. For you, every year is a good year, no matter how the markets perform. That's because the same very important thing happens to your investments every single year no matter what. *You own more shares of your selected funds at the end of the year than you did at the beginning,* and that's all that really matters!

TWO OF YOUR MOST IMPORTANT ALLIES

Every investor, no matter how disciplined or experienced, needs to turn to trusted advisors from time to time—and so do you. As described earlier, the exact makeup of the team that you'll collaborate with will vary based on your own circumstances. But I want to introduce to you to two members of your team right away. These two team members play an invaluable role in protecting you from right brain–inspired investment mistakes: your financial planner and your 911 rescuer.

1. **Your financial planner.** If you haven't already found this out, let me explain something about job titles in the financial services industry: they aren't too helpful. Whether you're looking at a business card, a directory, advertisements, or Internet search results, the terms and titles used are just as likely to bewilder as to enlighten. If you need help with your long-term investment strategy, should you work with an investment advisor, a personal finance coach, a wealth management

professional, or what? Anyone might call themselves any of these, so the titles themselves aren't much help. I'm going to arbitrarily use the single term *financial planner* just for simplicity. I'll explain shortly exactly what to look for; just understand that the kind of person you're looking for might not use the title *financial planner* and that just because someone uses that title doesn't mean that they're the type of professional you're looking for.

First, though, let's talk about who you *don't* want help from. A certain category of financial professionals out there want your business, but in general, you should avoid them. The short description of this category is salespeople—and they come in many varieties. Some are paid on a pure commission basis; the more you buy and sell, the more they're paid. Some charge you a percentage of the size of your investment account; you're not interested in such a guaranteed fee growth arrangement. Some are employed by firms that will try to steer you toward specific investment products and will compensate their salespeople more if they sell you those products. Some professionals and/or firms "lock you in." This means that if you want to change firms or advisors, you'll be forced to sell your shares, which is definitely not in keeping with our strategy. So as a general rule, you're not interested in any of these sales-oriented types. Some of these people may be top-quality professionals with high integrity. But the problem has nothing to do with their qualifications or character; instead, it has to do with whether they are in a position to put your interests first. (Although this is a general rule, there might be some circumstances where you'd want to consider an investment advisor from a full-service firm. It's easier to understand whether those circumstances apply to you after you've read the next few chapters. So we'll revisit this point at the very end of chapter 20.)

So who are you looking for? *You want a fee-based, independent, credentialed financial planner. Fee-based* means that you are paying for a specific service: developing an investment plan and offering independent advice on it. The fee can be either on a per-hour basis or a single flat fee. The fee should have nothing at all to do with the size of your account, what specific investments end up in it, or how they end up performing. *Independent* means that the planner has no vested interest whatsoever in advising you in one direction or another. An independent financial planner has no conflicts of interest, so he or she is in a position to offer undivided loyalty to your interests, first. Finally, titles may not mean much, but specific, formal credentials do. You're looking for either of two very specific credentials: certified financial planner (CFP) or personal financial specialist (PFS). These two certifications are very similar; the main difference is that a PFS is also a CPA (certified public accountant), and can be expected to bring credentialed tax expertise to the discussion as well. CFPs and PFSs have expertise in a comprehensive range of personal finance: not just investments but also other financial topics like mortgages, budgeting, and credit. Financial planners like this can be found in a variety of business structures. It might be a person operating alone, or it might be a small team or partnership, or even a large organization divided into various specialties. But beware: just because a financial planner is credentialed does not automatically mean that they are fee based and independent. You want somebody who meets *all three* criteria.

Once you've narrowed it down to those who meet the fee-based, independent, and credentialed criteria, how do you make a final choice? My recommendation is to focus on three things: price, compatibility, and chemistry. You're not necessarily looking for the rock-bottom lowest-priced planner, but the rates should be competitive. In addition, there should be no game playing or ambiguity on the part of the planner about what you're going to be charged. After an initial conversation with you, a reputable planner should be able to give you a straightforward quote or estimate. Compatibility means that you'll want someone who completely understands and supports the type of long-term investment strategy that we've been describing here. You should directly state that you're interested in very low-cost equity index funds, bought at regular, frequent intervals over a long period of time—and then look for a reaction. If you get anything other than a clear indication of affirmative support and understanding, then keep looking. But remember, compatibility works in both directions. You're looking for a financial planner who is willing (and ideally, eager) to work with a brand-new investor like you. The final element is chemistry. This is someone that you'll be putting a lot of trust in, so you'll want to be comfortable in the conversation. You'll want someone who is clearly knowledgeable but is also good at clearly explaining his or her thoughts to you without being condescending or mysterious about it.

Considering everything that you're looking for, it may take a fair amount of research for you to find the right financial planner. You might be thinking that this sounds like a lot of work, or that there is no need to pay someone to develop a plan that you could generate yourself with a little research. Remember, though, your financial future is at stake, so I don't recommend going it alone. You might be right about being able to do it just as well yourself—but you might be *dead* right. If you're more of a do-it-yourself type, go ahead and give it a try. But instead of immediately implementing your proposed strategy, arrange at least one consultation beforehand with the kind of planner I've been describing to review and critique it. My bet is that you'll learn a thing or two if you do, and that you'll end up deciding that it's quite worthwhile to continue working with the planner.

2. **Your 911 rescuer.** It's going to happen. Count on it. No matter who you are or how committed you are to sticking to your long-term investment strategy, or how financially knowledgeable and experienced you are, your right brain's persistence will find an opening sooner or later. Some form of greed and/or fear (perhaps in disguise) will convince you that the right course of action is to break with the plan. If you wait until then to decide how to deal with it, it will probably already be too late. Instead the better course of action is to expect that it will happen and to have a plan already in place to use when it does.

It may or may not seem like an emergency at the time; it might just occur in the form of a really smart idea that you've been increasingly considering. But regardless of the form that it takes, any time you're contemplating making an unplanned change to your investment strategy, it's a full-scale, four-alarm, red-alert investment emergency! And just like any other kind of emergency, your plan to deal with it can't be complicated, time consuming, or poorly defined. It's got to be as simple and clear as "Call 911!"

The first step in developing the rescue plan is identifying exactly who you are going to contact in the event of an investment emergency; we'll call this person your *rescuer*. Remember, it's you that you need protection from. You need someone to rescue you from your own bad ideas, so the ironclad rule is that your rescuer can't be you.

So who should it be? There are three criteria. First, it should be someone who fully understands and supports your long-term investment strategy—ideally, someone who invests this way as well and/or advises others who do. Second, you're looking for someone whom you trust, respect, and will listen to. Finally, you need to select someone who can be depended upon to respond promptly to your 911 call.

It is important to give this decision some careful thought. For most of you, the financial planner you end up working with will be the natural choice. I separated financial planner and rescuer for dramatic effect; I did that because I wanted to emphasize that these are two quite different types of roles and not necessarily performed by the same person. Being a rescuer isn't a "job" that you would formally hire someone to do—it's more like a favor. Most people would be honored that you've shown willingness to place such a high level of trust in them and would take the responsibility seriously. Your relationship with your rescuer should feel more like mentor–student than service provider–customer. So before automatically asking your financial planner to play the rescuer role, think about whether you might know other candidates. You might even want to select someone as a backup rescuer in case your primary rescuer is unavailable.

In any case, once you've identified your rescuer and secured their willingness, make sure that you have all of their current contact information in a place where you can quickly access it. I am literally recommending that you keep their phone number in your wallet or purse, prominently displayed in the contact lists that you use most often, and on your speed dial.

What happens when you get in touch with your rescuer in your moment of fear-or-greed-induced weakness? If you've chosen the right person, they'll talk some sense into you, that's what! But don't take it personally: your rescuer is doing you a great favor, which is exactly why you chose them. Remember, having these kinds of bad ideas is perfectly normal and doesn't make you a bad investor—but *acting* on them will.

TAKE THE PLEDGE

Let's close this chapter with a pledge. As I've emphasized repeatedly, you *will* be tempted to deviate from the plan. When the market is going up, you'll be tempted to take advantage, and when the market is going down, you'll be tempted to pull back or maybe even bail out altogether. These outsmart-the-market strategies might even work the first few times you try them, which is the worst thing that could possibly happen. But make no mistake: the surest way to succeed in the long term is to stay with the strategy, year after year, no matter what the market is doing.

To help you remember this, before you invest even one dollar, you're going to take a pledge. Raise your right hand, uncross all your fingers and toes, and repeat aloud the pledge shown below. I'm not kidding! Saying it out loud will help to make sure that this critically important point sinks in.

THE DISCIPLINED INVESTOR'S PLEDGE

I am a disciplined, long-term investor. I have a proven plan and I'm going to stick to it no matter what. My plan is based on very long-term trends, and it is the safest and surest way to get strong long-term results. I have the discipline to stick to my plan even when popular opinion and my own emotions tell me not to. When the market is going up, I am going to resist the idea that I can increase my gains by changing my plan to take advantage. When the market is going down, I am going to resist the idea that I can cut my losses by abandoning my positions. Just to be safe, I have identified a trusted expert who fully understands and supports my investment strategy and whom I will contact immediately if I am ever tempted to deviate from my plan.

SUMMARY

1. The recommended investment strategy is simple to understand, but it will work only if you stick with it—which isn't always easy. Your right brain can be counted on to generate all kinds of reasons to deviate from the plan.

2. If you have any preconceived ideas about the mindset required for successful long-term investing, throw them out. The mindset that you want to adopt is one of patience, consistency, rationality, and discipline.

3. Fear and greed are the most common emotions that cause major investment mistakes. Fear can compel you to lose sight of the long term and sell at a loss when you could be buying for the best prices. Greed can compel you to overbuy at the highest possible prices.

4. Occasionally some of these emotionally driven decisions pay off—temporarily. This is the worst thing that can possibly happen, because it encourages you to continue, or even accelerate, in the wrong direction. This is virtually guaranteed to end badly.

5. Following the never-ending ups and downs of the market through the financial media is not just irrelevant, it is potentially harmful. Therefore, you actively avoid regularly following the market and the associated media coverage. You get all the information you need from checking your investment account once a year or so.

6. Regardless of what the market does, *every year is a good year* for your investments. That is because *you own more shares of your selected funds at the end of every year than you did at the beginning.*

7. You'll need expert help in designing and implementing your long-term investment strategy. We're calling such an expert a financial planner, but this is simply an arbitrary designation, because the actual titles used in the financial services industry vary widely.

8. The type of financial planner you're looking for should be fee-based, independent, and credentialed (CFP or PFS). Once you've narrowed down the candidates using those criteria, make your final selection based on price, compatibility with your investment strategy, and personal chemistry.

9. Before you begin investing, identify a person to be your rescuer in case you get tempted by fear and/or greed to make any unplanned change to your investment strategy. If you're tempted, contact this person right away to get straightened out.

10. The Disciplined Investor's Pledge (go ahead, say it out loud one more time!)

   I am a disciplined, long-term investor. I have a proven plan and I'm going to stick to it no matter what. My plan is based on very long-term trends and it is the safest and surest way to get strong long-term results. I have the discipline to stick to my plan even when popular opinion and my own emotions tell me not to. When the market is going up, I am going to resist the idea that I can increase my gains by changing my plan to take advantage. When the market is going down, I am going to resist the idea that I can cut my losses by abandoning my positions. Just to be safe, I have identified a trusted expert who fully understands and supports my investment strategy and whom I will contact immediately if I am ever tempted to deviate from my plan.

· 18 ·

Your Portfolio

*E*nough already with the right brain. It's time to get your left brain engaged. As simple as our long-term investment strategy is, some elements deserve more thorough explanation than we've covered so far. Over the past few chapters, we've consistently been using a nine-word phrase that is a real mouthful: "broad mix of very low-cost equity index funds." It is time to explain exactly what that means and why that's what should be in your portfolio. That's exactly what this chapter is about, and it's definitely left brain friendly.

Before we start, I need to reissue the same warning that I have previously: this strategy is intended for those in the 1st third of their financial lives, who have no debt and a full cash bucket, have been following all of our previous recommendations, and who have a decades-long investment horizon. If this doesn't describe you, then I do not recommend this strategy for you. The reason I'm putting the warning at the top of this particular chapter is because of the widespread misconception that portfolio selection is all that matters, so I expect that anyone just skimming will probably jump right to this chapter. The truth is that portfolio selection is one of several very important elements of a successful long-term investment strategy, but not the *only* important one.

The idea that the specific investment you choose is everything is prevalent for lots of reasons. One major reason is that it's in the interest of the army of investment salespeople to convince you that their offering is right and that any other choice is wrong—and they spend a lot of money in advertising to repeat that message. Another reason is that comparing and contrasting alternative investment choices is a perfect subject for the financial media. Champions of each choice heatedly engage one another in debates. New statistics every trading day thicken the plot, and it is natural for us to get drawn into the high-stakes competition. All in all, this topic makes for outstanding entertainment, which after all is the business of the financial media. Besides, discussions about tax strategies and frictional costs are surefire ratings losers, even though *you* know that these topics are vitally important.

The point is this: it's important to keep the portfolio selection frenzy in its proper context. A perfect portfolio, purchased at sporadic and irregular times, placed in a tax-unfriendly, high-frictional-cost account won't get you or anybody else very far. Almost *any* broad mix of equity index funds—even one that is just okay—will do quite nicely if all of the other elements of the strategy are strictly followed. With all that said, as long as you're going to be investing this way, it still definitely makes sense to think it through carefully and to do the best job you possibly can in selecting the right set of funds to invest in.

A VERY FAST INTRODUCTION
TO THE WORLD OF INVESTING

Since we already know where we're heading (the nine-word phrase we've been mentioning repeatedly), we won't spend too much time covering anything else. But first, a brief introduction to the overall world of investing is in order, along with some basic vocabulary. The subject of investing is an immense one, and even if we limit the discussion to the purely financial choices (as opposed to investing in racehorses or an art collection), you can invest in a staggering variety of things. These investment choices are called *financial instruments, investment vehicles,* or sometimes just *assets.*

A fundamental consideration in investing is that each choice requires a trade-off between *return* and *risk.* (You'll hear this referred to as the risk-and-return scale or continuum, the risk/reward relationship, or the choice between safety and return—among many others.) Remember that investing involves inherently uncertain prices at some future time, so we're talking about probabilities rather than certainties. So a more technically accurate way to describe the trade-off is between probable or expected returns vs. probable or expected risk. You know what return means; that's the gain or loss that you earn from holding an investment. Investors usually annualize rates of returns for easier comparability; when investors say that a 10% return is expected, it is understood that this means you can expect to earn 10% if you hold that investment for exactly 1 year.

What about the risk part of the trade-off? Risk is generally measured by *expected variability* of return. Investments A and B may have identical 10% expected returns, but A might be expected to only ever vary from 10% by a point or two, while the expectations for B might be all over the map, with an *average* of 10%. In such a comparison, we say that B is higher risk, or more volatile. If you had to choose, you'd pick A every time—it's a no-brainer. But what if the very safe A had an expected return of 4% and the wildly volatile B had an expected return of 12%? Now the choice is tougher—and a more realistic representation of what the trade-off is about. Naturally your choices would be a lot simpler if there were such a thing as very high expected return investments with very low expected risk. There aren't, of course: that's what makes it a trade-off.

For our purposes, we're going to divide all the possible financial invest-ment choices into four broad categories. (These are different from what inves-tors formally define as *asset classes*, but this categorization is close enough and fits our overall discussion better.) The four are:

1. **Cash and cash equivalents.** This is the pure currency in your pocket, plus checking and savings accounts, CDs, and a few other similar choices. These are extremely low on the risk-and-return scale. The low risk is why you hold your cash bucket in this category.

2. **Bond funds.** A bond is an IOU from a company or government en-tity. *Funds* are collections of individual instruments, so, for example, a bond fund is a collection of individual bonds. These are relatively low on the risk-and-return scale. Although it is possible to lose money in a bond fund, it isn't particularly likely—but you aren't likely to earn a high return, either. You'll probably hold a small percentage of bond funds in your portfolio as a way of tempering its overall volatility and gradually increase this percentage over time.

3. **Stock or equity funds.** No doubt you already know what a stock is—a share of ownership in a company that is publicly traded. *Equity* is just another term for stocks. Equity funds are relatively high on the risk-and-return scale. It is not only possible to lose money in an equity fund, it is common. It is also quite common to earn very high returns. The majority of your long-term investment portfolio will consist of equity funds.

4. **Everything else.** The list of instruments in this category is very long and includes things like commodities, futures, options, foreign currencies, hedge funds, IPOs, real estate investment trusts, anything where the terms *derivative* or *leveraged* are used in any part of the investment's definition, and a host of others. This category even in-cludes *individual* stocks and bonds (as opposed to stock funds and bond funds). Some of these choices might make sense for you in the 2nd or 3rd thirds of your financial life. But for right now, *don't touch any of these*. They are only appropriate for completely different types of investors, so you're not interested.

YOUR THREE FORMS OF PROTECTION AGAINST RISK

You might be thinking, "Now hold on—you're telling me that the majority of my long-term investments are going into a category where it's quite common to lose money? I thought you said this was safe. What are you thinking?" Good! I'm glad you're thinking that way. It means that you understand a very important truth about investing: the money you're putting at risk has been built up from your own hard work, discipline, and sacrifice, and your financial future depends on how wisely you invest it. But I'm not about to steer you in a high-risk direction. Throughout this book, we've taken the wise, prudent, and conservative direction at every turn—and long-term investing is no exception. The reason that equity funds are safe for you is that you're going to invest with not just one or two, but *three* ironclad layers of protection. Although I would like to take credit for developing this ingenious three-pronged approach, the truth is that all three elements have been well known to investors for literally hundreds of years, if not longer. Here they are.

1. **Diversification.** Investing in one individual stock is just about the riskiest thing you can do; you'd be risking your entire portfolio on the performance of a single company. Let's say you bought shares in XYZ Cola Co. You might buy XYZ just as their main competitor, ABC Cola, launches a highly successful campaign, sending XYZ downward. Okay, then, what if you buy some XYZ *and* some ABC? Now, no matter who wins the cola wars, you've got the winner. Still pretty risky, though. What if the cola-drinking public suddenly takes a huge liking to fruit juice and stops buying cola altogether? Better buy shares in *every* beverage-producing company.

   You can see where this is going: the more different kinds of stocks you own, the more protected you are against more different kinds of risk. Well, you're headed toward funds that contain *hundreds* of stocks—and not only that, you'll own *multiple funds*. When you do that, you don't care at all about the risk of each individual stock or even each individual fund—you only care about the risk of your entire portfolio. A broad mix of equity funds is like investing in the entire stock market, but you can slightly tilt your portfolio in a risk/reward direction that you like by specifying the exact mix of funds (more on this later). It's like betting on every horse in the race or ordering the entire menu at a restaurant. All the really good performers tend to cancel out all the really bad ones, and you're left with the overall performance. You've heard "don't put all your eggs in one basket." In our strategy, you'll own just about *all* of the eggs and baskets!

2. **Frequent, regularly timed buy and sell points.** Let's say that you bought exactly the kind of investment portfolio I'm recommending, but you didn't spread your purchase out over a long period of time. Instead you just made one huge, lump purchase, on one particular day, and then held it for 40 years. This is much, much more risky than dollar cost averaging (DCA). Here's why: we know that virtually all investments go through up and down business cycles. That means that there are good times to buy (at the very bottom of a price valley) and bad times to buy (at the very top of a price peak). The problem is that you don't know for sure whether you've bought at a good or a bad time until well afterward. We also know that even highly acclaimed experts can't "time the market" this way with any consistent success. So whichever kind of starting point you had—good, bad, or average—would end up skewing your overall return in that one direction. But you aren't going to do that. Because you'll be using DCA, you'll be buying at regular, frequent intervals (probably payday), regardless of market conditions, investing a little bit at a time. You won't be locked into any *one* entry or exit price point or even any cluster of them—you'll have a huge *variety* of entry and exit price points. You'll own the good ones and the bad ones, so they'll average out. And this has a very favorable effect on your overall portfolio risk.

3. **Time.** As we discussed earlier, your wonderfully long investment horizon gives you a huge advantage over other investors, because you'll be able to compound your returns longer. The main reason your long horizon is an advantage is that it gives compounding a long time to work its magic, but a second effect is also very important—your long horizon lowers your risk. Here's how: once again, imagine you bought exactly the kind of investment portfolio I'm recommending, but in this example, your investment horizon is only 1 year. Your portfolio performance in that year might be good, bad, or average. You are completely rolling the dice, because once that year is completed, "game over." But if your time horizon is decades long, you're not completely dependent on any one year's performance. Your portfolio return consists of the *collection* of good years, bad years, and average years that will occur over this very long period of time, and you know any bad years you experience will be offset by good ones.

Any one of these three risk-protection tools will lower your exposure substantially, but you're going to use all three of them *simultaneously*—always. This triple protection allows you to swim among the sharks with no danger. You'll be enclosed in three completely independent shark cages; even if the sharks manage to get through one of them, you're fully protected by the other two. You can enter the high-risk, high-return world of equity funds with very high safety, but only if you use all three tools, every time. Even when all three tools are used, risk is not completely eliminated, but the combination of the three puts the odds overwhelmingly in your favor.

BREAKING DOWN THE EQUITIES

We've just learned that equities, taken as a whole category, are higher on the risk-and-return scale than the bond and cash equivalent categories. But the equity category itself is huge; many thousands of stocks are available on the world's exchanges, which can be combined in countless ways into funds. So as a way to make some sense out of this, investors like to break the vast equity category down into subcategories and then compare how these subcategories perform compared to one another and to the overall equity average. Of course, investors are mainly interested in the risk-and-return characteristics of the subcategories. There is no limit to the ways that equities can be divided up into subcategories, but here are four of the most widely used breakdowns.

1. **Country (or group of countries).** The U.S. equity market is the largest in the world and accounts for a little less than half of the total. But investors often go one step further and break the non-U.S. markets into *developed* (like the European countries with larger, more mature markets, plus Japan, Canada, etc.) and *emerging economies* (China, India, Eastern Europe, Latin America, etc.). The United States is relatively lower on the risk-and-return scale, and the less predictable, more volatile emerging countries are relatively higher.

2. **Company size.** The way that investors measure size is by market capitalization, or *cap* for short. You'll often hear references to large cap, mid cap, and small cap; this just means big, medium, and small company subcategories. As you might expect, the large-cap group is lower on the risk-and-return scale than the small-cap group.

3. **Industry.** An industry is a group of companies that operate in the same general business, usually in competition with one another, like the automotive industry. Stable, mature industries (like textiles, for example) are lower on the risk-and-return scale than newer, more volatile ones (like biotechnology).

4. **Growth vs. value.** This way of classifying is based only on the *financial* characteristics of stocks. Growth and value are two contrast-ing methods investors use to pick the winners out of the thousands of choices, and they use very different criteria. Without going into a lengthy description, suffice it to say that both growth and value sub-categories have been known to significantly outperform the market average—but rarely at the same time. This alternating performance characteristic makes these two a good risk-lowering combination; in-vestors like to hold growth and value funds simultaneously, knowing that this puts them in a position to benefit from a broader variety of future market conditions.

INDICES

An easy and useful way to measure how any group of stocks is performing is to create what is called an *index*. Example: if Holly and Molly (our friends from part I) wanted to see how the balloon industry as a whole was perform-ing, they'd identify all the balloon companies, look up the stock prices for those companies, give the larger companies heavier weighting than the smaller ones, and simply add up the prices. The resulting total wouldn't mean any-thing, *except as a benchmark*. If the total—now called the Balloon Index—was 10% higher this week than it was last week, they'd conclude that the balloon industry was doing 10% better.

Investors absolutely love to use indices! There is an index for virtually every conceivable way of slicing and dicing the equity markets, and market analysts eagerly study them, looking for trends and trying to identify the win-ning and losing market subsets. Probably the most popularly known index is the Dow Jones Industrial Average (DJIA); when a news report says that "the market was up 2% today," it is probably referring to the DJIA. The DJIA consists of only 30 well-known stocks, though, and investors often prefer a broader measure, such as the Standard and Poor's 500 (S&P 500). This index tracks the performance of 500 large-cap stocks representing leadership in all major U.S. industries and accounts for about 70% of the total value of U.S. equity markets. Remember all of the categorizations described in the section above? There are indices for small caps, large caps, and everything in be-tween—indices for every means of subdividing the globe, for each and every industry, and for a wide variety of growth and value stocks. There are dozens more, but here is a key point: indices are analytical tools, not financial instru-ments. You can't invest *directly* in an index.

ACTIVE ("BEAT THE INDEX") VS.
PASSIVE ("MATCH THE INDEX") EQUITY FUNDS

Here is where we start to close in on our target. Even though you can't invest in an index, you can invest in funds, which are collections of stocks designed to either match or beat some specific index. For example, you can't "buy" the S&P 500 directly, but dozens of funds have been designed specifically to meet or beat the performance of the S&P 500. Investors pore over historical data to see which of these many funds has the best track record in doing so. Likewise, for each of the other widely used indices, a set of funds is designed to meet or beat its performance.

While most funds compare themselves to a specific index, there is a critically important difference between those trying to *beat* the index performance and those simply trying to *match* it. Beating the index is really hard! It requires depth of understanding, extensive research, sophisticated technology, and probably a large staff overseen by an experienced and (hopefully) talented fund manager. Beating the index requires frequent buying and selling, year-round. Funds that attempt to beat their respective indices are called *actively managed* funds. In contrast, just matching the performance of an index is much easier. It is an overstatement to say that any well-trained computer can do it, but that's almost the case. Matching an index simply requires knowing which stocks are included, and their weights, and then buying shares in that precise proportion. Funds that seek to simply match an index are *passively* managed (as opposed to actively) and are often referred to simply as *index funds*. Bingo! At last we've found the financial instrument we've been hinting at all along. A fund that seeks to match the performance of an equity index is an *equity index fund*.

The obvious question is, what's so great about equity index funds? Why have we been so quick to rule out the actively managed funds? Wouldn't it be better to *beat* an index than simply to match it? Can't a highly experienced and talented fund manager, backed by a skilled research staff, beat a simple computer algorithm every time? The answer is, *actively managed funds usually do not outperform the index they are trying to beat*. In fact, they usually fall short of even matching it. Any given active fund will beat the index in some years, and some funds will do better than others for extended periods, but study after study shows that taking the sure thing of matching the index every single year is the better choice in the long term. This comes as a surprise to many people, partly because the actively managed funds are heavily advertised and marketed products. Still, the fact remains that the "boring" index funds are the better-performing choice over any long period of time. This is partly because actively managed funds are saddled with a built-in cost disadvantage and partly because consistently picking correctly which stocks to include and which to throw out isn't as easy as it may sound.

I want to make sure that the point here is clear. As a group, the actively managed funds consistently underperform the passively managed index funds. But that doesn't necessarily mean that *each and every* actively managed fund will *always* underperform a comparable index fund. Some actively managed funds are very definitely better than others. You may be able to do quite well with an actively managed fund over a long period of time, but only if you select from among the lowest-cost funds, and from those with a well-respected fund manager who has a long record of solid performance. The number of choices that meet these criteria is small, but not necessarily zero. Having said all that, I still definitely recommend the passively managed index funds for you. Why take on the extra risk of trying to pick out the right actively managed fund, when a much safer alternative is readily available?

FRICTIONAL COSTS

What about the very low-cost part of the recommendation? This is where frictional costs come in. As you'll remember, frictional costs are the cost of doing business when investing and include expenses like fees and commissions. Frictional costs come in many varieties, but they can all be divided into these two categories:

1. Frictional costs associated with the specific fund that you invest in
2. Frictional costs charged by the fund seller (or broker)

Of course we want to minimize both sets of frictional costs. We'll talk about the second category—seller-related frictional costs—later, in chapter 20. But at the moment, we're discussing what goes into your portfolio, so we'll discuss fund-specific frictional costs now. When we say a "broad mix of *very low-cost* equity index funds," we mean that our goal is to invest in those equity index funds that have the lowest fund-specific frictional costs.

The two main types of fund-specific frictional costs are *loads* and *expense ratios*. Loads are sales commissions, pure and simple. Some funds charge loads, and others don't. The ones that don't are called *no-load funds*. You will only invest in no-load funds. (This will be an almost-automatic result of selecting passively managed index funds; loads are much more characteristic of actively managed mutual funds.)

In contrast to loads, expense ratios are fees that you pay *each* year for as long you own the fund. Expense ratios are expressed as a percentage of the value of your investment and can run as high as 3%. These fees are intended to cover the ongoing expenses of managing the fund; that's why the fees are ongoing, too. As you might expect, the expense ratios of actively managed funds are generally much higher than those of passively managed funds. Let's say you bought a fund with a 3% expense ratio, owned it for a year, and during that year its value grew 10%. Did you actually make 10%? No! That 3% comes right out of your investment return; you made only 7%, because you paid 3% in fees. This difference—the direct result of the expense ratio—*compounds* year after year. Incredibly, many investors don't seem to care too much about expense ratios—but you do. The absolute highest expense ratio that you're willing to consider is 1%. Anything higher is immediately ruled out. In fact, for most of the funds that you'll consider, you should be able to do much better than 1%. At the time of this writing, perfectly good index funds that track the S&P 500 are available for as low as 0.09%. So now we have a much more complete definition of *very low cost*: passively managed no-load index funds with expense ratios lower than 1%.

As a final note, some index funds are sold as mutual funds and some as *electronically traded funds,* or ETFs. Which is better? Since virtually all index funds match their respective indices extremely closely, you don't need to compare the performance of index funds to decide which to buy, because their performance will be virtually identical. So all that is left to care about is cost. You don't really care whether you buy your index fund as a mutual fund or an ETF. You just choose whichever is available at the least frictional cost. Your financial planner can help you evaluate the various forms of fund-specific frictional costs to ensure that you select from the very lowest-cost ones.

VERY LOW-COST EQUITY INDEX FUNDS: WHY?

I'm sure it's no surprise to you that very low-cost equity index funds are the recommendation for your portfolio. After all, I've been conspicuously dropping hints about it since part I. It's good that we're completely clear on *what* goes in your portfolio, but let's make sure that you understand *why*. You might be perfectly happy to take my word for it, but I know that at least some of you might need a little more convincing. Besides, more so than the other recommendations in this book, this one is quite likely to be challenged by people you know. Even though there is nothing new or revolutionary about investing in equity index funds, they don't get nearly the publicity that other investment alternatives do. In case a colleague or family member puts you on the spot to justify your strategy, I want you to have a solid rationale to offer.

We saw earlier that one of the main obstacles we must overcome is *inflation*. Inflation robs you of your investment returns, and its effect *compounds*. So the only way to beat inflation is to overpower it with a portfolio that consistently taps into the power of compounding at greater rates than inflation does. All investing involves some element of risk, and no one knows what the future holds, but looking at financial relationships that have held true in the past can provide a lot of insight. The longer we can look back, the better, because we want to understand how inflation and investment returns have been affected by a wide variety of economic conditions.

The two things we want to compare are inflation and returns from investing in equities. You know what inflation is—the increase in consumer prices as measured by the Consumer Price Index, or CPI. When it comes to looking at equity returns, the best index to use for our purposes is probably the S&P 500, since it is very broad and has a long history. Fortunately, CPI and S&P 500 statistics have been reliably kept in the United States for roughly the past 100 years, more than long enough for our purposes. Let's find out what we can learn from the past century.

Take a look at figure 18.1. The graph starts in the year 1914, which is as far back as we have solid data for both items. The very thin lines show the inflation (dotted line) and S&P 500 (solid line) results for *each individual year*. The year-by-year results are a mess! The vertical axis has been shortened to show only the range between -10% and +20%, but if it hadn't been, you'd see individual years ranging from about minus 50% to plus 50%. It doesn't happen very often, but there are plenty of individual years when the S&P 500 does not outperform inflation. But we don't care about individual years; that's

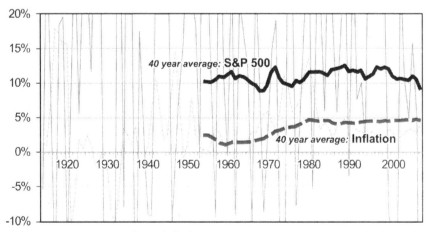

Figure 18.1.   S&P 500 and U.S. inflation since 1914.

for short-term investors and the drama-driven financial media. We care about long periods of time, like 40 years or so.

The thicker lines show the 40-year compound average annualized growth rates; they don't begin until the mid-1950s (40 years after 1914). The thick lines show us what we really want to see, by filtering out all the "noise" of the volatile short-term results that are shown by the thin lines. These thick lines show what the results would have been for our recommended investment strategy—buying broadly based equity index funds and holding them over long periods of time, like 40 years. Any time the solid thick line is above the dotted thick line, it means that the S&P 500 has beaten inflation. Well, looking at all these 40-year periods on the graph, the S&P has *always* beaten inflation, and inflation has never even come close! A century's worth of history tells us that the S&P 500 has very steadily averaged roughly 10% per year (when held for 40-year periods), while inflation has averaged just 4%. That means that equity investment returns have averaged 6% per year, after inflation.

In case you're thinking that 6% doesn't sound very high, remember the power of compounding. Here's an example: let's say that you manage to invest $6,000 per year. (That's 20% of a $30,000 annual income, or 10% of $60,000.) An investment program like that sustained for 40 years would appear to yield about $3 million. That's what your investment account statement would show, reflecting the before-inflation compounding rate of 10%. But the *purchasing power* of that account balance would be much less than that because of 40 years of rising prices. Even so, the after-inflation purchasing power of that investment would *still* be considerable: about $1 million, in current-year dollars.

Remember that the S&P 500 consists of large-cap, U.S. stocks. So compared with other available equity choices, an S&P 500 index fund would be relatively *lower* on the risk-and-return scale. Adding some small- and mid-cap investments and/or some international choices to your portfolio would increase its volatility but would also increase the return. In other words, our 6% after-inflation historical benchmark is definitely on the conservative side, historically speaking.

If you've noticed that the most recent S&P data has dipped below 10%, this reflects the recent very serious U.S. economic problems. But long-term investors look at it a little differently. Even acknowledging the seriousness of recent economic performance, look what has happened each *previous* time that the average dipped below 10%—it doesn't stay below 10% for very long. Over long periods of time, up and down cycles inevitably occur, but the 10% average has been maintained despite all the ups and downs, no matter how extreme. (And look what happened in the early 1970s, 40 years after the Great

Depression. That's right—equity investors got an unusually high payoff from investing at the bargain depression-era prices.)

Just because this has been the financial history over the past century doesn't necessarily mean that you can count on this happening during your own financial life. Some of you might view current world conditions with deep concern and expect a more pessimistic financial future. Of course, nobody knows what the future holds, but consider this: the past 100 years weren't exactly a picnic, either. That period included the most crippling depression in U.S. history, two world wars, and many other serious conflicts, crises, and disasters—and the S&P 500 U.S.-based equities *still* managed to average a 6% return after inflation.

Very low-cost equity index funds are recommended for your portfolio. To summarize the reasoning behind each one of the key parts of the recommendation:

1. I recommend *equities* because they very reliably beat inflation, while the cash equivalent and bond categories do not.
2. I recommend *index funds* because they very reliably match the equity indices, while the actively managed alternatives that attempt to beat the indices usually fail to consistently do so.
3. I recommend *very low cost* because nearly all index funds reliably match their indices, so there is no point in paying any more than necessary for identical performance.

I've emphasized that there is nothing new or revolutionary about the recommended long-term investment strategy. But since this strategy doesn't get much publicity in the financial media, there is a good chance that it's completely new to you. If it is, it might be reassuring if you could confirm it with someone who has had very considerable investing experience and success. Why not start at the top? If you conducted a survey in the investment community to identify the world's most successful living investor, there is little doubt who would emerge on top: Warren Buffett. He is the CEO of the investment company Berkshire Hathaway, which he has built up to a $200 billion-plus business over four decades. You can investigate his various and growing list of qualifications on your own, but trust me: they're impressive. (In case you're wondering whether Buffett is aware of the power of compounding, one of the many biographies written about him is partially titled *The Snowball.*)

Buffett is paramount among *professional* investors, and most of what he has to say publicly is primarily applicable to other professionals—but not always. Sometimes he is asked what advice he might have for the amateur investor, like you. His response is remarkably consistent. This is exactly the question we want answered, and we have the world's most successful investor delivering the same very specific response to it time after time. So what is his advice? *Very low-cost equity index funds, bought at regular, frequent intervals over a long period of time.* (As he told one young questioner during a Q&A session, "I'd just put everything into low-cost index funds and go back to work.")

Buffett's advice obviously carries more weight than anyone else's, but he is hardly alone in giving it. Many, many other experts are in agreement and have been for a long time. This is exactly what I recommend for you; it fits your situation ideally. Why? It is a very simple strategy to implement and maintain. It requires only a little ongoing monitoring or adjustment; the strategy remains completely unchanged in times of recession or boom. Because of the emergence of lower-cost technologies now widely available in the investment business, it has never been easier or more cost effective for the very small investor to pursue this strategy. But it works best for those with a very long investment horizon. Hey, wait—*that's you!*

YOUR ASSET ALLOCATION

Your *asset allocation* is a listing of the fund categories that you'll include in your portfolio and the targeted percentages for each category. An example might be 50% U.S. large caps, 20% U.S. small caps, 20% international, and 10% bond funds. Deciding on your asset allocation is a key step; this is where you actually finalize the exact risk-and-return trade-off that you're going to be taking in your long-term investment strategy. Since I've been very specific in my recommendations so far, you may be expecting me to tell you exactly what the ideal asset allocation is for you—but I'm not going to do that. This is something that's best for you to work out individually *with your financial planner.* (In fact, that's one of the most important things that financial planners do.) I can't just supply a single ideal allocation, because different investors have different ideas about what ideal means, mainly because people have different comfort levels with risk.

If you have some concern about risk and volatility, I can assure you this: if you use all three risk-protection tools described earlier, you are perfectly safe investing at the average risk-and-return scale within the equity category. But some of you might want to be a little more aggressive than that; if you're comfortable with a little more risk, you can shoot for a higher return, if that's your goal. The way you can achieve this is by assigning higher percentages to the higher risk-and-return equity categories in your asset allocation. For example, to aim for higher-than-average returns (and risk), go a little heavier on small caps and/or non-U.S. stocks and a little lighter on large caps, U.S. equity funds, and bonds. In any case, even though I'm not providing you with your own specific asset allocation, I can give you a few rules to follow in developing your own.

1. **Use broad categories**. As we've discussed, indices come in all shapes and sizes, and therefore so do the funds that attempt to beat or match them. Some of these represent relatively tiny subsets of the market. To get the full benefit of diversification, you want to avoid these narrowly defined or specialty subsets. Instead shoot for categories that represent *big, diverse cross-sections* of the market.

2. **Include a healthy proportion of international equity funds**. Even though the United States is the largest equity market, it still represents less than half of the world's equities. The U.S. market may be the one that is most familiar to you, but it is dangerous to load up too much on any one part of the world. History shows that the overall global economy doesn't move as sharply up and down as it does in any one country or region, so you'll want the evening-out effect of owning a good balance of U.S. and non-U.S. funds.

3. **Include bonds in your allocation.** Bond funds are lower on the risk-and-return scale than equities, but a small proportion will provide some beneficial stability to your overall portfolio. Specifically, in very occasional years *all* equities will go down sharply; if you have bonds in the mix, your portfolio won't go down as far, so you won't have as big a hole to climb out of. A traditional rule of thumb is that whatever your age is, that's the percentage of your portfolio that should be in bond funds. That rule may be a little out of date, but the idea behind it is still solid: as time goes on and your investment horizon gets shorter, the bond fund proportion in your portfolio should gradually increase. Since you're just starting out, the percentage of bond funds in your allocation will be quite low for now; that's why we've been using the phrase *equity index funds*. It would have been technically more accurate to have said "a broad mix of very low-cost index funds, heavy on the equities but with a dash of bonds, too."

4. **Avoid overlapping categories.** What would be wrong with an asset allocation of 50% U.S. large caps, 30% U.S. technology industry, and 20% U.S. growth stocks? The answer is that quite a few individual stocks would be contained in *all three categories*. This is not at all what you want. By having three different categories, you might think that you're diversifying—but if there is overlap, then the diversification is just an illusion. The categories you select should track indices

that are different from one another and that respond independently to various economic conditions.

5. **An effective allocation typically includes between three and seven categories.** You'll want at least three categories so that you include U.S. equities, international equities, and a bond fund. (At least at the time of this writing, there is no such thing as a total world stock market index fund. However, there are individual funds that track the total U.S. and total non-U.S. markets.) Having more than seven adds unnecessary complexity to your portfolio; you're likely to become vulnerable to overlap, and you'll be more vulnerable to higher transaction-based frictional costs.

6. **Rebalance your portfolio regularly.** Let's say that your asset allocation was the example that we gave earlier: 50% U.S. large caps, 20% U.S. small caps, 20% international, and 10% bond funds. Now suppose that U.S. large caps just had a fantastic year, but international equities' year was awful. Guess what has happened by the end of the year to your carefully planned 50–20–20–10 split? That's right—it has drifted way off the plan, and now might be something like 60–20–10–10. Your portfolio needs to be reset back to the original percentages, which investors call *rebalancing*. Sometimes new investors have a tough time with this idea. "You're telling me I need to get rid of my biggest winners and go buy more of my biggest losers?" Yes, that's exactly what I'm telling you; your portfolio will perform better in the long run, and with lower volatility, if you do. However, there are low- and high-frictional-cost ways to rebalance; your financial planner can help you with this.

TARGET DATE FUNDS

A relatively new—and very interesting—type of *fund package* has become increasingly popular. These go by various names, such as target retirement date funds, life cycle funds, or age-based funds; we'll just collectively call them *target date funds*. The fact that these funds are increasing in popularity is good news for you. As I've been reminding you, your investment objectives are distinctly different from the majority of other investors', and therefore most market offerings aren't designed to meet your needs. But target date funds are right up your alley! As long as you are careful about selecting the right one, a target date fund can be an extremely simple, convenient, and low-cost way to successfully invest. We'll close the chapter with this discussion, because explaining how they work is a good way of bringing together many of the key ideas we've just covered.

The fund seller Vanguard was the first to really develop this market, with their Target Retirement Fund family, but they've been joined by Fidelity (Freedom Funds) and T. Rowe Price (Retirement Funds). Even more sellers may soon enter. All three of these are no-load, work in about the same way, and represent exactly the kind of investing that we're recommending. I'll use the Vanguard fund as an example to explain how these work.

The first thing you do is pick a target retirement date. Precision isn't important, and your idea of retirement can be slow or gradual. All you need to do is make an educated guess about when you think you'll be entering the 3rd third of your financial life. Let's say that you choose the year 2048. Vanguard offers a choice of funds in 5-year increments, so you'd pick the Vanguard Target Retirement 2050 Fund, which goes by the symbol VFIFX. This investment is a package that consists of *three index funds*. Its asset allocation (right now) is roughly 72% total U.S. equities, 18% international equities, and 10% in a broad bond fund. This covers all the bases that we've been recommending, and it does it in just about the simplest way possible. As time goes by, won't you need to remember to slowly increase the percentage allocated to the bond fund? No—when you invest in this fund, Vanguard makes that adjustment for you, automatically. Won't you have to remember to rebalance the funds periodically if the allocation drifts away from what you want? No—again, Vanguard does this automatically for you.

Here is the great advantage of target date funds: all you have to do is keep buying the fund on a regular schedule—and that's it! Everything else is taken care of for you, automatically. When you do so, you are following each one of the six asset allocation recommendations that we just made, and you are fully utilizing all three risk-protection strategies. This is just about as close to "set it and forget it" as you can get.

Because of all the sophistication and automation in an investment like this, it must carry a really high expense ratio, right? Wrong! VFIFX is a no-load fund, with an extremely low expense ratio of 0.2%—way below our 1% maximum. This very low expense ratio is the reason that I used the Vanguard fund as an example of how time-based funds work. The Fidelity and T. Rowe Price funds work similarly but carry substantially higher expense ratios of 0.8%, making Vanguard the low frictional cost choice. So if it seems like I am pushing the Vanguard fund, I'll just say that I will be happy to push *any* high-quality target date fund with the lowest expense ratio. Markets can change, though, and sometimes very fast. Be sure to research all the choices carefully before making a selection.

SUMMARY

1. Portfolio selection has a popular reputation as being the *only* thing that really matters when it comes to long-term investing. The truth is that it is one of several very important elements, but not the only one.

2. All financial investments involve a trade-off between probable or expected returns vs. probable or expected risk. Simply put, the higher the average returns you want, the more risk you have to take on. Return is the gain or loss that you earn from holding an investment, and investors usually annualize rates of return for easier comparability. Risk is measured by the range of variability of return, sometimes referred to as volatility.

3. The very lowest risks and returns are in the cash-equivalent investment category; the low risk is precisely why we choose this for our cash bucket. Bond funds entail low to moderate risk and return, while stock (or equity) funds are highest on the risk-and-return scale. There are many other kinds of investments beyond these three types (including individual stocks or bonds), which range widely in risk and return; but these aren't recommended for beginning investors.

4. Three very powerful and well-known risk-protection tools make it safe for you to invest in equity funds, but only if you use all three tools, all the time. These are diversification, frequent and regularly timed entry and exit points, and holding each investment for a long period of time.

5. Because the equity market is so huge, investors use a variety of ways to break it down into subcategories. Four of the most common ways to break down the equities include by country (or groups of countries), by company size (as measured by market capitalization or cap), by industry, and by growth vs. value.

6. An index is an analytical tool used to track the price performance of any particular group of stocks. A great many indices are available, but some are followed much more widely than others. The most popularly known index is the Dow Jones Industrial Average (DJIA); within the investment community, the Standard and Poor's 500 (S&P 500), which includes large-cap stocks representing over 70% of the U.S. equity total, is favored as a broad measure of market performance.

7. Investors cannot directly invest in indices, but they can invest in funds. Funds can be actively managed (which means that their goal is to *beat* a particular index) or passively managed (their goal is to *match* an index). These passively managed funds are often called index funds. The actively managed funds generally *don't* consistently beat their targeted index, but index funds virtually always match it.

8. Frictional costs directly associated with funds include loads (one-time sales commissions) and expense ratios (ongoing fees paid each year, charged as a percentage of the investment's value). Index funds are usually no-load and have generally much lower expense ratios than comparable actively managed funds.

9. Over the past 100 years or so, equities (as measured by the S&P 500) have increased in value by about 10% per year and by about 6% per year after inflation. This performance may or may not hold true in the future, but even if the performance is less, equities are still the highest-probability choice to consistently outpace inflation.

10. An asset allocation refers to a list of fund categories held in a portfolio and the target percentages of each. Because of differing attitudes about risk, as well as potential choice limitations (in the case of employer-sponsored retirement savings programs), it is best to work out your own best asset allocation with the help of your financial planner.

11. General recommendations regarding asset allocation are (1) use only broad categories; (2) include bonds (which you'll gradually increase in proportion over time); (3) include a healthy proportion of non-U.S. equity representation; (4) avoid overlap (the same underlying stocks within multiple selections); (5) stay between three and seven funds; and (6) rebalance your portfolio regularly (when proportions drift away from the original targets, take steps to reestablish them using the lowest-frictional-cost means possible).

12. A *target date fund* is a special type of fund package that automatically rebalances, and gradually includes more bonds, as you get closer to your prespecified retirement date. As long as you are careful about selecting the right one, a target date fund can be an extremely simple, convenient, and very low-cost way to invest successfully.

· *19* ·

Protecting Your Investments from Taxes

$\mathcal{I}$n the last chapter, we covered what you should invest in to maximize the long-term gain in your portfolio. Now the question is, how much of that long-term gain would you like to actually keep? If you answered something like "as much as possible," then this chapter is for you.

I've got bad news and good news. Positive investment returns, sooner or later, result in income to you—and in the United States, income gets taxed. That's the bad news. The good news is that the U.S. government *wants you to save and invest*, especially for your retirement, so they have provided some very big tax incentives designed to encourage you to do just that.

It is vital for you to understand that these tax incentives are a *very big deal.* Why? If you do everything else just as we've recommended—consistently save and invest at least 10% of everything that you ever earn, invest in a broad mix of equity index funds, and discipline yourself to buy only at frequent and regular intervals—then your investment program will eventually result in a very large gain. How wisely—or not—you make use of these tax incentives will determine how much of that gain you get to keep. The difference between using these incentives—or not—to shield your investment gains from unnecessary taxes is not a minor one, measured in a few percentage points. Far from it—if you haven't planned carefully, when you approach your retirement, unnecessary taxes can wipe out *huge chunks* of your gain.

Still, lots of people who could benefit from these tax incentives don't do so and end up paying lots of taxes that they could have easily avoided. Why? You probably already know: when it comes to taxes, a lot of people find it hard to get motivated to spend time studying a subject that they know ahead of time will be fairly complicated and filled with jargon, and where the all-important details seem to change every time you look at them. That's exactly

263

what I thought the first time I heard about tax shields, and it might be what you're thinking right now. Well, I won't sugarcoat it—the tax incentive language and rules are guilty as charged. They *are* complicated (at least initially), jargon filled, and subject to relatively frequent change. The incentives themselves go by a very unappealing list of names, such as 401(k), 403(b), IRA, Roth plan, and TSP. The official language that explains them reads like it was written by a huge bureaucracy. That's because it was—the U.S. Congress. The main incentive that a lot of people get, especially young people just starting out, is to just forget all about them!

But if you allow yourself to get intimidated or discouraged by all that, you're making a big mistake. The U.S. government is giving you a wonderful and very valuable gift. Don't throw this gift away just because of the bureaucratic wrapping paper. If you take the time to learn how to properly open the gift, you'll find a VIP pass from the IRS. Best of all, you don't need to be a VIP to use it—just about anyone who invests is eligible. Still, I am sympathetic to the difficulty in getting motivated, so I'll try to cover the topic as clearly and succinctly as possible. In that spirit, here is a clear and succinct recommendation: *whatever you do, never, ever begin a long-term investment program without first determining a tax strategy, based on thorough, current, and careful research and in consultation with your financial planner.*

TAX SHIELD BASICS

A few notes before we get started: *tax incentive* is a broad, generic term. Terms with a similar meaning include tax shelter, tax-privileged or tax-advantaged investment, or even loophole. The term I'll use is *tax shield*, because many of these other terms come with baggage that I'd prefer to avoid. Because these programs are products of a political body, the rules governing them tend to be somewhat subject to change. That's why I'm not going to describe them in great detail here; by the time that you read this, many of the details could easily have changed. The thing to remember is that the basic structure of these tax shields has now become pretty stable; only the detailed rules change frequently.

New investors are sometimes confused about investment tax shields, so let's first clarify what a tax shield is not: it is not something that you invest in, it is not a style or type of investing, and it is not—all by itself—an investment strategy. Instead, a tax shield is an *account* that you open with a financial services company, like a bank, a broker, a fund seller, or the administrator that your employer has selected to run their retirement savings plan. This account is *where* your investment portfolio is held, and the investment activity that happens inside a tax-shielded account is taxed very differently than if it had taken place in a normal account. The choices of the type of account (tax shielded or not) and what specific financial instruments (like equity index funds) to buy are entirely separate decisions. So if you hear someone say, "I know I need to start investing, but I can't decide whether to open an IRA or to buy some stock," then the best thing for you to do is to loan them your copy of this book. (That's like saying, "I know I want to take a trip, but I can't decide whether to go to Baltimore or to travel by car.")

But what about the whole alphabet soup of tax shield choices? Relax—you definitely won't have to learn about all of them, because you're only eligible for one or two choices at any one time. It mostly depends on where you earn your income. The most commonly known tax shield is a 401(k) plan, offered by most private employers. The typical setup is that your investment is made via an automatic payroll deduction. Your employer selects a plan administrator, which is a financial company, and you hold your investment account with the administrator, not your employer. The arrangement is similar for 403(b) plans (for those working in public education and certain nonprofit organizations) and thrift savings plans (also known as TSPs, for government employees, including armed services). And if you are self-employed or your employer doesn't offer a plan (or if you don't like your employer's plan), then you can set up an *individual* retirement account (IRA) on your own.

So you want to do all of your investing in a tax-shielded account, if you possibly can. Under certain circumstances, you might be forced to put a part of your portfolio in a normal (or unshielded) account as a temporary measure, or as a last resort. That's fine; it's still better than not investing, and there are ways to invest in an unshielded account that will minimize taxes, too—just by not as much. But the point is, *anytime you have a choice, your long-term investments should go into a tax-shielded account.*

Earlier we noted that although the rules that govern tax shields change frequently, the basic structure has remained fairly stable. So what is this basic structure? The tax shields come in two varieties: you can either get your benefit early (as you invest) or later (as you withdraw). The early-benefit shields are called *tax deferred* (or sometimes *traditional* because they were the first type offered). The later-benefit shields are called *Roth* plans, after the senator who originally sponsored them.

THE COLD, CRUEL WORLD OF UNSHIELDED INVESTING

To understand the value of the tax shields, you first need to understand the somewhat unforgiving tax life of an *unshielded* investor. The first tax principle that applies in the unshielded world is that nothing happens until you sell—and then everything happens. Let's say that in January, you buy 100 shares of XYZ stock for $5 per share, a $500 investment. This initial purchase price is known as your *basis*. In February, the price skyrockets to $1,000 per share. Your statement confirms that your investment has ballooned to a value of $100,000. But because you haven't sold, from a tax point of view, nothing at all has happened. In March, XYZ encounters tough times, and the stock price falls to 1 cent per share. You sadly note that your entire account is now worth all of 1 dollar. Again, though, you haven't sold, so tax-wise nothing has happened. Finally in April, the share price reaches $6, and you decide to sell your XYZ stock. From a tax point of view, this is all that matters: you've made a profit of $1 per share, for a total of $100. That $100 profit is called a *capital gain*, and in the United States all capital gains are taxed. The only question is, by how much?

The answer is, it depends on how long you held the investment before you sold it. Capital gains are broken into short-term and long-term categories. The dividing line between short term and long term is currently 1 year, but this required holding period is changed by Congress from time to time, so do a search on "long-term capital gain holding period" to find out what it is at the time that you're reading this. Long-term gains are taxed at a special, low rate, but short-term gains are taxed at whatever your tax bracket rate is. So just remember that *long-term capital gains are always taxed lower than short-term gains*. Why? The tax laws are designed to reward long-term investors (who, in the view of legislators, provide the capital required by businesses to grow, which benefits everybody), as opposed to short-term speculators (who are only out to make a quick profit for themselves and thus don't deserve special treatment). Under today's rules, if you were in the 25% tax bracket, you would pay a $25 tax on your $100 gain, because you only held your investment in XYZ for a few months. If you'd held it for longer than a year, though, you'd pay a lower rate.

You're probably thinking that this example isn't too relevant, because your strategy is to hold on to your investments for decades; therefore, you'd always qualify for the lower long-term capital gains rate—right? Not so fast. The example was for individual stocks, but you're going to be buying *funds,* and funds are trickier. Remember that a fund is a collection of underlying financial instruments (an equity fund is a collection of individual stocks, and a bond fund is a collection of individual bonds). If you buy an equity fund, even if you don't sell it, the fund manager is regularly buying and selling the *underlying* stocks that go *into* the fund. The selling part of this behind-the-scenes activity generates a tax liability for you. This tax liability may be short term or long term—it depends on how long *the fund* has held the stocks, not you.

If you own and hold an equity fund in an unshielded account, you will get a formal statement at the end of the year explaining just how much of this has gone on during the year, and you'll be required to pay taxes as a result of it, even though you never sold any shares of the fund itself. This phenomenon is known as *tax leakage* (among other names, some a little more colorful).

Certain kinds of funds are much leakier than others. Actively managed mutual funds tend to buy and sell underlying stocks quite frequently; as new information becomes available, active fund managers are constantly repositioning their holdings in an attempt to beat their targeted index. Index fund managers, on the other hand, operate passively; they only need to buy or sell when the index definition changes, which is a relatively minor and infrequent occurrence. As a result, when you are investing without a tax shield, actively managed funds are typically much leakier—and generate more tax liability for you—than index funds.

The final point about unshielded long-term investing: whatever you decide to put in your portfolio, you'll need to stick with it. Why? Compounding. If you sell early, you will interrupt the compounding cycle by the amount of the resulting taxes. This is probably the *most* unforgiving aspect of unshielded investing. It is very difficult to select an asset allocation, and keep it balanced, that you can stick with over a 40-year period without doing quite a bit of selling. If you have to sell for any reason over that period, the resulting taxes come directly out of funds available for compounding. It's like paying the same tax over and over again every year, in the form of lost compounded value.

To sum it up: *never invest unshielded if you can help it. But if you must, hold your investments long enough to qualify for capital gains treatment, select relatively less leaky index funds, and stick with whatever investments you initially select.* We could talk about a lot more from the world of unshielded investing; CPAs have entire shelves of books on just that. But what we've covered is enough to give you the idea that it is indeed rough out there. Still, that's the world that many investors choose to live in, either because they don't know any better, or they find the tax shields too confusing or intimidating. But not you!

ROTH PLANS

Get ready to step out of the cold, cruel world of unshielded investing and into the simply wonderful world of Roth shielded investing! Roth plans are relatively recent, but we'll cover them first (before the tax-deferred shields), because they are so simple to understand. Are you ready? Here goes: you save and invest at least 10% of whatever you earn, just as we've been discussing.

The key part is this: you hold your investments in a Roth account (a Roth 401[k] or a Roth IRA). Then when you reach the 3rd third of your financial life and begin selling some of your index funds and withdrawing money from your account, you pay no taxes at all—ever. What about when your funds sell underlying stocks, which causes tax leakage in the unshielded world? No taxes. What about selling required to rebalance your portfolio? No taxes. How about selling big parts of your portfolio halfway through your investment horizon to include some different instruments more suited to the 2nd third of your financial life? No taxes. Ever. Period. That's it! Isn't that simply wonderful—and wonderfully simple?

There's got to be a catch, right? Not really. The closest thing to a catch is that with any tax shield, there are rules to follow. The rules can be a little complicated and change from time to time. The rules for Roth IRAs and Roth 401(k)'s are different from one another but cover the same general types of things: the maximum amount per year that you can contribute, the age that you must reach before you can begin withdrawing, and the types of penalties you face if you're forced to withdraw early. Your tax professional, along with your financial planner, are both indispensable members of your team in helping you establish, and fully understand, a Roth plan account. But now that you know how dramatically better Roth plans are than unshielded investing, you look at a little bit of homework and a few appointments with your support team as minor speed bumps on the investing highway, not intimidating obstacles.

TAX-DEFERRED PLANS

With a tax-deferred tax shield, you get your tax break *now*, as you invest, not later as you withdraw. Compared with a Roth, you see your investment balance grow faster, but when you look at your investment balance, you will have to remember that it's not all yours; you will have to pay income taxes on it as you withdraw. In other words, you got your tax break on the way in, so you won't get another one on the way out. The end result can be just as valuable, though—the difference is in how you arrive there. These tax shields have been around quite a bit longer than Roth plans. Because they are older, they are also more common. For example, only some employers offer you a choice between a Roth 401(k) and a traditional or tax-deferred 401(k)—the rest offer only the tax-deferred version.

Here's how tax deferral works: as you invest, every dollar that you contribute is tax deductible in that year. This current year's tax deduction is not a detail or a nice freebie: the tax deduction is the *entire point* of a tax-deferred tax shield. The deduction allows you to save taxes in the year that you invest, and the whole idea of this tax shield is for you to take those saved taxes and reinvest them on top of your other investments. These on-top investments, which are then compounded over a long period of time right along with your original investment, are what make tax-deferred investing so much better than unshielded investing.

This requirement is vitally important for you to understand. *In order for you to get the value of this tax shield, you must reinvest the current year's tax savings that the shield generates.* If you just go out and spend these saved taxes, then you haven't accomplished much by utilizing this tax shield. You'll only be a little bit better off than investing without any shield. But nobody will require or remind you to do it; it's up to you to realize that that reinvestment is the key, and then to do it.

Because this is so important, let's take a simple example. Let's say that you make $40,000 per year, that you have selected your employer's tax-deferred 401(k) as your tax shield, that you are contributing 15% of your income to this 401(k), and that you're in the 25% tax bracket. That means that you're contributing $6,000 per year. But that contribution is tax deductible, which saves you $1,500 in taxes (25% of $6,000). Instead of going out and spending that $1,500, you want to put that $1,500 right back into the 401(k). In this example, you can think of it like this: every year, you invest $6,000, and then the U.S. government throws in another $1,500. Since you're going to make sure that you reinvest that $1,500, your 401(k) contributions for the year now total $7,500. (You've still invested 15% of your income; but with the tax savings added, the *total* contribution into your investment account is now 18.75% of your income.) This $7,500 is the amount that is going to be subject to all the benefits of compounding, but the sacrifice to you only "feels" like a $6,000 sacrifice, because the extra $1,500 comes out of tax savings, not out of your own potential spending. If you simply spend that $1,500 instead, then you'll miss out on all the years of compounding that that money could have earned for you.

If any of this is a little hard to follow at first, don't let that discourage you. It may help to go over this in a more individualized way with your financial planner. The main thing to remember about this type of tax shield is that you can see its benefits, in the form of a higher balance, in your investment account as soon as you start using it. However, your taxes on the gains aren't eliminated—they are simply deferred until you begin withdrawing funds from the account. When you do (which won't be until decades' worth of compounding has occurred, and you're ready to retire), you'll pay tax on your withdrawals at ordinary income tax rates. But thanks to the tax savings in all of those years when you contributed, and thanks to compounding, you will still come out much further ahead than if you'd invested without this shield.

TAX DEFERRED VS. ROTH—WHICH IS BETTER?

First of all, you may not have a choice. Your employer may only offer one type of plan. But if you do have a choice, the simplicity of the Roth plan is very appealing. There is no requirement to remember to reinvest tax savings, you just invest and forget about it. But most of you would probably be willing to trade a little simplicity for a better return. So the real question is, how do the Roth and tax-deferred tax shields compare with one another in terms of delivering the best return? Mathematically, they are virtually identical. The only difference between the two comes to light if there is a difference between your current tax bracket (while you are investing) and your future tax bracket (while you are withdrawing). The short explanation is this: you're trying to decide whether you want your tax break *now, or later*. Well, the higher your tax bracket is, the more a tax break is worth to you: so if you think that you're in a higher tax bracket now compared to what it will be in your retirement, then you want your tax break now—tax deferred. On the other hand, if you think you're in a lower tax bracket now than you will be in retirement, you want your tax break later—Roth.

Very helpful—except how are you supposed to know what tax bracket you'll be in 40 years from now? Of course, you *don't* know. But for most of you, the safest assumption would be to lean toward a Roth plan. Since you are just starting out in your financial life, the odds are that your current tax bracket is as low as it is ever going to be throughout your working life—and maybe ever. And while we don't know what tax rates will be decades from now, history would seem to indicate that the overall rate structure is more likely to drift upward than downward. Both those factors point toward a Roth plan. (Someone like Buck and Penny might reach the opposite conclusion. Their current tax bracket is probably higher than what they'll face in retirement, so for them, tax deferred is probably the best choice.)

I highly recommend that you work all this out with your financial planner and/or your tax professional. For most of you, the conclusion will be that it is a better decision to go with the Roth. Your current low tax bracket plus a simpler process make it a winning combination.

EMPLOYER MATCHES—PURE GOLD!

It's not only the U.S. government that wants to encourage you to save and invest for your retirement—most employers do, too. There are two ways that employers encourage this. The first is to offer a tax-shielded retirement savings plan for their employees. Most employers offer a tax-deferred plan, but more and more are offering Roth-type plans, too. But many employers go further than that—they offer *matching contributions* on top of what you invest. These employer matches are pure gold! Think of it—if you are willing to save and invest for your own retirement, your employer will give you free money! The catch is that you only get the free money if you are willing to place it in your long-term investment account, but that's exactly where you would want to put it anyway. What could possibly be better than getting free money? Only one thing could possibly be better—free money that compounds tax-free for decades, which is exactly what you get when you qualify for an employer match. Why would employers do such a thing if they weren't required to? For the simple reason that they know that a matching program makes them a highly preferred employer. Any company with a strong matching program will have their pick of the best potential employees.

How does it work? It's just about as simple as it sounds: you contribute money into your tax-shielded retirement plan, and your employer contributes to it, too—on top. Employer matches are completely voluntary on the part of each individual employer, so their willingness to match—and by how much—varies tremendously. There may be no match at all, or the amount of the match can be 10% of whatever you contribute, 50%, or even higher. The employer may apply this matching percentage to every dollar you contribute, or only up to some cap amount. The matching may begin immediately upon your participation in the plan, or there might a waiting period before the matching begins (designed to keep you from leaving).

Bottom line: *if your employer offers a match, take advantage of it to the fullest extent that you possibly can. This is simply the best long-term investment plan possible.*

In fact, investing in a tax-shielded account with an employer match is such a fantastic opportunity that it is the one and only exception to the fill-your-cash-bucket-first rule. Filling your cash bucket is extremely important, and you should be on financial red alert until you have it completely full. On the other hand, taking advantage of an employer match is such a great deal that it would be senseless not to take full advantage of it—it would be like walking away from free money. (Wait . . . it *is* walking away from free money!)

So what do you do if your cash bucket isn't full, but you qualify for an employer match? Use a 50–50 plan. Take 50% of your savings and use it to fill your cash bucket, and invest the other 50% in your retirement savings plan. Once your cash bucket is full, immediately switch to 100% funding of the investment plan. An even better idea is to cut your spending back even more than you already have. If you've been saving 10% of everything you earn, shoot for 20%

instead. That way, you can continue filling your cash bucket at the same rate and participate in the matched investments at an equal rate. Instead of a 50–50 plan, that's a 100–100 plan, made possible by lowered spending.

MINI CASE STUDY: IRA SHIELD

Meet Ira Shield. Ira is 25, and plans to earn, save, and invest for around 40 years before he retires. He makes $40,000 per year and intends to invest exactly $6,000 each year (15% of his income), without fail. He is in the 25% tax bracket and expects to remain there even throughout his retirement. He has just hired Ruth Roth to help him sort through his tax shield options. Ruth is the perfect choice. She is a personal financial specialist (PFS), which means she has financial-planning as well as CPA skills.

The first thing that Ruth asked Ira about was his $6,000-a-year plan. "Right now, that is 15% of what you earn, which is very admirable," Ruth began. "But you'll probably earn more and more as you gain experience and skills. You could earn even more if you started investing supplemental income. Have you ever heard of the Ultimate Acceleration Strategy? That's where you freeze your spending level instead of your savings level. Then, as your income goes up, your savings and investment level can go up, too."

"Yes, I know about that," replied Ira. "And that's probably what I'll end up doing. But I want to keep my assumptions as simple as possible for now, because all I'm trying to do is make a comparison between different tax strategies. What I want to know is this: if I invest $6,000 a year, and if inflation keeps running at 4% and equity index funds keep returning about 10%, won't that be good enough even without one of those fancy tax shields? I know all about the power of compounding, so if I just save and invest, and let it all compound for 40 years, does a tax shield really make that big a difference?"

"This is amazing, Ira," Ruth replied. "You'll never believe this, but I just had a group of clients who all retired last week, after precisely 40 years of investing exactly the way that you just described. Almost everything they did was identical, *except* their tax strategies. But when it came to taxes, they couldn't have been more different from one another."

"Wow! Tell me more," replied Ira. "Did their tax strategies end up making any difference?"

"Normally, I would never disclose anything about the financial affairs of any of my clients. But they were so surprised by how different their results were that they actually want me to tell everyone how it came out. Let me find their file . . . yes, here it is, the Charmings . . . Prince and Snow Charming, and their seven associates. All nine of them invested exactly $6,000 per year

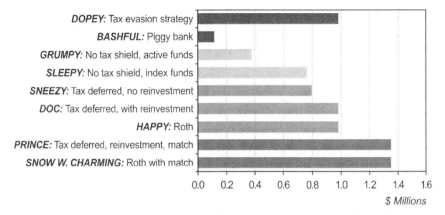

Figure 19.1. **Investment account value after 40 years (after tax and after inflation).**

for 40 years. And most of them—but not quite all of them—invested in equity index funds, just like you're planning to do. So it turns out to be the very thing you're asking about: the only difference between these nine people's investment results is their tax strategies. Take a look at the chart (see figure 19.1) to see how different their results are.

"So remember, the amounts that this chart shows are *after taxes and inflation*. Their investments all averaged a 10% return, but inflation averaged 4%, leaving them with about a 6% return. So let's start with Dopey. He was dopey enough to think he could get away without paying any taxes at all. He refused to follow my advice, and he chose to evade taxes instead of trying to avoid them legally. He found a very tricky way to earn the investment income without declaring any of it on his tax forms. Of course, he's in jail now, but he did manage to invest for 40 years before he got caught. The only reason I'm including him here is as a benchmark to compare everything else to. As you can see, investing this way with *no taxes at all* left him with almost $1 million—right before the whole balance was confiscated by the IRS.

"The next associate was Bashful. He was too shy to ask anyone for advice, so he was completely clueless about investing and tax shields. He ended up just putting $6,000 per year into his piggy bank; you can see what inflation did to him. I used dark bars to show Dopey and Bashful, because they each used strategies that I would definitely *not* recommend.

"Grumpy was quite upset about how complicated the tax shields were, so he decided against using any tax shield at all. Not only that, he thought that index funds were boring, so he went for one of the heavily advertised actively managed mutual funds. But when he started seeing how bad the tax leakage hurt his returns, he got even grumpier. Sleepy did a lot better, because he invested in less-leaky index funds, but still not nearly as well as if he'd been awake enough to have opened a tax-shielded account. Grumpy and Sleepy invested the right amounts and at the right times, but without tax shields; look how much it cost them.

"Sneezy *did* open a tax-shielded account—a tax-deferred one. But he didn't reinvest his tax savings every year. Since he was in the 25% tax bracket, his $6,000 investment saved him $1,500 in taxes every year. But Sneezy just went out and spent that $1,500 every year. His returns are nothing to sneeze at, but he didn't do nearly as well as Doc, who *did* reinvest his $1,500 tax savings every year. What about Happy? He did exactly as well as Doc, even though they used different types of tax shields. It just goes to show that you can do just as well using a tax-deferred account as you can with a Roth, but you do have to remember to reinvest. Look at the total investment value for Doc and Happy—nearly $1 million! The two of them made just a modest salary, but by using tax-shielded savings accounts, today they're both after-tax millionaires. That amount will last them a very long time. And they did it 100% legally. Dopey wouldn't have done any better even if he'd gotten away with his tax evasion scheme.

"Of course, Mr. and Mrs. Charming—their names are Prince and Snow—did the best of all. They did exactly what Doc and Happy did, but they happened to work for employers who offered a 50% match on all investments in their company's retirement savings plan. Now both of their accounts are worth over $1.3 million. Now that they have that much to compound, if they want to keep working, their accounts will be up to $2 million each, after taxes and inflation, in just 6 more years—from $40,000-a-year incomes, just like yours."

"I'm pretty sure I understand what *after taxes* means," said Ira, "but tell me exactly what *after inflation* means."

"Sure, that's very important to understand," replied Ruth. "Look at Happy and Doc, for example. The graph shows their account values at just about $1 million, after inflation. But that's not what it says on their statements. The actual amount in their accounts is almost $3 million. But because of 40 years of inflation, that $3 million will only buy about what $1 million would have bought 40 years ago, when they began saving and investing. Snow and Prince each have about $4 million in their accounts, but that $4 million only has the *purchasing power* that $1.3 million would have had back when they started. I graphed it this way to be conservative. I didn't want to mislead you or anyone else by making your jaw drop because of inflated future amounts."

Ira took a good long look at the chart. Finally he said, "Ruth, you've opened my eyes. I was just about to start investing like Grumpy or Sleepy. But that would have cost me hundreds of thousands of dollars of unnecessary tax.

When I really think about what this means, it isn't just the money, it's what the money really means. And what it really means is that I would have had to keep working for several extra years if I had invested without a shield. I guess these tax shields are no fairy tale!"

SUMMARY

1. The U.S. government wants you to save and invest for your retirement and offers you significant tax incentives for doing so. These tax incentives are a very big deal and can make an enormous difference in how much of your long-term investment gains you get to keep.

2. Whatever you do, never, ever begin a long-term investment program without first determining a tax strategy based on thorough, current, and careful research.

3. Tax shields are *accounts* in which you hold your long-term investment portfolio, and the investment activity that happens inside a tax-shielded account is taxed very differently than if it had taken place in a normal account.

4. If you invest long term without any tax shield, you'll be subject to capital gains tax when you sell. If you invest in funds, you'll be subject to tax leakage (more for actively managed funds) even if you don't sell. Never invest unshielded if you can help it. But if you must, hold your investments long enough to qualify for capital gains treatment, select relatively less leaky index funds, and *stick with* whatever investments you initially select. Any early selling interrupts the compounding cycle.

5. The tax shields come in two varieties: you can either get your benefit early (as you invest) or later (as you withdraw). The early-benefit shields are called tax-deferred plans, and the later-benefit shields are called Roth plans.

6. Roth shields are very simple to understand and operate. You receive no deduction when you invest, but you pay no taxes on your gains when you withdraw—or *ever*.

7. Tax-deferred shields allow you to treat your investments as tax deductions; this generates tax savings each year that you invest. These tax savings must be reinvested back into the tax-shielded account for you to receive the benefit of this type of shield.

8. For both Roth and tax-deferred plans, there are rules covering the maximum amount per year you can contribute, the age you must reach before you can begin withdrawing, and the types of penalties you face

if you're forced to withdraw early. These rules can be confusing and subject to frequent change, but the basic structure has remained fairly stable for several years.

9. You can either participate in the plan that your employer offers or establish a tax shield on your own. Your tax professional and your financial planner are both indispensable members of your team in helping you establish, and fully understand, a tax shield.

10. For most investors just starting out, a Roth plan is recommended over a tax-deferred plan because of its simplicity, and the probability that your tax bracket is likely to be higher than your current one in your retirement years.

11. If your employer offers a match, this is the best long-term investment plan possible. Take advantage of it to the fullest extent that you possibly can—even if your cash bucket isn't completely full.

· 20 ·

Long-Term Investing: Let's Do It!

$\mathcal{A}$t long last—it's time to start your long-term investment program! Investing is the centerpiece of your strategy to steadily and safely increase your net worth, year after year. Most of what we've covered throughout this book has been designed to put you in a position to invest successfully. And most of what we've covered in part IV has been designed to give you a deeper understanding of certain key aspects of investing, especially the ones that new investors can sometimes struggle with. So now, with all that behind us: *let's do it!*

Exciting, isn't it? But be careful. Now is the time to remember everything that we've learned about the mindset of the successful long-term investor. As you put the finishing touches on your long-term investment program, it's easy to get swept up into a whirlwind of anticipation of entering a new phase in your financial life; but if you allow emotions to take over, you'll be susceptible to all kinds of right-brain hijacking attempts. Remember, we're simply methodically planting trees, not going on a big-game safari.

To reinforce the importance of a disciplined, patient mindset, the approach that we'll take in this chapter will be to present a straightforward checklist. Our checklist will consist of fourteen sequential steps. Some of them will have an "A" and "B" to choose from, depending on whether you're going to invest through your employer's retirement savings program (such as a 401[k]) or on your own through an IRA. Most of what we cover will be review; in this chapter, we're bringing all of these now-familiar ideas together into a specific sequence. Let's begin!

THE FIRST THREE STEPS: MAKING SURE YOU'RE READY

A key thing to remember is that once you begin your long-term investing program, the idea is that you're not going to touch that money for decades. Doing so would interrupt the compounding cycle and might also result in early-withdrawal penalties. These savings are intended for your *future* self, not your current self. By the time you see them again, they'll have compounded to incredible proportions, and you'll barely recognize them. So say goodbye to these dollars for now, knowing that you'll have a happy reunion with them someday a few decades from now. The first three steps in our checklist are designed to make sure that you're really ready to say goodbye for now.

1. **Ensure that you are financially ready.** No surprises here—before you begin, it's a must that your primary means of earning an income is solidly in place and that you have a well-established First Rule program of saving a bare minimum of 10% of everything you ever earn. You should also be free of any debt, with the possible exception of a mortgage on your primary residence (see step #2). If you have any outstanding car loans, credit card balances, student loans, and so on, these should all be paid off first before beginning your investment program. Finally, your cash bucket should be completely full; depending on your own circumstances, this means 4, 6, or 8 months' income. If you do have any debt, or if your cash bucket is not full, then you should be on financial red alert, spending the absolute least and saving the absolute most you can to resolve these conditions as quickly as possible.

   As we've discussed before, there is *one* exception to the cash-bucket requirement: if your employer offers a tax-shielded program with a match, and you qualify for it, then you should begin participating even before your cash bucket is full. In that case, use a 50–50 plan as discussed in the last chapter. As soon as your cash bucket is full, devote all of your savings to your employer's program.

2. **Resolve your housing situation.** We discussed renting vs. buying in part III, and by now you've reached some type of decision about it. If you've decided that buying is for you, *and* if you've met all nine of the readiness tests, then I advise you to buy a house first, before beginning your long-term investment program. Saving for a down payment and closing costs is a major undertaking; focus on that first before turning your attention to investing. On the other hand, you may have decided that buying a house is definitely *not* for you. If that's

the case, then you're renting (as cheaply as possible, of course), and you can begin your long-term investing *now*.

It can get tricky, though, if you're somewhere in between. There are all kinds of reasons to temporarily be in a "not now, but maybe later" status when it comes to buying a house. Maybe you're leaning toward buying, but you want to wait until your income is higher. Maybe you're sure you want to buy, but you aren't in a situation where you can commit to staying in one place for 5 years. Whatever the reason, now that your cash bucket is full, you have a decision to make: where are you going to put your First Rule savings? If you invest your savings in a tax-shielded account, the money (probably) will not be available for buying a house, so you'll have to save up for that later, which will interrupt your investment progress. If you save *outside* a tax-shielded account, with the idea that you may or may not want to use that money to buy a house later, you'll miss out on all of the advantages of tax-shielded investing. And since your house-saving investment horizon is shorter than your retirement-savings horizon, you'd probably want a different kind of portfolio than the equity index funds we've been recommending all along.

As you can see, this type of situation can get a little complicated. That's why I recommend that you seek the help of a financial planner. The idea is to retain at least some flexibility, while still continuing to save and earn a solid return. Don't get discouraged if you're temporarily in an in-between status; this is actually a relatively good type of problem to have. Most people don't save enough to begin with, but you are, and now you're just trying to save in the wisest and most responsible way while still retaining some flexibility. Depending on how certain you are that you'll eventually buy a house, you might end up investing in a relatively low-risk portfolio in an unshielded account, or you might go for some type of 50–50 plan. With the help of your planner, you'll reach a sound decision.

3. **Hire a financial planner.** If you haven't already done so (because of an in-between status in step #2), now is the time—no ifs, ands, or buts about it. You want a fee-based, independent, credentialed financial planner. It is probably a good idea to go back and review our discussion on financial planners in chapter 17. I recommend that you establish an ongoing relationship with your planner. Ongoing might mean something as simple as a relatively short, once-a-year meeting just to make sure that you're on track and are considering all of your options. The fees you'll pay for this are a small price to pay considering what's at stake. But no matter your circumstances or

confidence in your own financial skills, I recommend in the strongest possible terms that you hire a financial planner as you proceed through the steps that follow, *for at least your first full year of investing.* These steps involve the building of your investment structure that will remain fundamentally in place for decades to come. You want this structure to be as solid as possible. Hiring an expert to advise you on the fundamentals of its construction is a must. Think of it as long-term financial success insurance.

YOUR TAX SHIELD

4. **Choose a tax shield.** Remember, every time you have a choice you want every long-term dollar that you invest to be placed in a tax-shielded account. So now the question we must address is, what kind? This decision might be very simple, or it might involve carefully weighing several factors. It all depends on your circumstances.

Let's say that you work for an employer who offers a terrific tax-deferred 401(k) plan, with a 75% match that you are immediately eligible for, which features a very broad menu of funds to select from. It's a no-brainer. Your research is over. The decision is made. That's your tax shield! On the other hand, let's say that you're self-employed or you work for an employer too small to offer a plan of any kind. There isn't much research to do here, either; you'll be using an IRA as your tax shield because that's your only choice. You will have to decide between a Roth IRA and a tax-deferred one, though. For most of you, a Roth will be the way to go, but you should still go through this carefully with your financial planner. You may have some out-of-the-ordinary aspects to your current or future tax situation that could tilt the scale in the other direction.

But as you might have suspected, sometimes it isn't such a simple choice. The details of the plans that employers offer vary all over the map, and the tax shield rules are quite subject to change, so there is some danger in making generalizations. Typically, though, the characteristics of an employer-sponsored plan that might make it a less-than-ideal choice would be a limited menu of investment alternatives, restrictions on eligibility, or particularly high frictional costs. Our ideal asset allocation includes a broad mix of equity index funds, along with a bond fund or two. But what if your employer's plan administrator only offers actively managed funds? That may or may not be a deal breaker, depending on what your financial planner can tell you about the quality of the funds offered and/or the extent to which certain frictional costs will be waived. IRAs offer virtually unlimited investment alternatives, including choices like the set-it-and-forget-it, target date funds. But IRAs have their own set of potential issues, like much lower annual contribution limits. (At the time of this writing, the upper contribution limit for an IRA is $5,000 per year; the 401[k] annual limit is more than three times higher.) In short, there are lots of factors to consider in making your decision—your employer's plan vs. an IRA, Roth vs. tax deferred—and you will definitely want expert advice. This is where your financial planner is indispensable.

As a final note, you might end up with *more than one* tax shield. For example, if your employer's plan has very limited investment choices and no match, that could be enough to cause you to choose an IRA instead. But depending on how much you're planning to invest, you might exceed the current IRA contribution limit. In that case, your best choice might end up being to choose an IRA as your primary tax shield, invest in it up to the maximum amount allowed, and then invest the excess amount through your employer's plan. Putting the excess in a less-than-perfect employer plan is probably better than the cold, cruel world of unshielded investing; and *both* are certainly better than not investing the excess amount at all. This is just the kind of scenario that your financial planner can help you navigate.

YOUR PORTFOLIO DECISIONS

Next we face three big decisions that you've known were coming: from whom to buy your funds, how to allocate your assets, and what specific funds to invest in. It turns out that the best order in which to tackle these decisions—as well as which of them require the most thought—depends on the tax-shield decision that you made in the previous step. So we'll go through these three decisions twice: the first time, assuming that you'll be investing through your employer's plan (we'll label these steps "A"), and then again assuming that you'll be opening an IRA (labeled "B"). Just read whichever set applies to you and skip the other one. (If you read them both, it's bound to get a little confusing—for example, the steps are in a different order.)

A. Investing through your employer's plan

> **5A. Choose a fund seller.** You'll buy your funds from, and hold your account with, your employer's plan administrator. Easy deci-

sion. Remember, though, that the frictional costs associated with employer-sponsored plans vary widely. Investing through a plan like this is usually relatively frictional-cost friendly, but not always. Be sure that you fully understand all the various kinds of frictional costs involved in your employer's plan.

6A. Determine your asset allocation. This is where you actually decide the exact risk-and-return trade-off that you're going to be making in your long-term investment strategy. Remember the six tips on asset allocation that we covered in the previous chapter, and work out a specific allocation with your financial planner. Even though you are only concerned with initial percentages at the moment, remember that your asset allocation will change over time, shifting gradually toward a higher bond fund percentage.

7A. Select the specific funds to invest in. Once you've determined your asset allocation, now your attention turns to the menu of investment options that your employer's administrator offers. The choices vary widely from plan to plan. Some plans offer very limited selections within each category, some offer many choices, and others offer everything in between. Some plans even offer target date alternatives. Whether your plan offers a narrow or a wide selection, the process for you is the same: working with your financial planner, evaluate the available choices within each of your asset allocation categories and choose the funds that best match your asset-allocation objectives at the least frictional cost. Even though these costs seem small, frictional costs are a direct reduction from your investment returns. Every dollar that comes out of your returns today is a dollar that cannot compound in the future. After 30 or 40 years, even small differences in frictional costs can make a distressingly large impact on your overall account balance.

B. Investing through an IRA

5B. Determine your asset allocation. This is where you actually decide the exact risk-and-return trade-off you're going to be making in your long-term investment strategy. Remember the six tips on asset allocation that we covered in the previous chapter and work out a specific allocation with your financial planner. Even though you're only concerned with initial percentages at the moment, remember that your asset allocation will change over time, shifting gradually toward a higher bond fund percentage.

6B. Choose a fund seller. Fund sellers come in all shapes and sizes. They differentiate themselves from one another based on the breadth and depth of services they offer, on the types of financial products they sell, on the speed and convenience they provide, and on frictional cost. By far, your most important criterion is cost. Your goal is to select the lowest-frictional-cost fund seller for the size, frequency, and kind of investing you're going to be doing. Why are we making cost the top priority? First and most important, frictional costs are a direct reduction from your investment returns. Every dollar that comes out of your returns today is a dollar that cannot compound in the future. An important lesson we emphasized in part I is that relatively small decisions repeated a large number of times will really add up. Although the individual cost per trade seems like a small number, you are going to be incurring it several times a year for 30 or 40 years. Eventually, even small differences in frictional costs can make a distressingly large impact on your overall account balance.

The combination of your very long investment horizon and your dollar cost averaging strategy makes you a very different—and less needy—type of investor. Most of the services offered by the various brokers are intended for investors with strategies that require much more active management, so you don't need to pay for them. The only advising you need will come from your objective, independent financial planner. The products that you're after are index funds, which are relatively simple and straightforward financial products. So all you need is an inexpensive, reliable, and reputable broker to buy them from—and nothing else. It is likely that you'll end up opening an account with one of the many inexpensive online brokers now available. Another possibility is that you'll open an account directly with the provider of a target date fund. The financial services marketplace is dynamic, and you and your financial planner should survey the choices thoroughly before making a final selection.

7B. Select the specific funds to invest in. Once you've determined your asset allocation and chosen a broker, the next step is to select specific funds. The low-cost online brokers typically have a very wide selection of index funds, and since your asset allocation categories are broad to begin with, you are sure to find excellent, low-cost choices for each category. Remember that frictional costs come in two categories: those associated with the fund *seller*, and those associated with the *fund itself*. In step 6B above, you've already chosen the seller based on least frictional costs. Likewise, since the performance of most index funds is virtually interchangeable, you select from among them based on least frictional cost of the *fund*. That way, you've minimized both sets of frictional cost. Your financial planner knows the ins and outs of how the various frictional costs are charged and is your invaluable partner in minimizing them.

Special opportunity to *combine* steps 5B, 6B, and 7B. We just went through steps 5B, 6B, and 7B one at a time to make sure that you understood the thinking behind each step. But there is a very convenient and effective way that you can combine all three steps into a single decision. Here's how: it's no secret that I'm a big fan of the target date funds that we discussed at the end of chapter 18, but I *especially* recommend them for you. Why? As an IRA investor, you don't have an employer-selected administrator discounting or even eliminating any frictional costs for you. That means that you're more vulnerable to these kinds of costs, which can come your way directly from the funds that you select, as well as from the seller. Well, when it comes to minimizing frictional costs for IRA investors, it's very tough to beat buying target date funds directly from the fund provider. As an example, at the time of this writing the Vanguard Target Retirement Date funds carry an ultra-low expense ratio of 0.2%. If purchased directly from Vanguard there is no per-transaction fee, so you can invest automatically each payday without worrying about running up frictional costs. There is a small annual fee, but this is waived if you sign up for electronic statement delivery, which you'd want to do anyway. There is a $3,000 minimum to begin. Whether you choose Vanguard or one of the other target date funds, you're likely to pay much lower frictional cost by investing this way than any other alternative. You'll also benefit from the set-it-and-forget-it convenience of automated asset allocation adjustment (increasing the percentage in the bond category as you get older) and rebalancing. I recommend that you give this approach strong consideration; it is a simple and very cost-effective way to cover all the bases at once on steps 5B, 6B, and 7B.

YOUR DCA PLAN

You remember from chapter 16 that you're going to be using a dollar cost averaging (DCA) approach. DCA means investing a relatively constant dollar amount on a fixed schedule, buying the same mix of investments over and over again, regardless of market conditions. We've reached the part of the checklist where you decide on the specific details of your DCA plan.

Before going on, be aware that you might run across a little bit of controversy about DCA. I want to assure you that the overall philosophy behind DCA isn't controversial at all. Nearly everyone seriously advising young investors like you recommends it. The debate is all about one very specific detail—what to do if you have a one-time, larger-than-usual amount to invest. A strict DCA policy requires exactly the same dollar amount to be invested every single time. For example, a by-the-book DCA proponent would say that if you come upon a windfall, or begin generating some temporary supplemental income, the right thing to do would be to slowly and gradually direct the additional money into your portfolio over a long period of time. My advice to you is to avoid getting distracted by this controversy; just follow the main idea behind DCA, which is to consistently invest, *roughly* the same amount at regular intervals, without fail. If you have some new or extra money to invest, contact your financial planner for advice. Unless the amount is truly large, he or she will probably just advise you to invest it right away.

8. **Decide on the exact amount to invest.** You've already been following a First Rule savings program for some time; the only difference now is that the savings amounts are headed into your long-term investment account, instead of into your cash bucket or house-related savings. So by now, the math is very familiar—10%, at a bare minimum, of the gross amount of everything that you earn. If you're investing through your employer's plan and your employer offers a match, be sure to take full advantage of it, even if it means saving and investing more than you have been up until now. Don't walk away from free money!

The remaining two steps in the DCA plan deal with how often to invest and how to automate the process. As before, the recommendation varies based on whether you're investing through your employer's plan or in your own IRA account. We'll use the now familiar "A" and "B" labels. Read the section that applies to you and skip the other one.

A. Investing through your employer's plan

9A. **Decide on how often to invest.** Since you're investing through your employer's plan, this step is easy—you invest every payday, through an automatic payroll deduction. The majority of employers who offer these kinds of plans allow you to contribute via payroll deduction without charging you a transaction fee. (Otherwise, you might choose to invest larger amounts, less frequently. Work this out with your financial planner if your employer's plan does charge a transaction fee.)

10A. Determine how to automate the process. Again, you can take advantage of the "all-in-the-family" nature of the relationship among you, your employer, and the plan administrator. Since your fellow employees who are participating in the plan are all investing on the same schedule with the same administrator, it's a safe bet that a simple and streamlined automation process is available. Just work with the plan administrator and/or your employer's payroll department to specify the exact funds that you want your payroll deductions to be invested in every payday, and you're done. The nice part about this process is that you know with complete assurance that you're responsibly taking care of your financial future with every paycheck. Because the investments are made for you without ever getting into your checking account, you are paying yourself first. You will never miss the money, and you won't be in a position to let fear or greed give you any "bright ideas."

B. Investing through an IRA

9B. Decide on how often to invest. How often you invest will depend on one particular frictional cost—transaction fees. Here's an example: let's say that you've selected six particular index funds for your portfolio. You've decided on an online broker for your IRA who charges $10 per trade. If you're paid twice a month, that's 24 paychecks per year. If you invest every time you're paid, that's six transactions per paycheck, 24 times a year, at $10 per trade: $1,440 a year in transaction costs! If you're investing $6,000 per year like Ira Shield and it's costing you $1,440 per year to do so, you're taking a 24% subtraction out of your investment returns every year: extraordinarily bad idea! What if you overreact in the other direction and try to completely minimize transaction costs by investing only once per year? Well, now your transaction costs are only $60 per year, but you've given up an entire year's worth of investment returns to achieve the savings. That doesn't seem like financial wisdom, either. Your intuition probably tells you that the best answer is somewhere in between, and your intuition is right. Your financial planner can help you work out exactly the best intervals for you to use for your

DCA plan to keep transaction costs reasonable while still capturing the majority of available investment returns.

10B. Determine how to automate the process. Instead of an arrangement between your employer and a plan administrator, you need to establish one between your bank and your broker. The most important consideration is to set this up in such a way that none of the money you're planning to invest ever appears in your checking account, tempting you to spend it. It may not be possible to prevent your investment money from *ever* appearing in your checking account, but if it does, you want its visit there to be the shortest one possible. Of course, you don't want to be tempted to spend it, but you should also be concerned that every minute it spends in your checking account is another minute that fear or greed could potentially give you an opportunity to mistakenly rethink your plan. You want your process to be as quick and automatic as possible. Exactly how this works will depend on what capabilities your bank has on the sending end and your broker has on the receiving end. Your financial planner can help you work with both parties to determine the best plan.

THE FINAL STEPS

11. Choose a 911 rescuer. For most new investors, this recommendation seems like overkill. But if you choose to skip it, you're underestimating the persuasive powers of your right brain, and you risk allowing one bad, impulsive decision to destroy everything you've worked so hard to put in place. Think of this step as simple—and free—insurance. You may never need it, but if you do, it can save your financial future. As we described in chapter 17, you'll want to choose someone who understands and supports your long-term investment strategy, whom you respect and will listen to, and who can be depended upon to respond promptly to you when needed. The most likely candidate for your 911 rescuer is your financial planner, but it doesn't have to be. You may have someone else in mind; the only requirement is that your rescuer meets all the criteria. Choose whomever you feel most comfortable with. Once you've asked someone to play this role and they've agreed, don't hesitate to contact them at the first sign of a "better" idea than your carefully constructed plan.

12. **Make your first investment.** You've done a lot to put yourself in a position to make your first long-term investment, and now it's time. Immediately afterward, go back and double-check that everything has gone exactly as you expected it to. Since your process is as automatic as possible, any glitches will just be automatically repeated until they are identified and corrected. Once you've determined that the transactions have been successfully performed, take some time to enjoy the moment. To go back to our analogy, all you've done is plant a single tree—but still, it's the *first* tree. Someday you'll return to find a whole forest, but even then you'll probably want to search for the very first tree you planted, the one that started it all. So enjoy and celebrate the moment; you're taking a very important step. Your own hard work and responsible approach have allowed you to enter a new and critically important phase of building a successful financial future for yourself and your dependents. Congratulations!

13. **Repeat.** One of the most important reasons for making the investment process as automatic as possible is so that this step requires no active thought or effort on your part at all. You want these investments repeated behind the scenes, without your awareness or involvement, like clockwork. You invest when the market is up, when it is down, and when it is flat. You don't watch the market, you don't listen to the financial media, and you don't hover over your account balance. The investment activity is steadily going on in the background, and you just simply *let it happen.* This will free you up to focus on your job and to seek fulfillment in the other areas of your life, confident that your financial future is being surely and safely built, one investment cycle at a time.

14. **Rebalance your portfolio as necessary.** As we discussed earlier, the various parts of your portfolio will grow at different rates at different times, and this will throw your asset allocation out of balance. The solution is to rebalance it, of course, but there are many different ways to go about this. The two main things to consider are frictional costs and potential automation. If it weren't for frictional costs, you could rebalance your portfolio every day if you wanted to. But because rebalancing involves buying and selling funds, a set of relatively small rebalancing transactions will cost you just as much as a normal investment set. You can get around this by rebalancing infrequently or by adjusting the amounts that you buy and sell on your next (or next few) normal investment cycles. This takes more active involvement on your part than is ideal, but rebalancing is fundamental and must be done somehow. Your financial planner can

help you determine an approach to rebalancing that is frictional-cost friendly. Some employers' plans, and some brokers, have automatic rebalancing capabilities, which certainly warrant investigation. And remember, one of the main advantages of the target date funds is automatic rebalancing; if you choose this type of fund, you won't have to worry about rebalancing no matter where you hold your account.

A FINAL THOUGHT: REVISITING THE FULL-SERVICE INVESTMENT FIRM

I've been saying all along that most other investors are doing a very different kind of investing than you'll be doing; they have bigger portfolios, a much shorter investment horizon, and a substantially more complex set of financial issues to deal with. The majority of these investors work with personal investment advisors from full-service investment firms—the kind with prominent local offices and big advertising budgets. I've steered you away from them specifically because of their high frictional costs and because our investment strategy is so simple that it doesn't make sense for you to pay for the kind of personalized service these full-service firms offer. So if I've been steering you away all this time, why am I bringing them up again now?

There are three important reasons to revisit our discussion of these firms. First, even though you may not formally do business with a full-service firm, under the right circumstances a full-service investment advisor might make an ideal candidate for your 911 rescuer. Second, you won't *always* be in the 1st third of your financial life. Someday you'll be in the 2nd and 3rd thirds; and when you are, your portfolio will be significantly larger and possibly more complex. At that time, a full-service firm might make perfect sense for you. Third, for a *few* of you a full-service firm might make sense now. Hold that thought—I'll come back to it shortly.

The key is selecting the *right* investment advisor from the *right* firm. This isn't easy because it is often difficult to tell the right advisors from the wrong ones, especially for an inexperienced investor like you. The right ones might work for small, medium, or large firms, so you can't tell them apart simply by the name on the building; you'll have to look for other clues. The right ones have 10 or more years' experience. This ensures that they've made this work their career and have been through at least a couple of full market cycles. Senior people like this, who handle the largest and most complex accounts, are in those positions for good reasons: they are experienced, and they have a deep knowledge of the investment markets. In addition, the right ones are fully familiar with, and highly supportive of, the investment strategy that I've outlined throughout part IV. They would sincerely love to see you succeed using just such a strategy—although they may have an enhancement or two to suggest. What about the wrong ones? Watch out! They may look and sound just like the right ones and might even work for the same firms. But what I've described as frictional costs to be minimized, the wrong financial advisor sees as fees to be maximized. A very big warning sign is a financial advisor who recommends a specific branded investment product, and the brand is the same name as the investment advisor's firm.

So if the right investment advisors are so hard to tell apart from the wrong ones, how do you proceed? One word: *referrals*. The best place to start is with people you already know and trust, who are in the 2nd or 3rd third of their financial lives and are in strong financial shape. That may be your parents, your boss, or a current or former teacher. Just ask them if they have a relationship with a full-service investment advisor and if they'd recommend that person as someone worth talking to. If so, see if you can arrange a short, one-time courtesy interview with the advisor, using your referral as an introduction. Your goal is simply to explain your investment strategy to the advisor and ask for feedback.

Now I'll let you in on something that you may find surprising; many of these advisors would be very happy to be your rescuer, and they'd do it for free. I've been fortunate enough to have access to several such professionals in writing this book, and when this subject has come up, their response has been remarkably consistent—they *really like* the idea of being an informal, occasional mentor for a young investor. Maybe it's because they made their own investment missteps when first starting out and would welcome the opportunity to explain some key things to a newcomer that they wish someone had explained to them. Maybe the young people in their own lives have shown little interest in listening to investment advice, so they'd be delighted to encounter someone just starting out who is sincerely seeking guidance. Maybe they are happy to do a favor for their long-time client who referred you, or they see you as a potential client yourself someday. Or maybe—some of them are just (gasp!) nice people.

Are you getting the picture? Highly experienced investment professionals, right in your own area, who would just love to offer you personalized advice and support, for free! Who better to be the voice of reason for you when you're in the midst of a temptation to stray from your carefully prepared investment strategy? If you are successful in arranging such a meeting, maybe nothing will come of it, or maybe you'll be shuffled down the hall to a junior associate. (If that happens, politely listen and learn, and then try elsewhere.) But maybe you'll end up with a very experienced and knowledgeable person willing to serve as your rescuer.

To be clear, for most of you I do not recommend that you actually open an account with a full-service investment advisor at this point in your financial life—and that's fine, because that's probably not what they want either. In most cases, it just isn't a good fit; your account is too small for them, and their costs are too high for you. But as I mentioned earlier, it might make some sense for a *few* of you to consider it. Which few of you? If the whole topic of long-term investing seems hopelessly intimidating to you, and/or if you have serious doubts about your ability to stick to the strategy regardless of market conditions—then you might be one of the few. And if you're using an IRA as a tax shield, as opposed to a plan offered by your employer (complete with a plan administrator to help guide your way), then that further qualifies you. *Understand that you will undoubtedly pay more in frictional costs if you invest through a full-service firm.* These firms charge on a per-transaction basis or as a percentage of your portfolio balance. Yes, it's an expensive way to go, and that expense will come right out of your investment returns. But if you believe that full-service is the only way that you can confidently invest, then for you it may be worth the extra cost.

NOW YOU'RE READY!

That's it! The fourteen-step process that we just reviewed will allow you to become a successful long-term investor, and it's the final piece of financial education in the book. There is only one way to properly close this chapter, and I'll bet you know what it is: that's right, one last time, let's recite the *Disciplined Investor's Pledge*. But this time, as you recite, you'll have a new and much more complete understanding of each of its points.

THE DISCIPLINED INVESTOR'S PLEDGE

I am a disciplined, long-term investor. I have a proven plan and I'm going to stick to it no matter what. My plan is based on very long-term trends and it is the safest and surest way to get strong long-term results. I have the discipline to stick to my plan even when popular opinion and my own emotions tell me not to. When the market is going up, I am going to resist the idea that I can increase my gains by changing my plan to take advantage. When the market is going down, I am going to resist the idea that I can cut my losses by abandoning my positions. Just to be safe, I have identified a trusted expert who fully understands and supports my investment strategy, whom I will contact immediately if I am ever tempted to deviate from my plan.

And now: **YOU ARE READY TO INVEST!**

SUMMARY

This chapter presents a methodical fourteen-step plan to guide you through implementing your long-term investment plan. However, some of the steps, as well as the sequence, will vary depending on whether you are investing through your employer's retirement savings plan or whether you are investing on your own via an IRA. So to keep everything clear, here are *two* summaries for this chapter, one for each scenario.

A. Investing through your employer's plan

1. **Ensure that you are financially ready.** Your income and First Rule plan are in place, and you have no debt, with the possible exception of a mortgage on your primary residence.
2. **Resolve your housing situation.** If you're a buyer, then complete the house-buying process first before beginning long-term investing. If you've decided to rent long term, begin investing now. If you are somewhere in between, then consult your financial planner.
3. **Hire a financial planner.** You want a fee-based, independent, credentialed financial planner. This is not optional as you go through the remaining steps and throughout your first full year of investing.
4. **Choose a tax shield.** If your employer offers a choice of plans, work with your financial planner to decide which choice matches you and your circumstances the best.
5A. **Choose a fund seller.** You buy funds from, and hold your account with, your employer's fund administrator.
6A. **Determine your asset allocation.** With your financial planner's help, decide on what categories of assets to hold and in what percentages. This allocation determines where your portfolio will most likely perform on the risk-and-return scale.
7A. **Select the specific funds to invest in.** You will be limited to the choices made available by the fund administrator; work with your financial planner to determine the best fit for you.
8. **Decide on the exact amount to invest.** Same as what you have been saving all along—10% bare minimum. If your employer offers a match, be sure to take full advantage of it.
9A. **Decide on how often to invest.** Simple—every payday.
10A. **Determine how to automate the process.** This is an easy decision; you'll set up an automatic payroll deduction, resulting in the automatic purchase of your preselected funds.

11. **Choose a 911 rescuer.** Choose someone who understands and supports your investment strategy, whom you respect and will listen to, and who can be depended upon to respond.

12. **Make your first investment.** You are entering a new phase in your financial life; congratulations! Carefully check it afterward, to make sure that everything went as planned.

13. **Repeat.** Just let it happen, paycheck after paycheck, like clockwork. Don't pay attention to the market, the financial media, or your account balance.

14. **Rebalance your portfolio as necessary.** Your plan may have an automatic rebalancing capability and/or offer a target date fund that doesn't require rebalancing. Otherwise, work with your financial planner to develop a frictional-cost friendly rebalancing plan.

B. *Investing through an IRA*

1. **Ensure that you are financially ready.** Your income and First Rule plan are in place, and you have no debt, with the possible exception of a mortgage on your primary residence.

2. **Resolve your housing situation.** If you're a buyer, then complete the house-buying process first before beginning long-term investing. If you've decided to rent long term, begin investing now. If you are somewhere in between, then consult your financial planner.

3. **Hire a financial planner.** You want a fee-based, independent, credentialed financial planner. This is not optional as you go through the remaining steps and throughout your first full year of investing.

4. **Choose a tax shield.** Work with your financial planner to decide between a Roth and a traditional IRA.

5B. **Determine your asset allocation.** With your financial planner's help, decide on what categories of assets to hold and in what percentages; this determines where your portfolio will most likely perform on the risk-and-return scale.

6B. **Choose a fund seller.** Since most brokers offer a wide selection of index funds, your primary consideration is lowest frictional costs.

7B. **Select the specific funds to invest in.** For each category in your asset allocation, choose the lowest-frictional-cost index fund, with the help of your financial planner.

8. **Decide on the exact amount to invest.** Same as what you have been saving all along—10% bare minimum.

9B. Decide on how often to invest. Each round of investing will incur frictional costs, so you don't want to invest too frequently; but if you invest too infrequently you'll miss chances for investment gains. Work with your financial planner to find the right balance.

10B. Determine how to automate the process. You'll need to arrange an automatic process between your bank (on the sending end) and your broker (on the receiving end) resulting in the purchase of your preselected funds. The idea is that any money earmarked for investment should spend the *least* possible time in your checking account.

11. Choose a 911 rescuer. Choose someone who understands and supports your investment strategy, whom you respect and will listen to, and who can be depended upon to respond.

12. Make your first investment. You are entering a new phase in your financial life; congratulations! Carefully check it afterward to make sure that everything went as planned.

13. Repeat. Just let it happen, investment after investment, like clockwork. Don't pay attention to the market, the financial media, or your account balance.

14. Rebalance your portfolio as necessary. Your broker may have an automatic rebalancing capability, or you may have chosen a target date fund that doesn't require rebalancing. Otherwise, work with your financial planner to develop a frictional-cost-friendly rebalancing plan.

WRAP-UP AND SUMMARY

Question and Answer Session

Congratulations! You completed all four parts of the book, and by doing so you've learned a tremendous amount about how to achieve a strong financial future. I'm sure you had a lot of questions about personal finance before you began reading, and that even more occurred to you as you progressed through the chapters. I hope that most of your questions about each individual topic have been answered as you continued reading. But now that you've had a chance to reflect on everything that you've learned, maybe some broader questions have begun to emerge in your mind. When I've taught the fundamentals of personal finance to others, I've found that some of the best learning takes place after some of this type of overall reflection.

To stimulate some of this deeper learning for you, imagine that you and a group of your fellow readers have gathered for a question-and-answer session with me. You've all been asked to come prepared with questions that have occurred to you about everything covered in the book. Further, you've been advised that since your financial future is at stake, this is no time to hold back; objections, challenges, and debate points are welcome, as well as comments and clarifying questions. Are you ready? Here is what such a question-and-answer session might sound like.

Q1: At various times throughout the book, you've talked about *financial red alert*. You even talked about times when I might be on financial red alert for more than one reason at the same time. So once and for all: what exactly does it mean to be on financial red alert, and when exactly am I supposed to be on it?

A: When you are in normal status—not at red alert—you save a minimum of 10% of everything you earn. You might choose to save more than that—20%, 30%, or even more—but 10% is the minimum. But when you are in financial red alert, you don't think in terms of minimum *savings* amounts anymore. Instead, the goal is to *spend the absolute minimum* amount that you possibly can, and therefore save the maximum amount. Sometimes you need to be on red alert for months, or even a few years, so obviously it isn't about just skipping some spending items once or twice. Instead, it means really committing to a lifestyle of minimum spending for a sustained period. It is also a time to be aggressively looking for any supplemental income you can find. Billy Bigshot went from overspending his income to saving 44% of it, and it wasn't nearly as hard as he thought it would be. And that was after only a week of thinking about it. I'm sure he'll be able to come up with even more savings later. *That's* financial red alert.

Two specific conditions trigger immediate financial red alert:

1. When you're in debt of any kind—a mortgage on your primary residence is the only exception—until you are completely out of debt.
2. When your cash bucket is not filled, until it is.

There are two other situations where financial red alert is optional, but strongly suggested:

3. When you are eligible for a 401(k)-type program with a match, until you have met the maximum contribution amount required. This is nothing less than an opportunity for free money, and it is highly recommended that you claim all of it that you are eligible for.
4. If you decide that buying a house is for you, the time you spend saving up for your down payment and closing costs can be shortened by going on red alert. This has the advantage of allowing the equity in your house to begin building sooner, and for you to begin your long-term investment program sooner.

And yes, it is possible to be in more than one of those conditions at the same time. If you are, the question becomes, which red alert do you deal with first? I recommend that you give them all top billing. The way that you do this is to *split* your monthly savings among your financial red alerts. For example, if you are in debt and your cash bucket isn't filled, then use half your savings each month to pay off your debt and the other half to fill your cash bucket. Continue in this way until one of the red alerts is resolved, and then devote all your savings to the remaining one.

Q2: Okay, a lot of us have student loans from the minute we begin our financial lives. Those are usually very low interest. Some mortgage lenders don't count student loans as much as other debts when you're trying to get a mortgage. As a matter of fact, some financial writers even say that if your student loan interest rates are low enough, you are better off investing instead of paying them off early. So since outstanding student loans aren't as big of a problem as other debt, you don't seriously mean to tell us that we're supposed to be in financial red alert until they are all paid off, do you?

A: Yes, that's exactly what I mean to seriously tell you. Debt is debt, and your ability to fully tap into the power of compounding is seriously limited until you get rid of all of it. The writers who tell you to go ahead and invest while you have outstanding student loans are technically right, assuming that you can actually find investments that can safely and consistently give you after-tax returns higher than your after-tax student loan interest rates. But they're right in a *dead-right* kind of way. It's like stepping on the brake and the accelerator at the same time and concluding that it is theoretically possible to move the car forward that way. You might move forward—a little bit—but you'll be fooling yourself. Because you see small positive gains, you'll be very unlikely to control your spending with the same urgency as you would under a financial red alert. The truth is that you're very unlikely to really get anywhere until you are completely free of all nonmortgage debt, period.

The only special treatment that student loans should get is that they are usually the ones you should pay off last. If you have multiple debts to pay off, pay off the highest-interest-rate debts completely first—which is usually credit card debt. Then move on to the next-highest-interest-rate debt, and so on. Since student loans are generally the lowest interest rate, those will probably be the ones that you pay off last.

Q3: Well, speaking of the high cost of a college education, you never covered how we are supposed to afford sending our kids to college. Tuitions are already very high and are increasing much faster than inflation. But I still feel strongly that a college education is extremely important for my children. So I would feel very selfish saving and investing for my own retirement before I had first saved and invested enough to pay for my kids' college expenses. Do you agree with that?

A: Well, no, I don't agree. But first let me explain why we didn't cover this in the main part of the book. For most people, your children's college falls into the 2nd third of your financial life, and we're focusing on the 1st third. Also, not everyone has children, and the ones who do may not share your conviction that it's the parent's responsibility to pay for 100% of a child's college education. But I'm glad you brought it up, because many people will at least start thinking about this in their 1st third.

I definitely applaud the fact that you place a high value on a college education. I do, too. The main part of your statement that I disagree with is that paying for kids' college should come *before* your own long-term investment program. I understand that this might sound selfish at first, but hear me out. Suppose you do save and invest for your child's education first, and that this causes you to fall short on your own retirement savings. If that's what happens, think carefully about what would happen next. If you are able to keep working, then that's what you'll be forced to do. And since you've sacrificed a few decades of compounding, you'll have to work many extra years for each one year that you didn't save and invest for yourself. In that case, your child will have to live with the knowledge that their elderly parent is working long past retirement age solely to pay for that child's college. But what if you aren't able to keep working? In that case, the very child that you put through college will be one of the leading candidates to support you financially. Neither of these scenarios sounds like you are doing your child much of a favor by shortchanging your own retirement savings. Isn't it a much better gift to your child to ensure that *you* are completely financially self-sufficient for life, so that your child will never have to worry about supporting you or watching as you work far beyond retirement age?

Don't misunderstand me—I am not saying that you should never pay for your children's college education. But I am saying that *your own retirement savings come first*. Once you've begun your long-term investment program, stay with it no matter what. But even while you are doing that, it might be possible to *also* save and invest for your children's college education. Here's how: the bare minimum for your own savings and investment is 10% of your income. If you can save more than 10%—say, 15% or 20%—then put the 10% minimum into your own investment program and the difference into a college savings fund. If you can save even more than that, you can make terrific progress on both fronts. If this seems like the direction you might be heading, then I strongly urge you to consider the Ultimate Acceleration Strategy that we discussed in part I—you're a perfect candidate for it.

People have many different opinions about paying for a child's college education, and there are many more aspects to it than the purely financial ones. A thorough treatment of all the angles would easily fill a book of its own, so I encourage you to approach it with a lot of research and careful thought. If you're going to devote some of your savings and investments toward a college savings program, by all means do it in a tax-shielded way. Several different kinds of tax-advantaged programs are specifically designed for college-related savings, but they are very separate from the tax shields we discussed in part IV. You'll need to involve your financial planner and/or your tax professional if you decide to go this route.

Q4: The whole book is about what to do in the 1st third of our financial lives—but then what? Do we do completely different things in the 2nd third and 3rd third? Will we have to buy another book for each one of *those* thirds, too?

A: The 1st third is for getting all of the important fundamentals in place, right from the start. This is where you get your financial river flowing in the right direction and establish all of the critical habits that we've discussed throughout this book. Because of the unbelievable power of compounding, there is an enormous advantage to beginning your long-term investment program as *early* in your life as possible. As you can now fully appreciate, there are some important things to take care of before you can begin investing, and some of those things may take some time. But here is the goal: by the time you leave the 1st third and enter the 2nd, if you've established all of the fundamentals that we've talked about and have your long-term investment program well under way, you will be in an *outstanding* position to build a very strong net worth.

In the 2nd third of your financial life, you *keep doing* every single one of these things that you put in place in the 1st third. They are now well established and on solid footing, so you just pour on the coal for the *entire duration* of the 2nd third. Think of it—that's roughly 20 years of saving and investing, probably with higher and higher income, month after month and year after year. Compounding probably got you to raise your eyebrows after the 1st third of your financial life—by the end of the 2nd third, your jaw will drop!

But something else usually happens during the 2nd third, also: your life will probably get more complicated. Your household size is likely to grow, with all the mostly happy "complications" that go along with spouses, partners, and/or dependent children. Later, your household size may shrink, which introduces a completely different set of complications—like college, which we just discussed. You may go through a divorce or split up with a longtime partner. You may play an increasing role in the care of your aging parents. Your income will probably grow along with your skills and experience but may well be accompanied by increased responsibilities and time demands. You may end up moving a few times, or even more. Keeping your health up to par may not be as simple and automatic as it once was. These kinds of factors combine to add complications to *all* aspects of your life, including your financial life.

It would be much more difficult to write a single book for people in the 2nd third of their financial lives. People's lives evolve and complicate in very different ways from one another, so the financial challenges become more individualized. It is quite possible that your investments will become more sophisticated and your portfolio more diverse. You may well find yourself increasingly relying on the advice of your virtual financial team—financial planner, tax professional,

302   *Question and Answer Session*

and others—because you need advice even more customized than it was before, from people who know and understand your situation.

I'm not trying to paint a gloomy picture of the 2nd third of your financial life. Complications can be good or bad, but they do make managing your financial life more, well—complicated. That's one of the main reasons why it is so important to get on the right track financially during the 1st third; compared with the 2nd third, it is simpler to do, and you have more time to do it. Even more to the point, if you haven't gotten your financial life completely squared away in the 1st third, then the 2nd third is likely to be characterized by financial crises at a time when you are least able to deal with them. The last thing you want in the 2nd third is for your financial condition to be a *source* of even more complications—especially not unexpected and unpleasant ones.

The 3rd third is when you'll have the most flexibility and choice. You've been practicing delayed gratification for your entire financial life. Well, the 3rd third is when you can finally realize the payoff from all of that patience and discipline. At this point, work is truly optional. You may have some new and different financial problems to solve, but most people *wish* they had high-net-worth issues to deal with, like estate planning and portfolio optimization. And speaking of your portfolio, the 3rd third is when you shift your asset allocation away from *growth* and much more toward *income*. The main point is that you'll have tremendous freedom to enjoy all the other aspects of your life because your finances are in excellent shape. If you want to buy some books about how to enjoy the 3rd third the most—well, you'll have plenty of money and time to spend on them!

Q5: This whole plan is just too demanding. Financial red alerts for months, or even years at a time? You have got to be kidding. What you're describing is the life of a cheapskate. Your ideas about spending and saving are way too tight. I'm sorry, but I don't see how you expect us to follow this kind of penny-pinching strategy.

A: Good! I'm happy you're asking the question that way, because I'm a believer in direct communication. The fact that you're asking it means that I've succeeded in getting across that this strategy *really does* require some sacrifice and discipline.

I'm making recommendations, but the choice is yours. I am not on a mission to get everyone to follow this strategy. But I *am* on a mission to *educate* as many people as possible, so that you can make informed choices. I would hope that you'd choose to follow the recommended strategy, but if you don't, then you're making that decision *consciously,* with a good idea of what the consequences are likely to be. So take the recommendations or leave them; all I ask is that you give them serious consideration. But before you choose to leave them, here is one more thing to think about. I am recommending that you live on no more than 90% of your income—and even less than that at financial red alert times. A large proportion of the world's population would be delighted to *live* on the 10% that I'm asking you to *save*. How big a sacrifice is 10% savings—really?

I'm not suggesting that you save and invest because I think that sacrifice and discipline are noble ideals. They are, but that's completely beside the point. Instead, I'm recommending that you save and invest because I think that there is a very good chance that in the future you'll end up needing it, and that there are unbelievably powerful ways that the "current you" can compound small savings into huge gifts for the future you. If so, the future you will be very grateful that the present you anticipated that and did something about it—and so will the future you's family and friends.

Q6: Hi, I'm Gloria Graphic, Gary Graphic's cousin. My question is about long-term investing. You're recommending that we put almost everything into equity index funds, but everything I read says that the stock market is very risky. I'm like my cousin, so I like graphs, but all the equity graphs that I've seen just show sharp ups and downs. Is it really safe to invest in equity index funds?

A: Gloria, remember that the great majority of other investors have much shorter investment horizons than you do. And for those much shorter-term investors, the stock market *is* risky! Since these other investors greatly out-number the very long-term investors like you, most of the articles you've read, and the graphs you've seen, emphasize the high risk and the relatively sharp ups and downs.

Compared to most other investors, we are much more interested in very *long-term* trends, and they tell a completely different story. I thought that some-body might ask about this, so I brought along a couple of graphs (see figures S.1 and S.2). Both of these graphs show the S&P 500 index, going all the way back to 1900. The data on the two graphs is exactly the same, except for the vertical axis. First take a look, and then I will explain the difference.

Figure S.1 shows the S&P 500 index with a normal vertical scale. The graph is completely accurate, but this way of looking at it can only give you limited insight into the long-term trends. The main things you can conclude from this graph are that the recent numbers are much, much higher than the earlier ones, and that the recent numbers jump around a lot. Nearly everything that the financial media covers is concentrated on the extreme right-hand side of the graph, and as you can see, there is definitely a lot of volatility there for them to comment on. If you had invested in an S&P 500 index fund for 5 years—or even 10—you might have made a lot on the investment, or you

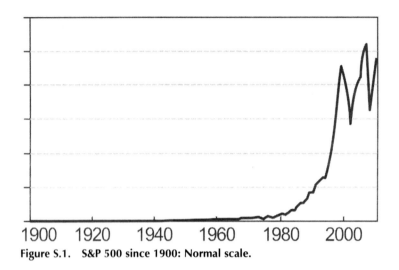

Figure S.1.   S&P 500 since 1900: Normal scale.

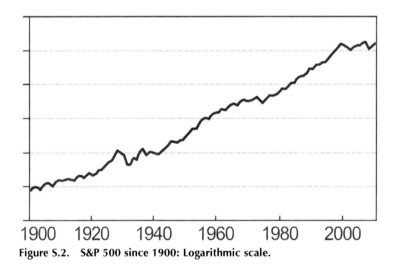

Figure S.2.   S&P 500 since 1900: Logarithmic scale.

might have lost a lot. As you can see, it all depends on exactly when you bought and exactly when you sold.

But what if you'd invested 30 or 40 years ago? Look at the prices in the 1970s and 1980s compared to the much more recent prices. The conclusion is very clear: *it really wouldn't have mattered exactly when you bought and sold*; you still would have made a huge gain! The risk is even less when you remember that you're not buying at any one, single time—you're buying a little at a time, continuously. The key is that you're holding your investments over a very long period of time.

But there is something misleading about the graph on the left. Because the earlier numbers are so tiny compared to the later ones, the human eye can't discern any trends at all in the early or middle part of the graph. That might make you conclude—incorrectly—that big gains from investing in the S&P 500 index have only been possible in the last 40 years or so. But that's not true. You would have made similar gains in *any* very long period of time on the graph. It just doesn't *look* like it, because of the scale.

To solve this visual problem, skilled graphics experts like your cousin use a technique called a *logarithmic scale* for the vertical axis. Here's how it works: instead of the second tick mark on the vertical scale being twice the value of the first tick mark (as it is on a normal scale), the second tick mark is *ten* times the value of the first one. The third tick mark is *one hundred* times the value of the first, and so on. When you look at figure S.2, which uses a logarithmic scale, you can see just how dependable and consistent the growth in this index has been as far back as we can go. So whenever you hear about the volatility of the stock market, and how risky it is, remember that you are among the very few investors who only care about very long-term trends. And those trends have been remarkably consistent for over 100 years.

Q7: You can show all the fancy graphs that you want, but they all have one thing in common—they look backward. Just because stocks have gone up in the past doesn't mean that they'll keep going up. I think we're heading for rougher times ahead, and I don't think that I want my money tied up in stock indices. What guarantees can you offer us that they will keep going up?

A: I can't offer any guarantee at all. You are completely correct in pointing out that investing in equities, even with all of the safeguards that we have put in place, does involve at least some element of risk. Studying the past gives us insights, but it doesn't give us guarantees. But there is a very, very big leap between saying "the future may not be like the past" and "therefore, I'm not going to invest in equity index funds."

Here is what I mean: the graphs that we just looked at were for the S&P 500, which is made up of stocks of relatively large companies operating in the United States. But remember, U.S. large caps are only one part of your portfolio. Your asset allocation will include medium and small companies, and it will include stocks representing many other countries, including some very high-potential emerging economies. Your portfolio won't be tied to any one industry, any one country or region, or any one company size. In other words, the investment program that we've outlined is really an investment in the continued economic growth and development of the *entire world*.

I agree that there may be rough times ahead, just as you stated. But the past has included some rough times, too. In the graphs we looked at, you can see when some of those times were. But even at the very roughest of those times—and even when the rough times lasted for multiple years—*eventually, growth resumed.* Keeping that in mind, as well as the truly worldwide nature of your asset allocation, stop and think just how rough the times would have to be in order to conclude that our recommended investment strategy is a poor one. Times would have to be *so* rough that the entire world's economic growth and development would have to stop cold and stay in a depressed condition for several decades. It's one thing to anticipate some rough times ahead, but what we're describing goes far beyond that: very long-term global stagnation. This is what some would call a doomsday scenario.

Few people are *that* pessimistic, but let's say that you're one of them. That leaves you with a problem: what are you going to invest in instead? Of course, you could invest in ultra-safe cash equivalent instruments, but your returns will be very low. (That actually *is* a guarantee!) Or you could try to construct a portfolio of stocks handpicked from industries that tend to do well in tough times, such as discount retailers, temporary agencies, or (believe it or not) providers of alcoholic beverages. You could invest in commodities like gold, which sometimes soar during times of economic turmoil. Or you could just conclude that since the future is so bleak, there's no point to investing in the first place.

Wouldn't you say that each one of these alternatives is pretty risky, too? I would.

Investing in equity index funds *does* involve some risk. But so do all the alternatives. Ultimately, our long-term investment strategy is based on this assumption: the future may not look exactly like the past, but over the long term, on a worldwide basis, economic growth and development will continue. It may not be evenly spread, and some periods will be rougher than others, but the overall long-term trend will be positive. We have mountains of evidence that tell us that holding equity index funds over very long periods of time has historically been an excellent way to earn great returns with relatively minor risk. Choosing any of the other alternatives means that you're betting your financial future on the assumption that the future will be completely unlike the past. That's just too risky, and I don't recommend it.

Q8: I've patiently listened to all of your recommendations, but I don't think I'm going to follow them. I'd rather invest in something else—myself! I want to be an entrepreneur and start my own business. If Bill Gates or Mark Zuckerberg followed your advice, they wouldn't be where they are today. Are you saying that starting your own business is a bad idea?

A: Not at all! In fact, I admire entrepreneurs. But I do advise you to think it through carefully. Successfully starting your own business takes a tremendous amount of talent, hard work, or luck—and usually plenty of all three. What I've outlined in the book is an approach that can work for *anyone*. In contrast, while the rewards of entrepreneurship can be great, it is definitely not for everyone.

One reason why the rewards are so high is that the risks are, too. Many new businesses fail within a few years. For every Bill Gates or Mark Zuckerberg there are many others who have tried and failed. And unlike those two examples, a high proportion of successful entrepreneurs had to go through a few failed attempts before finally succeeding. (Interestingly, one of the main lessons that new entrepreneurs often have to learn the hard way is the need to control spending and cash flow very tightly, so maybe some of the book's main recommendations will come in handy after all!) The odds are daunting, and the path is difficult. But still, for a few of you, the lure may be strong enough that you'll give it a try.

Whether to start your own business is a classic example of a decision involving both financial and nonfinancial aspects, as we discussed in part I. The advice given then definitely holds true: use a structured decision-making process and make sure that you carefully and objectively weigh all the factors, for and against. This protects you from making such an important decision impulsively or emotionally. You'll definitely want to talk your ideas over with others who have tried taking a similar route to get their insights. As we noted earlier, when you take a structured approach like this, sometimes angles and alternatives will occur to you in the process that you hadn't thought of before. For example, it might occur to you that starting your own business and safely investing for your future aren't necessarily mutually exclusive. You might decide to spend some or all of the 1st third of your financial life earning an income in a more traditional way, by seeking jobs that will ultimately give you the best preparation in the field that interests you. Then, after you've gone through the steps that we've described and gotten your long-term investment program well established, you can consider starting a business in the *2nd third* of your financial life. That way, you have ever-compounding investments to offset some of the risk of entrepreneurship.

If you take a deliberate, structured-decision approach like this, you'll be less likely to regret your decision, and you can approach whatever your decision is with confidence. After weighing everything carefully, if you still end up deciding to start a business right away, I wish you success!

Q9: There is something I've been wondering about from the beginning, but it's best to explain it with a couple of examples. In the chapter on cars, you tell us that certain makes and models are well known for holding their value better than others—but you don't tell us which ones those are. In the chapter on credit cards, you give a lot of advice about how to find websites that will independently and objectively help us find the right card. Why don't you just give us the websites? Better still, let's skip the whole research step altogether. Why don't you just tell us what the best credit card is?

A: I didn't list specific makes and models of cars, give out the credit card research websites, or recommend the best credit cards because I don't want this book to become obsolete in a few months or years. The right answers to questions like these are constantly changing, but the *principles* you've learned here will last you for a lifetime.

I've gotten specific in a few cases, though. I've directed you to the FICO and the *Kelley Blue Book* websites, for example, because these are sources of information that have been in place literally for decades and are highly likely to continue to be valuable. And I mentioned a very specific target date fund—Vanguard's Target Retirement Fund family—simply because Vanguard has done the best job, so far, of constructing a very low-cost investment product specifically designed for investors just like you're going to be. Beyond that, you're right—I've described the *principles* and then advised you to do the research.

A book isn't the right place for specific, up-to-the-minute financial recommendations on cars or credit cards, but the Internet *is*. Now that you know what to look for, you know how to find credible, objective recommendations on these and all kinds of other financial topics. I encourage you make a habit of this kind of research.

Q10: The case study chapter on Billy Bigshot seemed very realistically written. Is that because *you* spent some time in your early financial life being a Billy Bigshot?

A: Well, I—oh, I've just been told that we're all out of time for this session. Thank you for all your questions!

Your Financial Future

$\mathcal{A}t$ last, you've arrived at the end of the book! I think you deserve a reward for all of your hard work. Think of it as a thank-you gift, from me to you. So get ready, because we're going to go on a trip. This won't be any ordinary trip, though. We're not going to go to the mountains, or the beach, or to see any of the world's great attractions. Instead, we're going to take a trip *through time*. And the vehicle we'll be traveling in will be one of the most powerful and wonderful vehicles possible—your own imagination.

We're headed for a very specific destination in the future. Our trip will take us to the very day that you make the transition *out of* the 1st third of your financial life and *into* the 2nd third. Earlier we said that it isn't important to have the exact dates and ages figured out, and it isn't: the three phases of your financial life are conceptual tools to aid your learning, not actual times with strict boundaries. But for the purposes of our trip, I want you to imagine our destination as an actual, very specific date. Do whatever math you'd like in order to come up with a rough estimate. For most of you, it will probably be somewhere in your early 40s, but some of you might estimate an older or younger age. Now, only for our trip, turn your rough estimate into a specific calendar date and year. You'll have to just pick a date out of the air, completely arbitrarily—don't worry about it, that's exactly what we want. Say something like, "My destination is April 19 in the year 2034, when I will be just over 40 years old."

All right, do you have your exact date identified? If so, then engage your imagination and let's go! The trip will be best if you imagine everything as vividly as you can, so go ahead and invent all kinds of imaginary details. Use all your senses to bring the trip to life—see the sights, smell the scents, and hear the sounds around you on your arbitrary date. Imagine where you are and who is around you. There might be others on the scene you haven't even met yet. Now say—out loud—your destination in the present tense, like "Today *is* April 19 in the year 2034, and I *am* just over 40 years old."

Voilà—we are there! As tempted as you might be to spend time exploring what is going on in all of the aspects of your life, the purpose of this trip is to take a look at your *financial* life. And as soon as you think of your financial condition, you *smile*. Not a giddy, ecstatic ear-to-ear grin, but the kind of calm smile that comes from peace of mind. You aren't the wealthiest person in town, but your financial river is very definitely flowing in the right direction, and it is steadily picking up speed. You are a homeowner and have been for several years. All your bills are consistently and routinely paid. You owe no money whatsoever, except for the mortgage on your house. You carry appropriate insurance to guard against risk; for risks that aren't insured, you have a full cash bucket. You have a safe and effective tax-shielded, long-term investment program that you began years ago, shortly after you moved into your house. You've been steadily contributing to it ever since. In short, you've successfully built a very solid base of financial security for you and your dependents.

You are only one-third of the way through your financial life, and the hard part is already over! You aren't in the "set for life" category yet, but you are well on the way to it. You have already established the invaluable habits as well as the financial mechanisms to get you the rest of the way there. All you have to do in the 2nd third of your financial life is *continue* what you've already been doing. Setbacks and tough times may occur from time to time, but you're well prepared for them if they do. Of course there is more work to do, but your peace of mind comes from knowing that you already understand exactly what to do and exactly how to do it.

Your smile fades momentarily, though, as you realize that very few of your friends, family, and colleagues in your age group enjoy the kind of financial security that you do. Even many of those who make considerably more income than you do are on very shaky financial footing. And the irony is that some of them are worried about *you* financially. All they see is your modest lifestyle—you drive a used car, live in a house that seems beneath your means, seek out occasional ways to bring in supplemental income, and rarely seem to enjoy many of life's wonderful extravagances. Meanwhile, many of these people "feel" rich, either because of their high incomes or high spending rates, and they assume that *you* must be struggling. What they can't see is your financial bathtub, steadily filling up. Any of them could be doing much better if only they'd learned what you did, and put it into action right from the start—as you did.

You reflect on the key things you learned early in your financial life that led to such a successful 1st third. Of course you recall part I of this book, where you mastered the fundamental concepts that now guide your whole approach. Compounding[1] springs immediately to mind. [Note: the footnotes represent the chapter numbers where the footnoted subject was first introduced.] You were jolted when you first learned of its unbelievable power in personal financial management. You also learned what most of your friends and colleagues still haven't—that net worth[2] is what is important, not the faucet or the drain. You remember learning about the big picture,[3] and you thought at the time that it was just a fun little graphical exercise; but in hindsight, you can see that your habit of taking a long-term view has been a guiding light for your spending management since the beginning. You remember learning about the wonderful, but often financially dangerous, characteristics of your right brain.[4] And you realize that if you hadn't learned to recognize its tricks, you'd be much worse off today. You are especially grateful for having learned the Ultimate Acceleration Strategy[5]—you've used it, and that's exactly how you got so far so fast financially.

As for the part II lessons, it seems hard to believe that those were once unfamiliar concepts. After all, you've been regularly practicing those ideas for so long now, they've become second nature to you. Of course you follow the First Rule[2] of saving a minimum of 10% of all income, but you soon increased that percentage as a result of the Ultimate Acceleration Strategy. And of course you've done that all along by paying yourself first.[6] You never really saw that money as spendable to begin with, so that's why it never seemed like a sacrifice to save it. And now, your monthly budgeting cycle[6] takes less than an hour or so every month. The automatic downloads and flexible software make the number crunching in the *compare* part of the cycle simple. But you still make a point of ensuring that the decisions you make in the *plan* part are carefully prioritized and that you take advantage of all the opportunities in the *learn* part. It seems like ancient history now, but the first few budget cycles took a great deal longer. At first, you were quite surprised by the extent to which small transactions repeated a large number of times can really add up[6] and how much the subscription effect was silently draining from your bathtub.[6] And you learned how even a little research could save you lots of money by making you a smarter, better-informed consumer[6]. Maybe the most important lesson you learned was that the *combined* effect of all spending is what really matters; if you spend too much, it doesn't much matter whether each individual decision is sound or not. Now you realize that you wouldn't have learned any of these valuable lessons if you hadn't started budgeting.

Remembering the early budget cycles reminds you of your financial red alert[8] days as you were filling your cash bucket.[8] The red alert wasn't just for a few months; it was for a considerable period of time. Even though it sounded really grim as you were contemplating this "nothing but the bare necessities" lifestyle, now you look back at it with pride. You took it on as a challenge, even though nothing was forcing you to do that except your own determination, and you got through it just fine. You learned a lot, you surprised yourself with your own resourcefulness, and you were richly rewarded with increased confidence and peace of mind. Because you sacrificed *then,* at a time of *your* choosing, it is very unlikely that you'll have to face a similar level of sacrifice ever again.

Whenever you buy anything, you pay up front, never financing, paying installments, or any of the other names that borrowing goes by.[9] And when you pay, you almost always pay by credit card but never using credit.[9] You pay your balance in full, each month, without fail[9]. You still routinely check your credit reports, for free, three times a year to make sure that the credit bureaus' information about your financial activity is accurate and complete.[9] A few friends and family members have approached you for loans over the years, but in each case, you found a diplomatic (or even helpful) way to say no, while still maintaining good relationships.[9] You are in good standing with the IRS, but you never pay more in taxes than you legally have to.[10] You carry several types of insurance, and you review your coverage amounts and premiums on a regular basis to avoid overpaying or insufficient coverage.[10] As soon as you added financial dependents, you also added two other things: a will[10] and a term life insurance policy.[10] You will cancel your term life policy as soon as your net worth becomes large enough, and it's getting closer every year.

Now you look back at your big-ticket items. You're happy that you learned about cars[11] during part III, or you might have spent a lot of money unnecessarily at a time when you had the least to spare. The used car that you bought was several years old but had very low mileage. Because you'd carefully researched makes and models before you bought, you ended up with a car that held its value very well and operated economically. When you sold it several years later, you got back most of the price that you'd paid in the first place.[11] Not bad at all! You were so happy about that result that you pretty much just repeated the process for your next car.

The house that you bought has been a financial success, too—but it didn't happen overnight. First, there were the nine readiness tests[12] that you had to pass, just to make sure that you were in a position to buy. The readiness test that took the most time by far was the one that required you to first save up 27% of your target price.[12] That took quite a while, but you hastened it by renting as cheaply as you safely could in the meantime, by income growth,[5] and by keeping very tight control of your spending. Then you had to master a whole range of real estate and mortgage jargon,[13] but now you can use terms like *PITI, capital gains exclusion, prequalification,* and *underwater* in a casual conversation without skipping a beat. When you were finally ready to begin working with a buyer's real estate agent, you made sure to select one who had a lot of experience and local expertise and who understood that your top priority was *resale*.[15] (Yes, your agent brought up the three L's; and yes, you asked for them to be repeated in alphabetical order.) It took some looking, but you eventually found a house that met all your needs and had outstanding resale potential—great location, not too old or too new, with a style sure to remain popular among future buyers. This is the house that you still live in, and you make a point of keeping it in good repair. You've even done some remodeling, making sure to limit your projects to resale winners.[15] Your house doesn't have a stunning appearance, but every time you check its approximate resale value, you are delighted at the consistent increases in your equity. The equity gives you a preview of the big rebate[13] that you can expect when you finally sell.

The equity in your house is a big part of your net worth—but not the biggest. That distinction now belongs to your long-term investment portfolio,[18] which you learned how to establish during part IV. You invest a little bit at a time, with every paycheck. You are a *dollar cost averager*.[20] Whether the market conditions are good, bad, or anywhere in between, you continue accumulating shares of very low-cost, passively managed index funds,[18] which you buy from the lowest-frictional-cost fund seller[20] available. You hold your investments in a tax-shielded[19] account. Your funds are mostly a mix of equity funds, with a bond fund making up the balance. Everything is distributed according to an asset allocation[18] plan that you and your fee-based, independent, credentialed financial planner[17] established right at the beginning. You rebalance[20] your portfolio on a regular basis, using a timetable and method that you've worked out with your financial planner. And just as you planned, you are gradually increasing the proportion of bond funds[18] in your portfolio as you move through your financial life.

Your investment portfolio has increased 10% per year,[18] on average, which has far outpaced inflation. But now you have a much deeper, real-world understanding of the phrase "on average." The succession of individual years has been a wild ride, and on two different occasions, you were severely tempted to throw out your plan.[17] You are very happy that your 911 rescuer[17] talked you out of your emotionally driven ideas, because either one of those temptations would have left you much worse off than you are today. Once, when you'd had several good years in a row, you were completely sure that you could increase your returns by borrowing money to invest even more. If you had done that, you'd still be paying off that debt because the market took a very sharp downward turn shortly thereafter, and your losses would have been magnified. Then, as the market continued further downward for an extended period, you became convinced that equities were a terrible idea and were ready to sell everything. If you had jumped out the basement window as you were tempted to do, you would have thrown out some of your best bargains and missed the multiyear rebound that followed. Your 911 rescuer not only saved you from both of those potential disasters but also left you with some wise advice that you are now very happy to follow: you no longer pay any day-to-day attention to the financial markets.[17] And every once in a while, when you are sure nobody is watching, you still recite the Disciplined Investor's Pledge,[17] just to reinforce your investing philosophy.

You begin to reflect on everything that has been accomplished financially in the 1st third of your financial life. You know that the truest measure of financial success is net worth,[2] and yours has consistently increased, year after year. (The only exception was the year that you bought your house; it was close, but your closing costs[13] exceeded that year's savings.) At first, your net worth was tiny, and so were the annual increases. Slowly but surely, the increases became more noticeable; your net worth is now what some people would consider substantial. In fact, you've noticed that the annual increase in your net worth—driven mainly by the increase in your house's equity,[13] and even more by the increase in the value of your portfolio—is now getting to be more than half the size of your annual income. This realization makes you raise your eyebrows.

And then it hits you—that's the famous eyebrow-raise caused by compounding![1] The more you think about it, the more you truly understand that compounding is what is behind your excellent financial position. Real estate values are going up most years, causing your equity to increase at a compounding rate. The same is true of your long-term investments. Your habits of diligently budgeting, paying your credit card balance in full every month, and staying completely out of debt have all served to keep compounding from ever working against you. Compounding has been the key, after all. This must be why the author made that the very first chapter in the book. And the best part is that it's only a matter of time before the annual increases in net worth start to become really jaw dropping.

But wait a minute . . . has compounding been the key, or has there been something even more important? It may have been compounding that provided the financial magic, but it was *you* who had the foresight to learn about it, and *you* who took the initiative to apply it. It was *you* who practiced discipline and sacrifice through the financial red alert period, and *you* who diligently saved for a full 20% down payment, even though it would have been easier and faster (and much riskier) to have found a way to qualify for a lower one. It was *you* who did everything necessary to set up your long-term investment program, while others sat on the sidelines, claiming that they'd get to it eventually. It was *you* who stuck with the plan, even when it wasn't so easy to. *You* have been patiently and consistently financially responsible and have worked to provide for the financial future of yourself and your dependents. So *the real key to your financial success has been you* and your own hard work. You are only a third of your way through your financial life, and the future is looking strong and secure. You can feel justifiably proud of everything that you've accomplished.

I hope you have enjoyed our trip to your financial future! Now that you know how to use your imagination in this way, I'd like to suggest that you make another stop sometime. You see, someone is very eager to meet you. Actually, so are that person's dependents, and all *their* dependents, and—well, it's quite a crowd. I probably don't have to tell you who it is—that's right, it's the *future you*, living in the 3rd third of your financial life. And the future you can't wait to thank you, in person, for the fantastic, life-changing inheritance.

But now it's time to bring our trip to a close and return to the present. It has been my pleasure serving as your author and time-travel guide. I hope you have found this book valuable. The future that you just visited is *absolutely possible* for you to achieve—all you have to do is put what you've learned into action, right from the start. Congratulations on completing this book, and remember to pass along to others what you've learned. And most of all, best of luck to you in securing what is sure to be a very bright financial future!

Bibliography

Belsky, Gary, and Thomas Gilovich. 2010. *Why Smart People Make Big Money Mistakes and How to Correct Them: Lessons from the Life-Changing Science of Behavioral Economics.* New York: Simon & Schuster.

Bernstein, William J. 2010. *The Four Pillars of Investing: Lessons for Building a Winning Portfolio.* New York: McGraw-Hill.

Bogle, John C. 2007. *The Little Book of Common Sense Investing: The Only Way to Guarantee Your Fair Share of Stock Market Returns.* Hoboken, N.J.: John Wiley & Sons.

Larimore, Taylor, Mel Lindauer, and Michael LeBoeuf. 2007. *The Bogleheads' Guide to Investing.* Hoboken, N.J.: John Wiley & Sons.

Malkiel, Burton G., and Charles D. Ellis. 2009. *The Elements of Investing.* Hoboken, N.J.: John Wiley & Sons.

Siegel, Jeremy J. 2008. *Stocks for the Long Run: The Definitive Guide to Financial Market Returns & Long Term Investment Strategies, Fourth Edition.* New York: McGraw-Hill.

Stanley, Thomas J., and William D. Danko. 2010. *The Millionaire Next Door: The Surprising Secrets of America's Wealthy.* New York: Taylor.

Index

principal, interest, taxes, insurance
(PITI), 167–68, 177, 184, 190, 192
principal and interest (P&I):
deductibility, 182, 183; defined, 175;
fixed and variable rates affecting,
175–76; monthly payments, 177,
179, 184, *189*; Mortgageville case
study, 188–89, 194, 195; refinancing,
210
prioritization, 77–78, 81, 92
private mortgage insurance (PMI), 139,
177

real estate agents as allies, 200–201, 203,
206–209, 211–12, 313
rebates, 53–54, 58
red alert. *See* financial red alert
renting: advice against, 159–60; as
cheaply as possible, 170, 171, 312;
home owning as better choice, 170,
183; investing while renting, 292,
293; Mortgageville case study, 188,
190, 192, 193–98; passive income for
owners, 62–63, 64; renter's insurance,
138, 141; total cost of renting *vs.*
owning, *194*; while waiting to buy,
161, 165, 166, 168, 171, 185
retirement: Buck and Penny case study,
217–19; college education, saving
for, 299–300; IRAs, 265; Ira Shield
case study, 272, 274; long-term
investing, 216, 225, 226; matching
employer contributions, 271; net
worth, 43; portfolio income, 220;
redefined, 216; target retirement date
funds, 258–59, 261, 284, 308; tax
deferred *vs.* Roth accounts, 270, 276;
tax incentives, 263, 275; typical US
household, 38
right brain dangers: awkward financial
discussions, avoiding, 54–55;
borrowing, 116; budgeting, resistance
to, 75; buying high, selling low,
223; cash bucket, not filling, 110;
defined, 48–49; emotional decisions,

55–57, 145, 207–208, 277; fear
leading astray, 232, 239; financial
plans, derailing, 57–58, 229–30,
241; premature house buying, 169;
immediate gratification, justifying,
51–53; insurance fears, 136, 138;
long-term thinking, thwarting, 49–
50; letting others take charge, 50–51;
path of least resistance, 53–54; not
paying balances in full, 120
risk management, 133–34, 134–36, 141,
244–245, 246–48
Roth plans, 265, 267–68, 274, 275–76,
280–81

sacrificing, 6, 31, 32, 44, 96, 302–3,
312
saving: for a car, 146–47; cash bucket,
104, 106, 107, 113, 271–72; college
education, 299–300; compounding,
16, 20–24; *vs.* dissaving, 35; financial
red alert, 98, 106–7, 113, 116,
278, 297–98; first rule of saving
ten percent, 30–31, 32, 59–61, 68,
278; for a house, 165–66, 167–68,
169, 171, 185; investment accounts,
225, 285; net worth, 38, 43–45;
non recurring expenses, 79; paying
yourself first, 76–77, 83, 220;
responsible example, 41; ultimate
acceleration strategy, 60–61, 69
savings accounts, 73–74, 76–77, 83,
111–12, 113, 245
Social Security, 43, 217–19, 226
Standard and Poor's 500 (S&P 500):
beating performance of, 250; defined,
249; graphs to 1900s, 303–306; index
fund tracking, 252, 260; inflation,
253–55, 261; inflation chart, *253*;
normal and logarithmic scales, *304*
Stanley, Thomas J., 27
stocks. *See* equity index funds
student loans, 125, 278, 298–99
subprime loans, 166–67
subscription effect, 81–82, 84, 137, 311

About the Author

Chris Smith worked for Hewlett-Packard for 27 years, where he held a number of positions in finance before rising to the level of vice president of finance for two of HP's global business units, eventually playing a key role in HP's merger with Compaq. He has taught at Florida A&M's School of Business and Industry, where he was presented with an Outstanding Service Award for bringing real-life business experience into the college classroom. He is based in Seattle and is the single father of two college-age children.